Audiencemaking

SAGE ANNUAL REVIEWS OF COMMUNICATION RESEARCH

SERIES EDITORS

Suzanne Pingree, *University of Wisconsin—Madison*
Robert P. Hawkins, *University of Wisconsin—Madison*
John M. Wiemann, *University of California—Santa Barbara*

EDITORIAL ADVISORY BOARD

Books in This Edited Series:

Editors
**James S. Ettema
D. Charles Whitney**

Audiencemaking:
How
the Media
Create the
Audience

Sage Annual Reviews of Communication Research

Volume 22

SAGE Publications
International Educational and Professional Publisher
Thousand Oaks   London   New Delhi

Copyright © 1994 by Sage Publications, Inc.

For information address:

SAGE Publications, Inc.
2455 Teller Road
Thousand Oaks, California 91320

SAGE Publications Ltd.
6 Bonhill Street
London EC2A 4PU
United Kingdom

SAGE Publications India Pvt. Ltd.
M-32 Market
Greater Kailash I
New Delhi 110 048 India

Printed in the United States of America

Library of Congress Cataloging-in-Publication Data

Main entry under title:

Audiencemaking: How the media create the audience / editors, James S.
   Ettema and D. Charles Whitney.
       p.   cm. — (Sage annual reviews of communication research ; v. 22)
   Includes bibliographical references and index.
   ISBN 0-8039-4625-2 (cl). — ISBN 0-8039-4626-0 (pb)
       1. Mass media—Audiences.   2. Mass media—Economic aspects.
   I. Ettema, James S.   II. Whitney, D. Charles (David Charles), 1946–
   III. Series.
   P96.A83A95   1994
   302.23—dc20   94-10319

94 95 96 97 98 10 9 8 7 6 5 4 3 2 1

Sage Production Editor: Astrid Virding

CONTENTS

Chapter 1

THE MONEY ARROW:
AN INTRODUCTION TO AUDIENCEMAKING

James S. Ettema and D. Charles Whitney

AT THE BEGINNING of the 1970s, Wilber Schramm undertook the revision of a book, *The Process and Effects of Mass Communication,* that had served for nearly two decades as a constitutional document for our field of study. In his amended introduction to the volume, Schramm reported that half of all research on human communication had been conducted in the period between the composition of his original introductory essay in 1952 and its revision in 1970. Nonetheless, he saw no need to revise the fundamental "elements" and "actions" that constituted the field as he understood it:

> Whether face-to-face or mediated, whether immediate or removed in time or space, the communication relationship includes three elements and two kinds of action. The elements are the communicator, the message, and the receiver. . . . The communicator constructs, as best as he can, the signs which he hopes will call forth the desired responses—whether verbal or nonverbal, auditory, visual, or tactile. That is the first act of the communication process. A receiver selects among the stimuli available to him, selects from the content of the message he chooses, interprets it and disposes of it as he is moved to do. That is the second act of the process. The acts are separate, separately motivated, but brought together by the collection of signs we call the message. (pp. 15-16)

Schramm and his coeditor for the new edition, Don Roberts, elaborated this simple, generic model of communication into a conception of the field of mass communication with a selection of articles that can still usefully be studied. The revised edition included only four articles that had appeared in the first edition. Hadley Cantril's "Invasion from Mars" was one. Appearing for the first time were articles by Bauer, Boorstin, Hovland, Katz, Krugman, McLuhan, Lang and Lang, and Sears and Freedman. The volume can, then, be read as testament to the vigor of scholarship in a period when mass communication research allegedly was moribund.

With the passage of two more decades, however, we may be tempted to view Schramm's sense of progress in mass communication research with a touch of irony. We know now that so much more would happen so soon. As Schramm and Roberts were revising the book, Tichenor, Donohue, and Olien published "Mass Media Flow and Differential Growth of Knowledge" (1970); and soon after the book appeared, McCombs and Shaw published "The Agenda-Setting Function of the Mass Media" (1972). Such research signaled a shift in focus from affective to cognitive effects of media messages and infused new energy into the field with interesting theoretical formulations that mass communication research could claim as its own. Thus began, so our received history maintains, the paradigm shift that overturned the limited effects model inherited from Katz and Lazarsfeld (1955) and Klapper (1960). Soon, another paradigm shift—or, rather, paradigm split—would follow as critical and cultural studies gained voice in the field (e.g., Dervin, Grossberg, O'Keefe, & Wartella, 1989; Gerbner, 1983). And so, through the 1970s and into the 1980s, the "second act" of the communication process, as Schramm had characterized the reception of messages by the audience, was thoroughly rewritten.

In those same years, the first act was also under revision. In 1972 Herbert Gans published an article in the *American Journal of Sociology* decrying a "famine" in what he called "institutional studies" of mass communication but also acknowledging several recent articles on the topic. One of those articles, an application of phenomenological-interpretive sociology to news production, was Gaye Tuchman's (1972) "Objectivity as Strategic Ritual: An Examination of Newsmen's Notions of Objectivity." Another, an application of the sociology of complex organizations to the media business, was Paul Hirsch's (1972) "Processing Fads and Fashions: An Organization-Set Analysis of Cultural Industry Systems." This research signaled a shift in focus from individual "gatekeepers" to organizational routines and institutional arrangements, and it infused new energy into the field with interesting theoretical formulations from cognate fields of study.

This paradigm shift is, perhaps, best symbolized by two reassessments that appeared in 1977 of David Manning White's classic 1950 study of "Mr. Gates," the wire editor. Disputing White's conclusion that the editor's personal biases were the principal determinant of his story selections, both Hirsch (1977) and McCombs and Shaw (1977) concluded that wire service priorities, as reflected by the proportions of content allotted to standard news categories, were an important influence on news judgment. The point later was confirmed experimentally by Whitney and Becker (1982). Soon, critical and cultural paradigms would also proliferate in this corner of the field too (e.g., Fishman, 1980; Gitlin, 1980; Tuchman, 1978).

While the paradigmatic upheavals of the last two decades have produced new psychologies of audiences and new sociologies of professional communicators, Schramm's conception of communication, with its tidy separation of "elements" and its unidirectional progression of "actions," still captures rather well what most mass communication research is really all about. The predominant theoretical function of audiences is still to receive (i.e., "selectively attend to," "process information from," "make sense of," "be gratified by," "be socialized by," "be subjugated by," "offer resistance to," "ritualistically partake in," or just "veg-out with") media messages. And the predominant theoretical function of communicators is to make those messages (i.e., "report the facts," "distort the facts," "make the news," "repair the news," "represent reality," "invent reality," "manufacture popular entertainment," "create popular art," "process symbols," "produce culture," or just "put on a show") for the audience.

While the great flow of media messages *from* professional communicators *to* large audiences has always been a defining feature of mass communication as well as the central concern of mass communication research, Schramm did include a reverse flow of messages in his generic model of communication. He reproduced in his chapter several variations on Shannon and Weaver's (1949) encoder-signal-decoder formulation complete with the requisite feedback arrow. Although he said very little about that arrow himself, he followed his own chapter with one by Melvin DeFleur (1971) that featured a "Schematic Representation of the Mass Media as Social System." Among the array of arrows connecting the circles and boxes of the schematic diagram were several arrows pointing from "Taste-Differentiated Audience of Consumers" back in the general direction of "Production Subsystem." Some of those feedback arrows were unidentified; but one was clearly labeled. It pointed from "Consumers" toward "Financial Backers," who, in turn, were connected to "Market

Research & Rating Services" and "Advertising Agencies" and thence to "Production Subsystem." It was the "money" arrow.

AUDIENCEMAKING

The "money" arrow, along with those other, unlabeled arrows that Schramm would have understood to be "feedback," is the subject of the recent research assembled in this volume. The term *feedback* rarely appears, however, because the conception of mass communication elaborated here does not fit easily within Schramm's conception of communication as *essentially* a relationship devoted to the exchange of messages. Rather, the conception elaborated here subsumes content-oriented communication relationships into a larger and more complex set of socioeconomic and political—that is to say, institutional—arrangements.

A truly institutional conception of mass communication would not deny, of course, that messages flow between communicators and receivers. Rather, it would subsume these flows not merely into a "collection of signs that we call the message" but into the vast industrialized system of sign exchange for which DeFleur's boxes and arrows provided a rudimentary map. It would also subsume the connection between communicators and receivers not merely into a "communication relationship" but into a process by which the "production subsystem" actively constructs and carefully maintains a network of relationships with, among many others, that "taste-differentiated audience of consumers." Thus the conception elaborated here does not disregard Schramm's "elements" and "actions" of communication, but it focuses neither on how audiences receive messages nor even on how communicators make messages. Rather, it focuses on *how communicators make audiences.*

While, as we have noted, an institutional conception of mass communication has not been the predominant conception of the field, we do not argue that it is a recent conception. We might begin a review of its origins with Lippmann's *Public Opinion* (1922), which presented those famous "pictures in our head" as one manifestation of journalism as a sociopolitical institution. Certainly, we would trace its development through at least three important areas of study. We would trace it through media economics, whether neoclassical such as Owen (1975) and Owen and Wildman (1992) or critical political economy such as Schiller (1969), Murdock and Golding (1979), Dreier (1982), and Bagdikian (1990). We would also trace it through interorganizational analyses of media industry systems such as Hirsch (1972, 1977), Turow (1984), and Montgomery (1989). And, although mass communication as a political institution is not, per se, the focus of this volume, any complete account of the institutional conception would include examinations of the media not only, or even primarily, as the purveyor of political consciousness to the public (e.g., Herman & Chomsky, 1988; Paletz & Entman, 1981) but as the surrogate for the public in the policy process (e.g., Lang & Lang, 1983; Linsky, 1986; Protess et al., 1991).

This volume, like Schramm and Robert's revision of *Process and Effects,* does not, then, presume to announce a new conception of the field. Rather, it intends to elaborate a particular conception with an update on research. At the beginning of the 1980s, the editors of this volume assembled a collection of articles highlighting communicator studies conducted in the interstices of the individual and the organizational levels of analysis. The primary tasks for theory and research at that time included reconceptualization of both objectivity in journalism and creativity in the popular arts as organizational strategies and routines. The fundamental task of communicator studies as pursued in that volume, however, had not really changed from earlier gatekeeper studies. It was to explain how mass communicators, understood to be workers in complex organizations, manage the processes of message making. In this new volume, the editors offer an update on communicator studies by highlighting studies conducted in the interstices of the organizational and institutional levels of analysis. And here, the fundamental task of communicator studies has changed. It is to explain how mass communication organizations, understood to be components of industry systems, manage the processes of audiencemaking.

By the idea of audiencemaking, we do not mean the assemblage of individual readers, viewers, or listeners who receive messages. Such *actual receivers* may exist in mass communication theory as Schramm understood it, but they do not exist in an institutional conception of mass communication—at least, they do not exist as individuals. In an institutional conception, actual receivers are constituted—or, perhaps, reconstituted—not merely as audiences but as *institutionally effective audiences* that have social meaning and/or economic value within the system. These include *measured audiences* that are generated by research services, sold by media channels, and bought by advertisers. They include *specialized or segmented audiences* whose particular interests are anticipated—or created—and then met by content producers. And they include *hypothesized audiences* whose interest, convenience, and necessity are, presumably, protected by regulators. All such audiences exist in relationships with the media—or, more exactly, they exist *as* relationships *within* the media institution. However, any conception of these relationships that concentrates on the production and reception of "messages" (i.e., media content) and merely acknowledges "feedback" belies the complexity of the procedures by which the media construct and maintain those relationships.

This volume focuses primarily on the ways in which such audiences are constituted within the institutional arrangements of mass communication. We acknowledge, however, that effective audiences are not limited to such institutional analogues for actual receivers as the measured audiences produced by television ratings. Organizations—or, more exactly, the expectations, requirements, and demands registered by organizations—may constitute effective audiences. As Montgomery (1989) has shown, for example, the concern of various activist groups about the quality of television content often constitutes an effective audience for producers and programmers. And, as Hirsch and Thompson argue in this volume, the very lack of concern in the securities industry about the quality of newspaper content—but deep concern for return on investment—now constitutes an effective audience for publishers and editors. Thus the connection between capital markets and media corporations is also a "money" arrow connecting audience and communicator.

IMAGES OF AUDIENCE

To begin our elaboration of institutionally constituted audiences, we return to a recurring theme of communicator studies: the idea of audience image. Perhaps reflecting the Aristotelian admonition that communicators must know their audience, an occasional premise of communicator studies has been that professional mass communicators hold—or, at least, *ought* to hold—some image of their audience. The result of these studies invariably has been that professional mass communicators don't seem to have a very clear or complete image of their audiences (e.g., Burgoon, Burgoon, & Atkin, 1982; Gans, 1979; Schlesinger, 1978). Gans's (1979) observational study of national news magazine and network television journalists is illustrative:

> I . . . paid close attention to how the journalists conceived of and related to their audience. I was surprised to find, however, that they had little knowl-

edge about their actual audience and rejected feedback from it. Although they had a vague image of the audience, they paid little attention to it; instead, they filmed and wrote for their superiors and for themselves, assuming . . . that what interested them would interest the audience. (p. 230)

Not only is the image vague, but, as Gans suggests, it is not at all certain that a clearer image would matter much. Journalists report that their perceptions of the audience have a minor impact on their work relative to other sources of influence, according to Flegel and Chaffee (1971), who found that, among eight sources of perceived influence, journalists ranked readers' interests fourth behind such aspects of story content as unusualness, proximity, and importance. Journalists also ranked readers' opinions seventh behind their own opinions and their editors' opinions. Moreover, Flegel and Chaffee found that the "favorability" (i.e., slant) of story treatment correlated far more strongly with journalists' own opinions and their perceptions of editors' opinions than with their perceptions of readers' opinions. On the other hand, Pool and Schulman (1959) argued that journalists' "fantasies" about their audience did influence newswriting, based on an experiment demonstrating that student journalists who held views discrepant from those of their perceived audience tended to write less accurate stories. (For conceptual and methodological critiques of this study, see Darnton, 1975, and Whitney, 1982.) But even with these results, Pool and Schulman (1959) were compelled to acknowledge the importance of routine organizational practice for the production of news:

The author's fantasies are clearly not the only things that affect what he writes. An experienced professional newsman will have acquired great facility in turning out a standard product for each of the many kinds of routine story of which so much of the news consists. (p. 150)

In much the same vein, Espinosa (1982) argued, based on an ethnographic study of a television script conference, that audience interests and needs were actively considered by conference participants in the form of generalizations about audience preferences invoked in the course of discussions about the script. While these generalizations did implicitly reflect the perceived expectations of the audience, they explicitly concerned the structure and content of the script. This result reminds us that writers, whether newspaper reporters or television scriptwriters, along with most other creators of symbolic materials, learn and practice their craft not by internalizing an audience image but by acquiring and maintaining a "product image." As conceptualized by Ryan and Peterson (1982), a product image links together those who work on a cultural product down the production chain and assures the acceptance of the product as it moves down that chain by providing a shared image of "how it's done" or "what's hot." Ryan and Peterson distinguish product images from product conventions because product images can change quickly to meet changing market demands. Like the durable conventions of objective journalism, however, such product images are created by, and routinize the work of, media organizations (see Kapsis, 1986). Altogether, the research on production routines suggests that any audience images or fantasies found to be haunting professional communicators can be dismissed as harmless ghosts in the production machine.

The minimal effects model, it may seem, was exactly backward; mass communicators may affect (as well as effect) their audiences but audiences don't affect their mass communicators. We argue, however, that audience images vanish like ghosts only if we insist that they must be some sort of descriptive information (e.g., demographic information) stored in the heads of individual mass communicators to be used in the daily activities of message production. While newspaper reporters and television scriptwriters may not have audience images dancing in their heads as they write their stories, newspaper managers may have circulation and market research data and television programmers certainly have ratings data on their desks as they decide whether such stories should continue to be written at all. Thus "audience images" reappear, if we look for them, not in individual daily work routines but in organizational strategies and interactions within the overall arrangements of the institution.

In this volume, Webster and Phalen provide an example of such images with their analysis of the imagined or hypothesized broadcast audiences that have been constituted in the course of broadcast policymaking. The authors identify three audience concepts that "hide just beneath the surface" of the policy process in the form of assumptions held, and arguments advanced, by policy players. The concept of "audience as victim" reflects the hypothesis that audiences, particularly those thought to have special needs such as children and minorities, may be significantly affected by broadcast content over which they have little control. This concept has justified regulatory attempts to protect audiences from less desirable programming and to promote more desirable alternatives. The concept of "audience as consumer" assumes that audiences have well-formed content preferences to which broadcasters must respond. This concept has sustained the deregulation of the industry. The concept of "audience as coin of exchange" recognizes the economic value of audiences for broadcasters and has required regulators to deal with such issues as the "diversion" of broadcast audiences by cable channels and distribution of revenues through the Copyright Royalty Tribunal.

Similarly, Wartella enumerates in this volume some images of children-as-audience that have been constituted within the systems—both commercial and educational—for the production of children's television. While veteran commercial producers of television for children may take pride in that fact, they base their decisions on "gut instinct"; younger commercial producers such as those at the Nickelodeon cable network and educational producers such as those at the Children's Television Workshop conduct a good deal of research to assess children's responses to their offerings. More production organizations are, then, establishing procedures for "knowing their audiences"—or, more precisely, "knowing their audiences' responses to particular program concepts and content." As a result of this research (and, no doubt, much practical experience as well), a number of implicit audience assumptions, paralleling those found by Espinosa (1982), unite commercial and educational television production. Systems of children's television production, Wartella argues, are predicated on such assumptions as the following: "children want recognizable characters and stories" and "there are gender differences in what children like about television"—such assumptions constrain the ability of these systems to serve the interests of children.

TECHNOLOGIES OF AUDIENCE

In some measure, institutionally constituted images of the audience all depend *on* some measure. That is, they all depend on social scientific measurement technologies whether in the employ of developmental psychologists demanding better children's programs or ratings services documenting broadcasters' rights to royalties. Those employing measurement technologies usually claim that their methods provide accurate and detailed images of actual receivers so as to reveal, for example, the real information and entertainment needs of young children or the real program preferences of all those who watch television. Such claims are intended to maintain the credibility of the measurement technologies and, in turn, the effectiveness of the measured audiences as the institutional "coin of exchange." As Miller argues in this volume, however, such claims gloss over the fact that measurement technologies and the audiences that

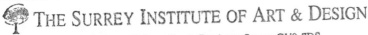

they construct always serve particular purposes and reflect particular interests.

Miller analyzes the trade-offs that audience measurement firms must make between the demands of media clients for extensive audience documentation, the needs of advertising agencies for efficient media-buying criteria, the willingness of respondents to provide the information in the first place, and, finally, the technical, organizational, and financial requirements of the measurement methods themselves. Measurement firms that negotiate a successful compromise in the form of a syndicated service (such as Nielsen's television ratings) create, in Miller's terms, a *social convention* that allows the institution to get on with the business of programming for audiences and advertising to them without worrying too much about who it is that might really be out there.

Audience measurement technologies most often come to popular attention as the arbiter of life or death for television programs. However, these technologies not only inform the day-to-day decisions of institutional workers, they help establish the enduring structure of the institution itself. The chapter by Barnes and Thomson in this volume demonstrates this process of institutional structuration by showing how changes in measurement technology along with changes in marketing strategy have produced an essential characteristic of media industries in what is often said to be "postindustrial society." That characteristic is content specialization.

Barnes and Thomson trace the arrival of many specialized magazines in the 1960s, along with the departure of some general interest magazines such as *Life* and *Look* in the early 1970s, to conceptual and technological developments in the advertising industry. One development was the concept of market segmentation that directed advertisers' attention toward more specialized advertising vehicles that would deliver smaller but more homogeneous and therefore more valuable audiences. Another development was advertising agency access to the computing power necessary to analyze the composition of the audiences offered by specialized publications and to allocate advertising expenditures among those publications. The conceptions of segmented markets and specialized audiences along with the technology necessary to more precisely describe those audiences were both necessary intermediaries linking the appetite of actual readers for specialized content to the publication of specialized magazines.

Barnes and Thomson go on to draw parallels between the magazine industry in the 1960s and 1970s and the television industry in the 1980s and 1990s. Advertisers remain interested in segmented markets and specialized advertising vehicles; and the development of the "people meter" measurement technology with its ability to generate more detailed images of smaller audiences promises to facilitate the growth of the more specialized cable television networks. Thus, the authors conclude, changes not only in content delivery technologies (e.g., the diffusion of cable) but changes also in audience measurement technologies are necessary for content diversification and institutional differentiation to proceed.

In technologically advanced societies, measurement technologies are an essential part of the apparatus for the social construction of reality. The chapters by Miller and by Barnes and Thomson show how particular contemporary measurement technologies influence the social conception of that which is measured (i.e., "the audience"). The chapter by Herbst and Beniger adds theoretical breadth and historical depth to the analysis of the relationship between measurement technologies and our conceptions of reality by reviewing three important moments in the history of the concept of public opinion. The authors argue that every polity displays a characteristic "infrastructure" or relationship between the technology for the assessment of public opinion and the conception of public opinion—indeed, of "the public" itself. One such characteristic infrastructure is that of prerevolutionary France in which *salons* were an essential mode of expression and assessment of public opinion, which was understood to be the conversation of political and intellectual *elites*. Another is that of nineteenth-century America in which newspapers were a characteristic means for registering public opinion, understood to be the agenda of partisan *groups*. The third is twentieth-century America (and other postindustrial societies) in which sample surveys, as conducted and portrayed by the mass media, are the characeric mode of expression and assessment of public opinion, which is understood to be the attitudes of a cross section of individuals—that is, an *audience* that both watches and is watched. Following Max Weber, Herbst and Beniger note the increasing rationalization of the technologies for the assessment of public opinion and the concomitant increasing effectiveness of those technologies as a means for social control of actual receivers.

THE AUDIENCE/MARKET

Actual receivers are not powerless but, as we have argued, they wield influence within the institution only when they have been constituted as some effective audience such as an identifiable and desirable market segment. In this volume, Wildman pursues the topic of the segmentation of the audience/market, and he finds, much like Barnes and Thomson, that segmentation strategies shape the structure of the institution in ways that have significant social and cultural implications. Specifically, Wildman examines the sorts of microeconomic incentives that result in temporal and spatial flows of media products. Temporal flows (e.g., hardcover to paperback to movie) reflect a strategy of segmenting audiences and employing the pricing and distribution policies that maximize the profit from the combination of segments. Spatial flows from larger audience segments (e.g., movie audiences in the United States) to smaller audience segments (e.g., audiences in most other countries) reflect a strategy of producing very high budget products for larger segments that often hold appeal for smaller segments as well. Lower budget products produced specifically for smaller segments often hold less appeal for larger segments, however, contributing to the often-criticized one-way media flows between nations.

The processes by which actual receivers come to be constituted as measured and segmented audiences, and, in turn, have their effect within the institution, are technically and organizationally complex, as the chapters by Miller, Barnes and Thomson, and Wildman all indicate. There is nothing necessary or automatic about the reconstitution of actual receivers as effective audiences nor is there anything necessary and automatic about the influence of these audiences within the institution. Under some conditions far more than others, media firms are responsive to their images of who the audiences are and what those audiences want.

One such condition is the degree of competition within a particular media industry. For example, DiMaggio (1977), Nord (1980), and Peterson and Berger (1975) all argue that the degree of competition within a culture-producing industry is related to the diversity of products offered by that industry. In highly concentrated industries, a few firms often compete for shares of an undifferentiated mass market with a few similar products. In more competitive industries, firms may find it more profitable to segment the market and offer specialized products to the various segments. Peterson and Berger (1975), for example, have demonstrated that periods of relative concentration in the recording industry have been marked by homogeneity in recorded music while periods of greater competition have served a greater range of musical tastes.

Another aspect of the economic structure that may make a media firm more sensitive to the audience, as that firm understands it, is public ownership. In this volume, Hirsch and Thompson argue that the "market-driven" mentality now taking hold in the newspaper business does not really reflect a decline in the economic prospects of the industry. Rather, the rush to create research-based, user-friendly information products, sometimes at the expense of traditional journalistic values, reflects the perceived need of publicly traded newspaper firms to maintain high share prices. To do so, these firms must demonstrate for the benefit of securities analysts a commitment to short-term financial performance. And so it is that the demands of the securities industry register with many newspaper publishers as one very effective audience. These demands usually include more attention to another effective audience: *the readership* as constituted through the analysis of market research, circulation data, and, of course, conventional wisdom. Ironically, we might note, those traditional journalistic values—especially objectivity—that now seem to be threatened by the market-driven mentality of some media managers are, themselves, the marketing strategies of an earlier business era (Carey, 1969; Schudson, 1978).

An institutional conception of mass communication does grant consumers (i.e., actual receivers) some power to assert their wants and needs. And in this volume, Cantor places the power of television audiences in its proper institutional context. She begins by examining the role of audiences as reference groups for media creators and finds that, under certain circumstances, television writers and producers do hold information about their audiences "in mind" when they work. She also examines the role of audiences as interest groups and finds that, from time to time, television networks have accommodated the demands of minorities, women, gays, and others. Like other authors in this volume, however, Cantor concludes that the primary means to make sense of "audience power" is to understand audiences as markets that really can exert power only in the aggregate—by refusing to watch.

But if an institutional conception of mass communication does not deny consumers all power to assert their wants and needs, it does grant media firms substantial power to exploit those wants and create those needs. An institutional conception takes as its primary concern the nature of such transactions and their implications for the political and cultural order. For example, Kaminsky (1985) and Schatz (1988) suggest how the form and content of film genres have developed through a long history of such transactions. Many films, each somewhat different, are produced, and those that are most successful present a product image to be learned, emulated, and eventually altered. Through this process, a genre evolves. Individual creators need not have a clear idea of who the actual receivers are or what they want. It is the industry system as a whole through the "feedback" of box office receipts, along with the track records of successful creators and the ever-mutating images of recently successful products, that attunes content to audience. While individuals produce, write, and direct specific films, the meaning and value of the genre cannot be allocated to the artistic vision of various individuals. The creative process is a function of the industry itself.

On the other hand, as Peterson shows in this volume, this process does not necessarily attune media content to audience desires very closely. The marketing strategies of culture industries are intended not merely to "know" audiences but to shape them into predictable and manageable markets. Peterson shows, for example, that the distinction between blues and country music does not so much reflect differing intrinsic characteristics of the music or differing tastes of the audiences for each genre as it reflects the racially based marketing strategies of the recording industry early in this century. Categorization of music for marketing purposes does not merely maintain distinctions among music genres, Peterson argues. Such categorization also enforces the boundaries of genres, making the attempts of artists to "break out" and "cross over" far more difficult. The musical formats of radio stations have the same effect. Thus marketing strategies do not inevitably and necessarily offer what actual receivers most desire. They do, however, provide what markets will accept and, in the process, shape and constrain the forms of cultural expression that are available.

HISTORIES OF AUDIENCEMAKING

Studies of two historically significant instances of audiencemaking conclude this volume. Siefert recounts how the talking machine was turned from a technological curiosity into a commercial music industry. A key step in the process was the legitimation of the recording device as a musical instrument, not only to the public but to dealers who would sell the machines as well as the cylinders and discs on which the music was recorded. Among the competing manufacturers, the Victor Talking Machine Company gambled on the musical genre of grand opera to gain this legitimacy and to differentiate its disc players from competing cylinder players. Opera never sold well in comparison with other genres, but, Siefert argues, it did help to ease sound recordings into genteel parlors and thereby to open the way into the home for other forms of mass-produced entertainment.

And, in conclusion, Snyder suggests that vaudeville really marked the beginning of the mass audience. In the nineteenth century, as New York-based vaudeville circuits sent entertainers around the country, it was possible for the first time to think of a nationwide audience for a common, popular culture. Even as a nationwide system developed, it was both stratified—better known acts played large theaters in large cities—and specialized—Boston really did get cleaner acts than some other cities. But vaudeville's great accomplishment was a degree of national standardization, legitimation (as vaudeville houses were cleaned up and made less rowdy), and popularization (as star performers became national figures). Thus vaudeville, too, helped pave the way for subsequent forms of mass culture.

CONCLUSION

In the conception of mass communication that comes to us from Wilber Schramm, the idea of "audience" has been richly elaborated. Effects researchers may see the audience as the beneficiary of the media's tremendous information gathering and dissemination capacity or else as victim of the media's distorted portrayals of reality. Market researchers may see the audience as decision makers, whether rational or irrational, who must make program choices in multichannel environments. Political theorists with a pluralist bent may see the audience as an electorate that must formulate its voting intentions. Political theorists who have taken a critical turn, on the other hand, may see the audience as an oppressed mass that has been depoliticized by mass-mediated hegemony or else struggles to create oppositional interpretations of media content. Some theorists of the postmodern see the audience as exacting revenge upon the social order by refusal of all meaning while others see the audience as desperately searching for meaning in a culture of voracious consumption.

Conceptions of the audience within these various theoretical traditions exhibit a number of similarities that cut across the traditions. Some of the time, critical theorists join administrative researchers to characterize the audience as subject: an autonomous agent that acts to find or create meaning. And some of the time, both critical and administrative scholars characterize the audience as object: a victim that does not act but is acted upon and thus suffers the imposition, or else destruction, of meaning. But most of time, these scholars examine the message-based communication relationships between media and audience with only cursory attention to the institutional arrangements by which those communication relationships are constructed and maintained.

"Communication" is our field of study, after all, and so it is hardly surprising that we should privilege the communication relationship in our conception of mass communication. However, in the theoretical relocation of "communicator studies" from the individual/organizational to the organizational/institutional level of analysis, the arrangements in which communication relationships are produced become the primary focus of study. This institutional conception seeks to incorporate, and then move beyond, the focus on the perceptions of gatekeepers and the routines of organizations. In such a conception, audiences are seen to be the product of something like a manufacturing process, but they also are seen to be the site of contestation among media firms, measurement services, advertisers, interest groups, government, and other agents of institutional power. The research reports collected in this volume all attempt to enrich our conception of the processes by which these agents construct and maintain their relationships with audiences. These reports can be characterized as research on the work of professional mass communicators, but they also should be understood as research on the life of the audience—studies of the institutional life rather than the personal life, to be sure, but studies of the audience, nonetheless.

REFERENCES

Bagdikian, B. H. (1990). *The media monopoly* (3rd ed.). Boston: Beacon.

Burgoon, J. K., Burgoon, M., & Atkin, C. K. (1982). *The world of the working journalist.* New York: Newspaper Advertising Bureau.

Carey, J. W. (Ed.). (1969). The communications revolution and the professional communicator. In *The sociology of mass media communicators* (Sociological Review Monograph No. 13, pp. 23-38). Keele, Staffordshire, UK: University of Keele.

Darnton, R. (1975). Writing news and telling stories. *Daedalus, 104,* 175-194.

DeFleur, M. L. (1971). Mass media as social systems. In W. Schramm & D. F. Roberts (Eds.), *The process and effects of mass communication* (rev. ed., pp. 63-83). Urbana: University of Illinois Press.

Dervin, B., Grossberg, L., O'Keefe, B., & Wartella, E. (1989). *Rethinking communication* (Vols. 1-2). Newbury Park, CA: Sage.

DiMaggio, P. (1977). Market structure, the creative process and popular culture: Toward an organizational reinterpretation of mass culture theory. *Journal of Popular Culture, 11,* 436-452.

Dreier, P. (1982). The position of the press in the U.S. power structure. *Social Problems, 29,* 298-310.

Espinosa, P. (1982). The audience in the text: Ethnographic observations of a Hollywood story conference. *Media, Culture and Society, 4,* 77-86.

Fishman, M. (1980). *Manufacturing the news.* Austin: University of Texas Press.

Flegel, R. C., & Chaffee, S. H. (1971). Influences of editors, readers and personal opinions on reporters. *Journalism Quarterly, 48,* 645-651.

Gans, H. J. (1972). The famine in American mass communications research. *American Journal of Sociology, 77*(4), 697-705.

Gans, H. J. (1979). *Deciding what's news.* New York: Pantheon.

Gerbner, G. (1983). Ferment in the field. *Journal of Communication, 33*(3).

Gitlin, T. (1980). *The whole world is watching: The role of the news media in the making and unmaking of the new left.* Berkeley: University of California Press.

Herman, E. S., & Chomsky, N. (1988). *Manufacturing consent: The political economy of the mass media.* New York: Pantheon.

Hirsch, P. M. (1972). Processing fads and fashions: An organization-set analysis of cultural industry systems. *American Journal of Sociology, 77,* 639-659.

Hirsch, P. M. (1977). Occupational, organizational and institutional models in mass media research: Toward an integrated framework. In P. M. Hirsch, P. V. Miller, & F. G. Kline (Eds.), *Strategies for communication research* (pp. 13-42). Beverly Hills, CA: Sage.

Kaminsky, S. M. (1985). *American film genres.* Chicago: Nelson-Hall.

Kapsis, R. (1986). Hollywood filmmaking and audience image. In S. Ball-Rokeach & M. G. Cantor (Eds.), *Media, audience, and social structure* (pp. 161-173). Newbury Park, CA: Sage.

Katz, E., & Lazarsfeld, P. F. (1955). *Personal influence.* New York: Free Press.

Klapper, J. (1960). *The effects of mass communication.* New York: Free Press.

Lang, G. E., & Lang, K. (1983). *The battle for public opinion.* New York: Columbia University Press.

Linsky, M. (1986). *Impact: How the press affects federal policymaking.* New York: Norton.

Lippmann, W. (1922). *Public opinion.* New York: Macmillan.

McCombs, M. E., & Shaw, D. L. (1972). The agenda-setting function of the mass media. *Public Opinion Quarterly, 36,* 176-187.

McCombs, M. E., & Shaw, D. L. (1977). Structuring the unseen environment. *Journal of Communication, 26*(2), 18-22.

Montgomery, K. (1989). *Target: Prime time, advocacy groups and the struggle over entertainment television.* New York: Oxford University Press.

Murdock, G., & Golding, P. (1979). Capitalism, communication and class relations. In J. Curran, M. Gurevitch, & J. Woollacott (Eds.), *Mass communication and society* (pp. 12-43). Beverly Hills, CA: Sage.

Nord, D. P. (1980). An economic perspective on formula in popular culture. *Journal of American Culture, 3,* 17-31.

Owen, B. M. (1975). *Economics and freedom of expression: Media structure and the First Amendment.* Cambridge, MA: Harvard University Press.

Owen, B. M., & Wildman, S. S. (1992). *Video economics.* Cambridge, MA: Harvard University Press.

Paletz, D., & Entman, R. M. (1981). *Media power politics.* New York: Free Press.

Peterson, R. A., & Berger, D. G. (1975). Cycles in symbol production: The case of popular music. *American Sociological Review, 40,* 158-173.

Pool, I., & Schulman, I. (1959). Newsmen's fantasies, audiences and newswriting. *Public Opinion Quarterly, 23,* 145-158.

Protess, D., Cook, F. L., Doppelt, J., Ettema, J. S., Gordon, M., Miller, P. V., & Leff, D. (1991). *The journalism of outrage: Investigative reporting and agenda building in America.* New York: Guilford.

Ryan, J., & Peterson, R. A. (1982). The product image: The fate of creativity in country music songwriting. In J. S. Ettema & D. C. Whitney (Eds.), *Individuals in mass media organizations: Creativity and constraint* (pp. 11-32). Beverly Hills, CA: Sage.

Schatz, T. (1988). *The genius of the system: Hollywood filmmaking in the studio era.* New York: Pantheon.

Schiller, H. I. (1969). *Mass communication and American empire.* New York: Augustus M. Kelly.

Schlesinger, P. (1978). *Putting "reality" together: BBC news.* London: Constable.

Schramm, W. (1971). The nature of communication between humans. In W. Schramm & D. F. Roberts (Eds.), *The process and effects of mass communication* (rev. ed., pp. 3-53). Urbana: University of Illinois Press.

Schudson, M. (1978). *Discovering the news.* New York: Basic Books.

Shannon, C., & Weaver, W. (1949). *The mathematical theory of communication.* Urbana: University of Illinois Press.

Tichenor, P., Donohue, G., & Olien, C. (1970). Mass media flow and differential growth in knowledge. *Public Opinion Quarterly, 34,* 159-170.

Tuchman, G. (1972). Objectivity as strategic ritual: An examination of newsmen's notions of objectivity. *American Journal of Sociology, 77*(4), 660-679.

Tuchman, G. (1978). *Making news: A study in the construction of reality.* New York: Free Press.

Turow, J. (1984). Pressure groups and television entertainment: A framework for analysis. In W. D. Rowland, Jr., & B. Watkins (Eds.), *Interpreting television: Current research perspectives* (pp. 142-162). Beverly Hills, CA: Sage.

White, D. M. (1950). The gatekeeper: A case study in the selection of news. *Journalism Quarterly, 27,* 383-396.

Whitney, D. C. (1982). Mass communicator studies: Similarity, difference and level of analysis. In J. S. Ettema & D. C. Whitney (Eds.), *Individuals in mass media organizations: Creativity and constraint* (pp. 241-254). Beverly Hills, CA: Sage.

Whitney, D. C., & Becker, L. B. (1982). "Keeping the gates" for gatekeepers: The effects of wire news. *Journalism Quarterly, 59,* 60-65.

Chapter 2

VICTIM, CONSUMER, OR COMMODITY?
AUDIENCE MODELS IN
COMMUNICATION POLICY

James G. Webster and Patricia F. Phalen

FOR THE BETTER PART of this century, the official goal of American communication policy has been to serve the "public interest, convenience, or necessity" (Federal Radio Commission, 1928). Putting aside the actual quality of service that the public has received, it's difficult to imagine a policy that hasn't somehow cloaked itself in "public interest." For those who deal with media law and regulation, the relevant public is often an audience. Hence, to argue for or against some law or regulation, one must invoke a vision of the audience that portrays its needs, its wants, its weaknesses, or perhaps its economic value. No single vision, however, has dominated the policymaking process. Instead, different, sometimes contradictory, models of the audience have been advanced at different times, allowing diverse concerns to claim the mantle of the public interest.

We should note at the outset that our use of the term *model* is a bit generous. A review of the policymaking process does not reveal clearly articulated, systematically applied audience paradigms. Certainly there are times throughout the history of communication policy when a coherent view of the audience can be seen to inform government actions. But more often, the audience concepts hide just beneath the surface of such actions. They are implied, but not explicitly stated.

AUTHORS' NOTE: We would like to thank Sandra Braman, James Ettema, Timothy Brennan, Rick Morris, and Steven Wildman for their many useful comments on this manuscript.

Nevertheless, audience models are real and remarkably durable. They support and constrain the actions of policymakers. They explain fundamental differences in regulatory philosophies. Indeed, we believe that audience concepts, unspoken though they may be, are among the most powerful determinants of public policy. Our purpose here is to draw them out so their implications can be more fully considered. In doing so, we will state the elements of each model more bluntly than even their proponents might wish.

A SHORT HISTORY
OF MEDIA REGULATION

To appreciate how audience models have animated communication policy, one should recognize the context in which they have been used. At the expense of greatly oversimplifying a long and complicated record of legislation, rulemaking, and court cases, this section identifies certain factors that have given rise to the disparate notions of "audience."

In the United States, media regulation is balanced between direct government control of the media and reliance on largely unregulated marketplaces to serve the public interest. For print media, the clear applicability of First Amendment protections to "the press," as well as the conventional wisdom that all who wished to publish were free to do so, have tipped the scales heavily in favor of the marketplace. For broadcasting and the electronic media, the balancing act has been much trickier. Two features of the broadcast marketplace, in particular, have opened the door for regulatory oversight.

Historically, the most serious deficiency in the broadcast marketplace has been a shortage of frequencies relative to the number of people who wished to use them. Because all were not free to "speak," so the reasoning went, those who were privileged enough to have a government license could be required to provide programming in the public interest. While some scholars maintain that the shortage of frequencies was always a fiction (Hazlett, 1990), the so-called scarcity argument has sustained considerable government regulation of broadcasting.

Broadcasters' heavy reliance on advertising for financial support has further rationalized government regulation. This method of funding took hold in the 1920s and, unlike that of the print media, has accounted for virtually all of the industry's revenues. While it has been argued that advertiser support is consistent with the public interest because it requires broadcasters to "give the people what they want," many are unconvinced. Critics have pointed out that broadcasters actually respond to advertisers, not to the wishes of the public. Stations therefore are unlikely to serve small or otherwise undesirable audiences, especially if there are only a few broadcasters in a market. Moreover, people have no way to express the intensity of their program preferences, as might be the case if they paid directly for the media they consumed.

The apparent shortage of frequencies, in combination with complete reliance on advertiser support, has created a medium that seems quite different than newspapers or magazines. Because of these peculiarities, broadcasting has been rife with incongruities and pretexts for government intervention. On one hand, stations were businesses expected to maximize their audiences and sell them to almost anyone willing to pay. On the other hand, they were privileged "trustees" of the airwaves expected to provide public services, even if it was not in their economic self-interest to do so.

Underpinning these different, and potentially contradictory, roles were very different ways of thinking about the audience. Audience members could be prospective victims who need protection from a system designed to serve commercial interests. They could be citizens of a democracy who depend on media to enlighten them. They could be rational consumers of media content capable of making appropriate program choices no matter what the media serve up. Or they could simply be a commodity to be bought and sold. Depending upon one's view of the audience, rather different policies could be prescribed.

Strangely enough, however, a broadcast system of scarce licenses and advertiser support often allows policymakers to avoid an explicit declaration of their model of the audience. If, for example, broadcasters only offer simple-minded entertainment catering to the "lowest common denominator," the audience can hardly be blamed for not choosing more uplifting fare. As long as the system is somehow faulty, a final judgment on the nature of the audience itself is easily deferred.

That situation, we believe, is coming to an end. The growth of broadband distribution systems and more efficient ways to use the spectrum have greatly diminished, if not completely eliminated, the scarcity problem. Other "pay-per-view" technologies have eased the reliance of electronic media upon advertising. As this happens, it seems likely that audience concepts that have been implied or fragmentary will have to emerge from beneath the surface and be considered in their own right.

THE EFFECTS MODEL:
AUDIENCE AS VICTIM

Throughout the history of communication policy, it has been common to represent the audience as the potential "victim" of the mass media. The notion that people are somehow affected by what they hear or see is as old as the media themselves. On one hand, this model of the audience has great intuitive appeal, as reflected in popular notions about the "power of the press." On the other, an "effects" model of the audience is validated by much social scientific theory and research, ranging from early work on propaganda and attitude change to more contemporary notions of cultivation and agenda setting. This potent combination has allowed policymakers to summon up an effects model of the audience with considerable success.

In its most general form, the model is based on the following assumptions:

1. Audience members are easily exposed to programming that may not be in their own best interest.
2. The media can cultivate an appetite for vulgar, hateful, or trivial programming.
3. The public interest is served by a media system that limits exposure to undesirable programming and promotes exposure to meritorious content.

These simple assumptions do not, however, produce an equally simple model of how an audience can be affected. Rather, there are at least three distinct kinds of victimization that have concerned policymakers. The first is focused on the harm that results from the audience being exposed to bad content. The second is concerned with the harm caused by the media denying people access to good content. The third addresses the harm that results when good content is available but underused by the audience.

The first version is the most obvious form of the effects model and manifests itself in regulations designed to protect the public from specific categories of harmful content. Among the offending materials are obscenity, violence, and certain forms of commercial speech—especially speech that is deliberately misleading. Government efforts to assess and control these have been well documented elsewhere (e.g., Lowery & DeFleur, 1987; Rowland, 1983).

The most apt example in contemporary policymaking is the FCC's on-again/off-again battle with indecency in broadcasting. Of course, the audience of greatest concern here has been children. Well before the arrival of broadcasting, children were judged to be a special category of people, particularly susceptible to harm. The easy accessibility of electronic media has only heightened anxieties about children as potential victims.

In the late 1980s Ronald Reagan's FCC, which had acted so vigorously to reduce government intervention in broadcasting, took several stations to task for airing indecent material. In doing so, the commission unsettled the easily understood, if simple-minded, body of law that prohibited broadcasting certain words at times of the day when children were likely to be in the audience (*FCC v. Pacifica Foundation,* 1978). Instead, the commission considered a blanket prohibition on indecency, which would have reduced the adult audience to hearing "only what is fit for children" (*Butler v. Michigan,* 1957, p. 383). Regulators argued that protective policies were especially necessary because of the intrusive nature of broadcasting: "Because the broadcast audience is constantly tuning in and out, prior warnings cannot completely protect the listener or viewer from unexpected program content" (*FCC v. Pacifica Foundation,* 1978, p. 748). Thus the specter of harmful content victimizing even vigilant members of the audience led the Congress to legislate a round-the-clock ban on indecency despite the fact that (a) indecency in the print media is constitutionally protected speech and (b) the scientific evidence of harmful effects on children, let alone adults, is equivocal. (See *Comments of Action for Children's Television* et al., 1990.)

The second version of the effects model is somewhat less obvious, but certainly no less important. Under the assumptions of the model, it is quite possible for audiences to be harmed if they are denied good programming. Stated more affirmatively, the audience can be conceived as a community whose interests are ill-served in the absence of programming offering diverse views, artistic merit, and educational benefit that all may share. In fact, this notion of the audience pervades government-owned systems throughout the world and is described by Ang (1991) as the "audience-as-public" construct: "The audience-as-public consists not of consumers, but of citizens who must be reformed, educated, informed as well as entertained—in short, 'served'—presumably to enable them to better perform their democratic rights and duties" (pp. 28-29).

For many policymakers in the United States, serving the public has meant providing the audience with access to diverse ideas. This particular concept of good service is grounded in First Amendment theory, which prescribes a free "marketplace of ideas" as the preferred mechanism for discovering truth and promoting democracy. The importance of creating such a public forum is evident in early pronouncements of the FCC:

> It is axiomatic that one of the most vital questions of mass communication in a democracy is the development of an informed public opinion through the public dissemination of news and ideas concerning the vital issues of the day. . . . Unquestionably, then, the standard of public interest, convenience and necessity as applied to radio broadcasting must be interpreted in the light of this basic purpose. (Federal Communications Commission, 1949, p. 1249)

Unfortunately, in commercial broadcasting this idealized marketplace seems easily compromised by the willingness of the media to cultivate and serve the more base appetites of the audience. As a result, American policymakers have often focused their attention on the harm that flows from denying people good programming and have advocated policies designed to prevent such victimization.

Nowhere are the elements of this version of the effects model given greater force than in Newton Minow's "Vast Wasteland" speech of 1961— arguably the most influential public address ever made by an FCC chairman. Minow (1978) takes as a given the "overwhelming impact" (p. 284) of broadcasting on the American people. While naming a few "good" television programs, he chides broadcasters for their slavish pursuit of higher ratings and asserts that "if parents, teachers, and ministers conducted their responsibilities by following the ratings, children would have a steady diet of ice cream, school holidays and no Sunday School" (p. 286). Throughout, he makes it clear that people are not served just by giving them what they want—"some say that the public interest is merely what interests the public. I disagree" (p. 283).

Minow seems a bit uncomfortable with how his own remarks portray the American people, for he is at pains to credit them with "good sense and good taste" and being "wiser than some of the broadcasters—and politicians—think" (p. 286). In the end, he finesses the issue by asserting that "most of television's problems stem from a lack of competition . . . with more channels on the air, we will be able to provide every community with enough stations to offer service to all parts of the public" (p. 290). In the early 1960s, at least, it was possible to indict commercial media without rendering a final verdict on the audience itself. Economic constraints in the marketplace were more easily blamed for the media's failure to give audiences what was best for them.

The rather abstract assertion that under limited channels the choices of the mass audience could result in an inappropriate mix of programming was translated into public policy through a succession of FCC actions and court cases sometimes known as the "radio format controversy." The central question of the controversy was whether the commission should preserve a unique radio format, such as classical music, even though the station's owner believed another format would be more popular. In 1974 the Court of Appeals provided its answer: "There is a public interest in a diversity of broadcast entertainment formats. The disappearance of a distinctive format may deprive a significant segment of the public of the benefits of radio, at least at their first preference level" (*Citizens Committee to Save WEFM v. FCC,* 1974, p. 262).

Like Minow, the court pointed out deficiencies in the marketplace that caused the absence of certain programming and the harm that could result. Once again, blame was placed on the system rather than the behavior of listeners. As long as these flaws persisted, it was the government's responsibility to protect the public interest by providing diversity in both news and entertainment. In reaching this conclusion, the court seemed fully in step with an earlier Supreme Court decision that proclaimed "the right of the public to receive suitable access to social, political, esthetic, moral, and other ideas" (*Red Lion Broadcasting Co., Inc. v. FCC,* 1969, p. 390).

Despite the recent ascendancy of more laissez-faire policies, which we will review shortly, this version of the effects model is still a force in policymaking. For example, in *Metro Broadcasting, Inc. v. Federal Communications Commission* (1990), the Supreme Court handed down a controversial decision affirming the constitutionality of certain broadcast policies that gave preferences to media owners based on their race. In doing so, the court reasoned that diverse ownership was likely to promote diversity of expression and that all segments of the audience would ultimately gain: "The benefits of such diversity are not limited to the members of minority groups who gain access to the broadcasting industry by virtue of the ownership policies; rather, the benefits redound to all members of the viewing and listening audience" (p. 3011). There remains, it would seem, a strong inclination on the part of policymakers to make good content available, lest the public be harmed by its absence.

The third version of the effects model is a subtle, but profound, variation on the second. Here again the audience is harmed by being unexposed to good content, but the source of harm is different. This condition occurs when there is good content available but the audience ignores it.

The possibility of such self-victimization became an issue in the 1970s when the commission contemplated the "television of abundance" offered by cable. As the FCC confronted the growth of cable, it recognized a potential threat to one of its most cherished objectives. The commission had long favored news and public affairs programming as well as "localism" in broadcasting. These biases were motivated, at least in part, by a desire to keep the people informed about issues of public importance. Cable television, however, seemed capable of undermining that function by diverting viewers to less uplifting fare. One passage in the commission's 1979 report on the economic relationship between cable and broadcasting (Federal Communications Commission, 1979b) is particularly revealing:

> Television may have an important effect in shaping the attitudes and values of citizens, in making the electorate more informed and responsible, and in contributing to greater understanding and respect among different racial and ethnic groups. . . . Historically, the FCC has encouraged particular types of programming—local news, public affairs, instructional programs—on these grounds. To the extent that a change in broadcast-cable policy would dramatically change the amount by which these programs are not only broadcast *but viewed,* these issues could be an important component of a policy debate. (pp. 638-639, italics added)

Despite these concerns, and evidence that cable does indeed divert audiences from local news, the FCC has never acted to enforce exposure to news and public affairs. In fact, with the possible exception of providing "equal opportunities" under Section 315 of the Communications Act, or some attempts at balancing content under the old Fairness Doctrine, few public policies have sought to affirmatively provide an audience for specific programming. American policymakers have been reluctant to compel people to watch what was "good for them."

In part this is because the same market deficiencies—such as scarcity— that justified government intervention rendered the need for such policies moot. With just a few channels available, simply requiring that a message be aired effectively guaranteed an audience. In such a world, the right to speak was, de facto, a right to be heard. That this will continue to be the case, however, is doubtful. If a multiplicity of channels allows people to avoid good programming, then this largely dormant, and unflattering, model of the audience may play an increasingly important role in public policy.

THE MARKETPLACE MODEL:
AUDIENCE AS CONSUMER

Although the effects model is still evident in the policy discourse of today, another model of the audience began to dominate policymaking in the late 1970s and 1980s. This view of the audience, the "marketplace model," casts people in the role of consumers who enter the marketplace and select the products that suit their tastes. Like the effects model, this concept of the audience has considerable intuitive appeal. Most Americans accept the idea that adults are capable of entering a market and shopping wisely. Additionally, the model is sustained by a powerful body of economic theory. As early as the 1950s, neoclassical economists began developing a theoretical position that, by the 1970s, was holding sway among many policymakers (e.g., Noll, Peck, & McGowan, 1973; Owen & Wildman, 1992; Steiner, 1952). The elements of the marketplace model are as follows:

1. Audience members are rational, well-informed individuals who will act in their own self-interest.
2. Audience members come to the media with well-formed program preferences that cause them to choose specific content.
3. The public interest is served by a media system that is responsive to audience preferences as revealed in their viewing choices.

This concept of the audience helped rationalize the move toward deregulation that began during the Nixon administration, continued through the Carter presidency, and reached its zenith during the Reagan years. No one argued the marketplace model with more conviction than Mark Fowler, chairman of the FCC during most of the 1980s. And nowhere is Fowler's vision made more plain than in his 1982 manifesto, "A Marketplace Approach to Broadcast Regulation" (Fowler & Brenner, 1982). There, in direct contradiction of Newton Minow, is the declaration that "the public's interest . . . defines the public interest" (p. 210).

The increasing popularity of the marketplace model is evident in a number of regulations and court decisions that rely upon the choice making of audiences to guide public policy. Once again, the radio format controversy illustrates the point. By the mid-1970s the commission was determined to test, and try to overturn, the requirement that it be involved in format selection. In a 1976 Memorandum Opinion and Order, which

made significant reference to a paper by economist Bruce Owen (see Owen, 1977), the commission wrote that

> the marketplace is the best way to allocate entertainment formats in radio, whether the hoped for result is expressed in First Amendment terms (i.e., promoting the greatest diversity of listening choices for the public) or in economic terms (i.e., maximizing the welfare of consumers of radio programs). (Federal Communications Commission, 1976, p. 863)

The commission went on to argue that the Court of Appeals' strategy to "maximize format diversity through regulatory fiat could very well result in a diminution of consumer welfare" (p. 684). While recognizing the imperfections of the marketplace, in 1981 the Supreme Court put the matter to rest by finding that the commission could rely "on market forces to promote diversity in radio and entertainment formats and to satisfy the entertainment preferences of listeners" (*FCC v. WNCN Listeners Guild,* 1981, p. 604).

The foregoing model is best thought of as an economic model in which audience members select the programs or formats to suit their tastes. Whether the same model of the audience is compatible with the "marketplace of ideas" is another matter. Given the popularity and power of this metaphor, one might imagine that the role of consumers in this marketplace was well understood. If, as First Amendment theory holds, the truth will ultimately emerge from a clash of ideas, surely the audience must play a crucial role in the process. Does this metaphor assume, like the economic model, that audience members will choose ideas to suit their tastes? Does the metaphor require people to hear diverse ideas? Does it further require that people engage in thoughtful reflection upon what they have heard? To such questions, policymakers have offered surprisingly few answers.

The most ardent proponents of the economic model are inclined to argue that these questions are largely irrelevant. All the First Amendment requires is that individuals have a "right to speak." According to Owen (1975):

> This very freedom to enter the market, to test consumer response, which is guaranteed by the competitive mechanism, may be all that is essential to freedom of expression (from a constitutional viewpoint) *provided consumers demand the right information about political matters.* Surely the framers

of the constitution did not have in mind an absolute right to survival in the marketplace for all potential purveyors of ideas. (p. 27, italics added)

According to this model, the audience is sovereign. If the audience demands diverse content, then the marketplace will provide it in its most appropriate forms, especially if people can pay for programming and no provider is prohibited from entering the market. If, on the other hand, the public does not demand diversity, none will be forthcoming. For true believers in the economic marketplace, that too is an acceptable policy outcome. Others would surely be less sanguine about such a result.

It is clear that the effects model and the marketplace model are based on distinct notions of what is good for the audience. The marketplace model defines the "best" result as whatever the audience wants to watch. The effects model, in contrast, sets up standards of "good" that are independent of audience preference. The tension is illustrated in a 1979 FCC report: "There are certain social, political, and moral goals in a society that are largely independent of market considerations. Thus, when markets respond efficiently to consumer wants, some persons may nonetheless judge that those wants are 'undesirable' and should not be satisfied" (Federal Communications Commission, 1979a, p. 496). This reasoning is central to the debate between proponents of the marketplace model, who have tended to favor deregulation, and those more concerned with the adverse effects of an unregulated marketplace.

THE COMMODITY MODEL: AUDIENCE AS COIN OF EXCHANGE

There is a third model of the audience that seems to coexist with each of the other two. On any number of occasions, the government has conceptualized audiences as a commodity, leaving aside questions of victimization or rational choice. A typical expression of this model is found in the FCC's 1979 document on the deregulation of radio: "In a sense the listener is not the consumer of radio but the product which broadcasters sell to advertisers. In other words, in radio broadcasting true consumer (listener) sovereignty does not exist insofar as advertiser wants do not correspond with listener wants" (Federal Communications Commission, 1979a, p. 600).

The commodity model is less wedded to any notion of audiences as individual decision makers and is more a reflection of the fact that, under advertiser support, they are a common coin of exchange. The assumptions of the model are as follows:

1. Audiences have an economic value that is expressed in measurements of their size and composition.
2. Commercial media must be allowed to create and sell audiences if the media are to exist.
3. The public interest is served by preserving the system of advertiser-supported media.

Most laws and regulations have some effect on the financial condition of the media and related industries. Because these policies have an impact on "the bottom line," they attract the attention of many participants in the policymaking process. Certainly the FCC cannot be oblivious to the economic consequences of its policies. After all, the commission is responsible for seeing to it that broadcasting serves the public interest. If broadcasters are driven out of business by some ill-conceived policy, it could compromise the commission's most sacred mandate.

While profit and loss statements would seem an obvious source of information for policymakers, these data are not always used. For one thing, the commission long ago stopped collecting financial statements from broadcasters. For another, economic injury might be too far advanced by the time it shows up on company ledgers. As an alternative, policymakers will often use audience information, especially ratings data, as a surrogate for industry revenues.

One of the most straightforward uses of the commodity model can be found in the workings of the Copyright Royalty Tribunal (CRT). Under compulsory licensing arrangements, cable systems must pay for the right to carry certain broadcast signals. Each year, this creates a fund worth hundreds of millions of dollars. The CRT's job is to determine how that fund should be divided among various claimants. Chief among the claimants is the Motion Picture Association of America (MPAA), which has argued that copyright owners should receive royalties in direct proportion to how much their programs were actually viewed.

To make the case that it deserves the largest piece of the pie, the MPAA annually commissions a special study from A. C. Nielsen, based on market-by-market ratings data. Nielsen provides the MPAA with a list of every qualifying program, the number of quarter hours it was broadcast, and the number of cable households that viewed each quarter hour via retransmission of "distant" signals (Motion Picture Association of America, 1988). While the CRT is free to allocate funds in whatever manner it chooses, the MPAA's approach has become the method of choice. In this application, audience size becomes a kind of weight that determines the distribution of revenues, as is the case in more direct exchanges between buyers and sellers.

A fascinating, if somewhat more convoluted, example of how the government has used the commodity model of the audience emerges in the cases of "economic injury." Here, the question before policymakers is whether competition for a broadcaster's audience can be so damaging as to require that the licensee be protected from harm. While the courts initially ruled that this was none of the government's concern (*FCC v. Sanders Brothers Radio Station,* 1940), by the 1950s the Court of Appeals had qualified that hands-off policy. The court reasoned as follows:

> To license two stations where there is revenue only for one may result in no good service at all. So economic injury to an existing station, while not in and of itself a matter of moment, becomes important when on the facts it spells diminution or destruction of service. At that point the element of injury ceases to be a matter of purely private concern. (*Carroll Broadcasting Company v. FCC,* 1958, p. 443)

While the court's motivation was to protect the public from being "victimized" by ruinous competition, it did so by recognizing the commodity value of the audience and preserving that commodity for the exclusive use of an incumbent licensee.

In practice, the commission made little use of this doctrine in granting or denying broadcast licenses. However, as soon as it seemed cable television might "divert" audiences from local broadcasters, the FCC applied the logic of economic injury with a vengeance. Through the 1960s and early 1970s, it implemented a number of measures that diminished cable's ability to compete for the broadcaster's audience (see LeDuc, 1973). These actions were largely preemptive and often taken in explicit recognition that some members of the public might be worse off as a result. As the commission noted in one of its early decisions denying a cable system the means to import a distant signal: "True, a grant of the instant application would permit the rendition of better service by the CATV, but at the expense of destroying the local station and its rural coverage. The CATV would permit the urban areas a choice of coverage, but the local station . . . serves a wider area" (Federal Communications Commission, 1962, p. 464). Through such rulings, the commission extended the use of the commodity model. Not only could audiences be quarantined for their own good, some members of the audience could be denied freer choice so their commodity value could subsidize service to rural areas.

More recently, the FCC has handled claims of audience diversion in the context of its rules on syndicated exclusivity. These rules, which went into effect in 1972, were intended to ensure that broadcasters who bought the exclusive rights to syndicated programming would not have that privilege undermined by a cable system that imported a distant signal with the same program. The imported signal, it was assumed, would divert some audience that rightly belonged to the local station. While the commission later dropped the rule, in 1988 it decided to reimpose syndicated exclusivity. During that proceeding, the parties at interest all submitted analyses of ratings data purporting to show that audience losses did or did not occur in the absence of the rule. In reimposing the rule, the commission reasoned that "the ability to limit diversion means broadcasters will be able to attract larger audiences, making them more attractive to advertisers, thereby enabling them to obtain more and better programming for their viewers" ("The Why's and Wherefore's of Syndex II," 1988, pp. 58-59).

Clearly, American policymakers have few inhibitions about conceptualizing the audience as a commodity. In fact, the arguments of some licensees and copyright holders imply that they actually own the audiences associated with their franchises. The commodity model, however, is not the simple handmaiden of an unfettered, fully competitive marketplace. It has often justified policies—such as preventing economic injury—that constrain competition in the name of preserving "good" programming. Even in a regulatory era that favors competition, the FCC has continued to voice concern about the economic viability of broadcast media. For example, as part of its reconsideration of ownership rules, the commission stated:

> Maximizing competition may provide many voices, but each might maintain such a minute fraction of the audience that it would lack an economic base sufficient to effectively serve the needs of the public. On a local level, we believe that stations separately owned will each tend to strive for the same core audience with roughly the same type of programming, while the same stations managed in common may have greater incentives to appeal separately to distinct segments of the audience with distinct programming. (Federal Communications Commission, 1991, p. 3276)

Thus the commodity model of the audience has a chameleonlike quality. It is a suitable companion to either the effects model or the marketplace model, which are themselves profoundly at odds. One may argue that audience choices are dangerous in their consequences, or that they are an appropriate expression of rational preferences, and still recognize that, in the aggregate, those choices create a commodity. One may also dispense with the first two models altogether and deal with the commodity value of the audience on its own terms. Under the commodity model, "good policy" is that which ensures that the economic base of the media remains intact.

CONCLUSION

While it is possible to distill three rather distinct models of the audience from the history of communication policy, one should not conclude that those who invoke a particular model recognize it as such or that they will advance that model consistently over time. While some are predisposed to a certain view of the audience, many players in the process will adopt whatever model suits their purpose at the moment. This is especially true of the private interests that vie for advantage in the arena of public policy. One can, for example, find broadcasters using a marketplace model to argue against any number of government regulations. Yet they are equally adept at invoking an effects model to argue for protection from ruinous competition that might ultimately victimize the audience. Such potentially contradictory views of the audience are surprisingly difficult to detect, especially given the structural idiosyncracies of the broadcast marketplace. Indeed, the fact that the same people use different models at different times has probably obscured the role of audience models in policy debates.

We have suggested, however, that technological developments are gradually minimizing flaws in the marketplace, and that as this happens the role of audience models will become increasingly clear. While we can expect the "blue sky" of technological abundance to be clouded over for some time to come, it is interesting to imagine how these models might be applied in a new media environment without structural limitations. Specifically we should consider what becomes of these models if (a) all who wish to electronically communicate to a mass audience are free to do so and (b) people can pay directly for the media they consume.

Strictly speaking, the commodity model of the audience exists only in a world of advertiser-supported media. To the degree that the new media environment features direct payments for programming, concepts about the commodity value of the audience will have to change. In all likelihood, though, this will be more a change in vocabulary than substance. Under either method of funding, the audience will still be seen as the determinant of revenues. The fact that one approach depends on the value of audiences to advertisers while the other depends on the ability of audiences to pay fees will not make a fundamental difference in applications of this model to public policy. At most, we might rename it the "money model" of the audience.

More interesting developments would seem to be in store for the effects and marketplace models. We suspect proponents of the effects model will have a more difficult time making their case in the new media environment. While it's safe to assume there will always be policies designed to limit people's exposure to harmful content, policies that champion diverse or meritorious content would become increasingly difficult to defend. On one hand, if a freely functioning marketplace produces the kind of pluralistic programming that many hope for, policies that require such programming are simply unnecessary. On the other hand, if that marketplace fails to "deliver the goods," then one is left with the unenviable task of remedying that deficiency in some meaningful way.

If the effects model is to have an important role in public policy deliberations, it will probably be as justification for more active government interventions. Robert Entman has suggested one such possibility based on the notion of the audience as a community whose best interests require the airing of diverse views. He does not advocate a public right to hear but a "right to be exposed to diverse ideas" (Entman, 1991, p. 2). While it's not clear how this right would be implemented, it could conceivably justify policies designed to encourage levels of exposure that would not otherwise occur. The FCC hinted at such a possibility when it considered the impact of cable television on local news viewership. Whether such paternalistic policies could ever gain widespread acceptance is another matter.

At first glance, it seems likely that the marketplace model will be even more preeminent in the new media environment. After all, it is for such an environment that the laws of supply and demand seem best suited. If anything, we might expect a greater sanctification of consumer choice in a market where sellers are free to come and go and buyers are free to express the intensity of their preferences in the prices they pay for programming.

The biggest challenge to this model will not be in its ability to rationalize economic choices, but in its perceived compatibility with the "marketplace of ideas." While some may insist the "right to speak" is all that either marketplace requires, we suspect many policymakers will put the marketplace of ideas to a sterner test. Specifically, they will ask to what extent the marketplace actually produces diversity. This is a test that the economic marketplace might fail to meet in one of two ways.

The most obvious, and traditional, measure of diversity is "diversity of content." Will the actions of buyers and sellers in this marketplace produce a diverse universe of programming for all who wish to partake? Skeptics argue that, because unpopular ideas are likely to be unprofitable, they will be undersupplied by the marketplace (Entman, 1991). Hence genuine diversity will go unrealized. But even if there is a diverse universe of programming, this marketplace of ideas might still be an empty shell.

Unfortunately, diversity of supply does not guarantee what might be called "diversity of consumption." Quite the contrary, as the menu of content becomes increasingly diverse, each individual is in a position to consume an ever narrower diet of programming. In fact, much of what we know about human psychology and audience behavior suggests that this is precisely how "rational" people are likely to deal with diversity (Webster, 1989). If increasing diversity of content means that each individual is actually exposed to less diversity of expression, it's hard to see how such a result facilitates the marketplace of ideas.

If the economic marketplace fails to achieve diversity in either sense, it will be difficult for its proponents to imply that it is at one with the marketplace of ideas. In that event, the broad appeal of this model will be diminished. That could set the stage for the reemergence of an effects model, and a more intrusive regime of regulation.

To us, the critical questions are those of audience. What is the public's appetite for diversity? How can that appetite be cultivated or satisfied? And in the future, what will be the most compelling ways of thinking about the audience? Will the models of the audience be altered? Will new models be formed? The answers to these questions will determine much about the conduct of communication policy in the decades to come.

REFERENCES

Ang, I. (1991). *Desperately seeking the audience.* London: Routledge.

Butler v. Michigan, 352 U.S. 380 (1957).

Carroll Broadcasting Company v. FCC, 258 F. 440 (1958).

Citizens Committee to Save WEFM v. FCC, 506 F. 246 (1974).

Comments of Action for Children's Television, American Civil Liberties Union, Association of Independent Television Stations, Inc., Capital Cities/ABC, Inc., CBS, Inc., Infinity Broadcasting Corporation, Motion Picture Association of America, Inc., National Association of Broadcasters, National Broadcasting Company, Inc., National Public Radio, People for the American Way, Post-Newsweek Stations, Inc., Public Broadcasting Service, Radio-Television News Directors Association, Recording Industry Association of America, The Reporters Committee for Freedom of the Press, Society of Professional Journalists. (1990). Filed before the FCC in the matter of enforcement of prohibitions against broadcast indecency in 18 U.S.C. s 1464, MM Docket No. 89-494.

Entman, R. M. (1991, April). *A policy analytical approach to the First Amendment.* Paper presented at the 1991 Research Conference for the Bicentennial of the First Amendment, Williamsburg, VA.

FCC v. Pacifica Foundation, 438 U.S. 726 (1978).

FCC v. Sanders Brothers Radio Station, 309 U.S. 470 (1940).

FCC v. WNCN Listeners Guild, 450 U.S. 582 (1981).

Federal Communications Commission. (1949). *In the matter of editorializing by broadcast licensees,* 13 F.C.C. 1246.

Federal Communications Commission. (1962). *Carter Mountain Transmission Corp,* 32 F.C.C. 459.

Federal Communications Commission. (1976). *In the matter of development of policy re: changes in entertainment formats for broadcast stations,* 60 F.C.C. 858.

Federal Communications Commission. (1979a). *In the matter of deregulation of radio,* 73 F.C.C. 457.

Federal Communications Commission. (1979b). *In the matter of inquiry into the economic relationship between broadcasting and cable television,* 71 F.C.C. 636.

Federal Communications Commission. (1991). *In re revision of radio rules and policies,* 6 F.C.C. Rcd 3275.

Federal Radio Commission. (1928). *Statement made by the Commission, August 23, 1928, relative to public interest, convenience, or necessity,* 2 F.R.C. Ann. Rep. 166.

Fowler, M. S., & Brenner, D. L. (1982). A marketplace approach to broadcast regulation. *Texas Law Review, 60,* 207-257.

Hazlett, T. (1990). The rationality of U.S. regulation of the broadcast spectrum. *Journal of Law and Economics, 30,* 133-175.

LeDuc, D. R. (1973). *Cable television and the FCC: A crisis in media control.* Philadelphia: Temple University Press.

Lowery, S., & DeFleur, M. L. (1987). *Milestones in mass communication research: Media effects* (2nd ed.). New York: Longman.

Metro Broadcasting, Inc. v. Federal Communications Commission, 110 S.Ct. 2997 (1990).

Minow, N. N. (1978). Address by Newton N. Minow to the National Association of Broadcasters, Washington, DC. In F. Kahn (Ed.), *Documents of American broadcasting* (3rd ed., pp. 281-291). Englewood Cliffs, NJ: Prentice Hall.

Motion Picture Association of America. (1988). *A guide to MPAA and cable copyright royalty distribution.* Washington, DC: Author.

Noll, R. G., Peck, M. G., & McGowan, J. J. (1973). *Economic aspects of television regulation.* Washington, DC: Brookings Institution.

Owen, B. M. (1975). *Economics and freedom of expression: Media structure and the First Amendment.* Cambridge, MA: Ballinger.

Owen, B. M. (1977). Regulating diversity: The case of radio formats. *Journal of Broadcasting, 21,* 305-319.

Owen, B. M., & Wildman, S. W. (1992). *Video economics.* Cambridge, MA: Harvard University Press.

Red Lion Broadcasting Co., Inc v. FCC, 395 U.S. 367 (1969).

Rowland, W. (1983). *The politics of TV violence: Policy uses of communication research.* Beverly Hills, CA: Sage.

Steiner, P. O. (1952). Program patterns and preferences, and the workability of competition in radio broadcasting. *Quarterly Journal of Economics, 66,* 194-223.

Webster, J. G. (1989). Television audience behavior: Patterns of exposure in the new media environment. In J. Salvaggio & J. Bryant (Eds.), *Media use in the information age: Emerging patterns of adoption and consumer use* (pp. 197-216). Hillsdale, NJ: Lawrence Erlbaum.

The why's and wherefore's of syndex II. (1988, May 23). *Broadcasting,* pp. 58-59.

Chapter 3

PRODUCING CHILDREN'S TELEVISION PROGRAMS

Ellen A. Wartella

SINCE THE PASSAGE of the Children's Television Act of 1990, there has been considerable growth in the production of children's television. In addition to the four commercial networks' block of children's programs on Saturday morning, and weekday afternoons for Fox, there has been increased interest on local independent stations and especially on cable networks (USA Network, the Learning Channel, the Family Channel, the Cartoon Network, and, of course, Nickelodeon) in children's programming. In December 1993, even the stalwart public television system announced a renewed commitment to an expanded daily block of 9 hours of children's programming.

All of this activity in the marketplace brings with it high expectations for a renaissance in children's television, akin to the so-called golden age of early 1950s children's TV (e.g., Melody, 1973). As in the 1950s, when children's programs were found throughout the broadcast week and in a wide variety of programming formats and content, children's television in the 1990s displays increasingly varied formats (quiz shows and news shows have returned to children's TV in the 1990s) as well as increased numbers of programs. In this chapter, we will examine research on how producers of children's programs view their audiences as well as research on the nature of programming for children at both the national commercial network and the public television network levels. This project has added urgency, for an explicit aim of the 1990 Children's Television Act is the promotion of more, and more diverse, programming for children. If the act succeeds, its success will depend on the extent to which constraints on production internal to the television industry are lessened. In this chapter, we will discuss both the changes in the external environment as well as the nature of internal constraints that need to be addressed if a renaissance is to occur.

In other words, this chapter works with an implicit model of the production of children's television. It suggests that, like the production of other television and other mass entertainment (see Ettema & Whitney, 1982; Turow, 1984), children's TV production is constrained by externalities—chief among them the regulatory framework and environment, the economic superstructure, and the industry structure of networks, cable networks, and independent producers—as well as internal constraints. Among these are producers' notions of their audience—what children are, what they like, how they watch, what they can and do learn—and the practices—technical and technological, creative, and political—producers use to make children's programs.

CHANGES IN THE EXTERNAL ENVIRONMENT FOR CHILDREN'S TELEVISION

The 1990 Children's Television Act is the first national legislation directed at children's television. It came after a decade of government investigations into children's television and at least a half dozen congressional hearings dealing with children's programming (Kunkel, 1991). Since the establishment of Action for Children's Television (ACT) and its 1970 Federal Communications Commission petition to examine the quality of children's television, there has been vocal criticism of the nature of children's television fare and the inadequacy of the television industry's attempts to serve child audiences. Moreover, the 1990 act is an important reaffirmation of the requirement that broadcasters serve the "public interest, convenience, and necessity" (Sec. 315, Federal Communications Act, 1934) after more than a decade in which the Federal Communications Commission has insisted that marketplace competition adequately services television audience needs.

The act was intended to "increase the amount of educational and information broadcast television programming available to children" (Children's Television Act of 1990). Two of its provisions are of most importance for the future of children's programming. First, broadcasters must provide television programming that serves the educational and informational needs of children. Broadcasters may be held accountable for their actions with regard to children in license reviews every 5 years. In implementing the act, the FCC (1991, p. 2114) has stated that content will qualify if it "furthers the positive development of the child in any respect, including the child's cognitive/intellectual or emotional/social needs." Either programming that is aimed at a general audience, or programming specifically designed for children, will be considered and it is up to the broadcasters to identify which programming meets their obligation to child audiences.

Second, the act established a National Endowment for Children's Educational Television, housed within the National Telecommunication and Information Agency in the Department of Commerce, through which new programming ventures can be funded. In its first round, for $2.4 million, the endowment funded 12 projects, in various stages of development, focusing on programs aimed at children ages 8 to 12. While only $1 million was authorized for fiscal 1994, increased allocations for the endowment are anticipated in 1995 and 1996.

Early expectations for the act were high, that this first piece of national legislation would promote more and better children's television. However, watchdog consumer groups quickly found evidence of a lack of sincerity on the part of broadcasters. For instance, in 1992 the Center for Media Education, in cooperation with the Institute for Public Representation of the Georgetown University Law Center (Center for Media Education, 1992), reviewed broadcaster compliance with the act by examining license renewal applications of all commercial stations in the first eight states where stations were required to file renewals (Arkansas, Indiana, Kentucky, Louisiana, Michigan, Mississippi, Ohio, and Tennessee). The reviewers were particularly interested in the degree to which broadcasters were creating new programming intended to meet children's specific educational needs. They found that, overall, television broadcasters were not making a serious effort to service these needs: Minimal information about the children's requirement was included in license renewals, and although "some" new programs had been developed to meet the FCC children's requirement, the vast majority of stations were redefining old programs and claiming they had informational or educational potential. Specifically, of the 58 station renewals examined, only 10 reported production of locally originated regularly scheduled programs and only 1 reported in its renewal application that it created a show to meet the act requirement. Rather, stations claimed that general information programs such as news shows had informational content for children and were recasting traditional Saturday morning cartoon fare (e.g., *GI Joe,*

The Jetsons, and *Leave It to Beaver*) as having prosocial themes and thus meeting the FCC requirement. Dale Kunkel's analysis of 48 local commercial television stations' license renewal documents from 1992 reinforced the earlier study. He found that, although the stations claimed an average of 3.4 hours per week of programming "specifically designed" to meet the educational needs of children, many of the programs were of dubious educational merit, such as *GI Joe* and *Teenage Mutant Ninja Turtles.* Moreover, nearly 2 out of every 10 stations failed to demonstrate how any of their shows were specifically designed to meet children's educational needs, and 3 out of 10 stations failed to provide the basic required information—that is, brief program description and time, date, and duration of the show—for the FCC to assess their programming for children (Kunkel, 1991).

In spring 1993 the FCC called for an inquiry to determine whether the broadcasting industry was meeting the mandate of the Children's Television Act. The surrounding discussions of the act made it clear that the definition of programming for children that meets children's information and educational needs itself needed further clarification. And it became clear that the way broadcasters conceive of children as an audience for programming, as well as the process through which children's programs are produced and developed, needed scrutinizing. By summer 1993, the industry magazine *Broadcasting and Cable* reported that, while "the original FCC implementing rules gave broadcasters wide latitude in determining what is educational and informational programming and how much is enough to meet their statutory obligation" (p. 72), criticism from public interest groups and Congress had led the commission to consider the requirement of a minimum of 1 hour per day of children's programming. Furthermore, in 1993 the FCC was considering further definitions of educational programming. Clearly, under attack was the attachment of a prosocial message at the beginning or end of an entertainment program and the definition of core educational shows. According to *Broadcasting and Cable,* the FCC was considering that,

> to avoid definitional problems, we believe it may be appropriate to specify that the primary objective qualifying core children's programming should be educational and informational with entertainment as a secondary goal. In other words, we believe broadcasters should focus on programming that has as its explicit purpose service to the educational and informational needs of children, with the implicit purpose of entertainment, rather than the converse. (McAvoy, 1993, pp. 42-43)

The ensuing debate regarding the nature of "educational and informational programming" gives some clues as to how commercial broadcasters view child audiences. For instance, in filings before the FCC, the National Association of Broadcasters (NAB) (1993) requested that the FCC not impose quantitative mandatory programming requirements and not define core programming with a secondary entertainment perspective. First, the NAB suggests that short programming segments (such as informational drop-ins at the beginning and end of shows) should be allowed to meet the FCC children's programming requirement. Moreover, the NAB (1993) made assertions about the nature of child audiences:

> The NAB believes . . . that the Commission should not propose to specifically "label" short segment programming as only secondarily important. If that were done, NAB would fear that, as is discussed above with regard to requiring specific amounts of programming, this valuable type of programming might be discounted by both broadcasters and the Commission. Rather . . . short segment programming is well suited to children's short attention spans and can often be locally produced with acceptable production quality and thus may be a particularly appropriate way for a local broadcaster to respond to specific children's concerns. Short segments also can be effective in reinforcing particular messages and, when placed in or adjacent to popular entertainment shows, can reach large numbers of children. NAB suggests that this important form not be discounted by the commission or broadcasters, but rather be encouraged.
>
> Similarly, NAB believes it would not serve the goals of the ACT or the needs of children to relegate to "implicit" or "secondary" status the entertainment value of educational and informational programming. We would assert that any kind of children's programming must have high entertainment value to be watched and assimilated. (pp. 18-19, 21)

Two assumptions about the child audience—the importance of short segments of information and the need to be entertained—thus are clearly articulated in the justification of broadcasters' view of Children's Television Act requirements.

Another element of the external environment that must be acknowledged is the growth in the 1980s of the children's advertising market. During the 1980s a mini-baby boom of children born to increasingly affluent Yuppies fueled an unprecedented growth in marketing to children. As of 1990 there were 32 million U.S. children aged 4 to 12. In a 1984 study, McNeal (1987) found that children between 4 and 12 had an annual income of $4.7 billion, and by early 1992 he revised his estimate and reported the income of children to have risen to nearly $9 billion. In 1993 industry sources claimed that children under age 12 spend or influence the spending of $100 billion annually (*Broadcasting and Cable,* 1993, p. 37). Such a market clearly was desirable to advertisers wanting to sell a range of new products.

According to Kunkel and Gantz (1991), during the 1980s children's advertising extended beyond network Saturday morning fare to a host of independent television stations with first-run children's syndicated shows to air as well as cable networks eager to reach child audiences. While toy, cereal, and sugared snack/drink products predominated as products advertised to children, they were joined by running shoes, jeans and other clothing, travel and vacation locales such as Disneyland, and information services such as videotapes and telephone 900 numbers. But the greatest impact came with the development of toy company-television production arrangements, or what are known as program-length commercials or toy-based programming, which by the end of the 1980s became the mainstay of children's television.

The external environment of regulation of children's television and scrutiny of broadcaster's practices must be interpreted within the host of implicit practices for developing children's television shows. Furthermore, the various rules of thumb by which children's television producers and programmers "know" when they have good ideas for children—that is, the unwritten and sometimes unspoken expectations of what sells in the uncertain environment of television programming—are far more likely to have an impact on what is developed for children's television than the specific external environmental conditions.

In the next two sections, we will consider these internal constraints and programming practices for producing children's television, which tell us much about children's program producers' view of child audiences. First, we will consider national network programming practices and, second, local broadcaster practices.

NETWORK PRODUCTION FOR CHILDREN

In an early study of children's television producers, Muriel Cantor pointed out that those producing Saturday morning network fare in the late 1960s had two audiences to please: network programming executives and the viewing audience of children. She also noted:

At this time the reality of the marketplace is: If a producer wishes to make television shows to be shown on commercial television, he must please both of his two audiences, first, the buyers of the film, and eventually, the viewers. If a series is to be shown, the buyer is necessarily the most important audience, and he does have the most direct interaction with the producer. No show can ever be judged by the general audience unless it first pleases a buyer. In most cases, the buyer is the network.

There are other reasons why pleasing the viewing audience is a secondary consideration. Producers feel that direct expressions of approval or disapproval, such as letter writing, do not represent the large, heterogeneous audience commanded by television series. Their children and those of their friends are not representative of the audience. Indirect measures, such as market research and rating services are methodologically inadequate, telling nothing about reactions to content. In any case, since television shows appear on the air long after they are made, they could not be changed to reflect audience feedback. The only direct feedback is from the network representatives who watch each step of the production process. Especially with children's programming, the network itself is the primary audience; the content is directed to its desires and its mandates. (Cantor, 1974, p. 116)

Twenty years later, when Edward Palmer conducted his research on network children's television production, he found a very similar situation, with strong network control over the production of children's television in the five or six animated production houses regularly used by network television (Palmer, 1987). According to Palmer, by the 1980s the process of development of children's television programs at the network level was influenced by the previous 20 years of controversy. For instance, when Cantor was conducting her research in the late 1960s, children's television production came under the purview of the network daytime programmer. However, by 1972 each of the three major networks had appointed a vice president for children's television, at least partly in response to the inquiry into children's television conducted at the FCC between 1971 and 1974 (see Wartella, 1988). The addition of the children's television executive at the network changed the profile of who was making children's programming decisions, and, again according to Palmer (1987), these programmers, many of whom had come through government investigations into children's television in the 1980s, considered a background in and understanding of child development principles important. He quotes one network programmer:

I think it is important. I find it a real important part of my background . . . understanding children and really focusing and caring about the kids, staying in tune to the audience, their likes and dislikes, fads, understanding their phases of development and how they watch television, and the logic of what goes on in a typical household on Saturday morning. (Palmer, 1987, p. 115)

A second new element added to the children's television decision-making process was advisers for children's programs, both at the network level (NBC has a Social Scientific Advisory Committee composed of educators and experts in child development, ABC consults with the Bank Street College of Education in New York, and CBS has hired different individuals) and for individual programs (psychologist Gordon Berry consulted on *Fat Albert and the Cosby Kids*). The role of the adviser is to consult on the age-appropriateness of various content themes and portrayals. One network programmer describes the use of consultants:

We rely on the judgment and insights of individual consultants and have our advisory panel. They're down to earth and can tell me on a kids' level, for example, how I can simplify this idea. For example, in *The Smurfs*, one of our story editors pitched the idea of a story on death. Our initial response to the idea was negative—as being inappropriate for these young children. We took it to the social science advisory panel and really hashed it out. We still wouldn't have done it, but we were swayed by them. (Palmer, 1987, p. 117)

That year, NBC received an Emmy Award for *The Smurfs*' program on death.

A third element introduced in earnest by the 1980s was the use of market research to discern children's interest in program characters and, most important, the toys through which most children's shows are intimately linked today. As Engelhart (1986) tells the story, the development of the program-length commercial—that is, programming based on toy characters in which the program is part of an overall marketing strategy to sell toys and other licensed products—began in earnest with *HeMan Masters of the Universe*, which in 1983 was syndicated directly to local stations on a first-run basis. *HeMan* began the process by which toy manufacturers, children's television producers, and either first-run syndicators or networks develop children's programs together as part of an overall marketing strategy. Central to this process is ongoing market research with children to test the attractiveness of the toys, the characters based on them, the story lines, and the settings. By the late 1980s (Wartella, Heintz, Aidman, & Mazzarella, 1990), toy-related children's television programs dominated Saturday morning network television as well as first-run syndication. As Engelhart (1986) notes:

> With so much at stake, corporate managers have hedged their bets by attempting to discover beforehand what children will like in toys, in TV shows, in characters, in fantasy. But this "research" itself seems to be little more than a closed loop proving that variations on what already works will work—until eventually they no longer work . . . [I]n the hands of present-day corporate toy managers, however, such research does help direct companies into increasingly frenzied cycles of recombinant planning as bizarre in their own ways as in the widest attempts at genetic recombination could be in the world of biology. Corporate research, for example, showed that although Mattel's HeMan was aimed at boys aged four to eight, about 30 percent of those watching the TV show were girls. What to conclude from that? Well, why not mix a bit of Wonder Woman with a sizable dollop of HeMan, add lots of Barbie, and Lo you have HeMan's sister Adora, alias She-Ra, Princess of Power from Mattel, or Golden Girl from Galoob—two fashion action figurines for girls. (p. 80)

These three elements—the establishment of a network programmer specifically for children's shows, the addition of child development expert advisers to review scripts and suggest programmatic themes, and the increasing involvement of market research for describing the overall marketing strategy for the new toy-related children's programs of the 1980s—had an impact on the process of moving from script idea to on-air television programs. The process is very similar to that found for network entertainment fare (Turow, 1984).

Palmer (1987) has described the annual production cycle. In the 1980s only about a half dozen major production houses were producing children's television for the commercial networks and these were primarily small houses, such as Filmation, DIC, and Marvel. These have now been joined by larger production houses such as Warner, Disney-Buena Vista, and the Fox Network's own production house. As described by Palmer, the annual cycle begins in September or October when production houses pitch program ideas to network programmers. The very general "shopping list" of ideas is mutually discussed and the network programmer then may buy a development option. ("In effect the network buys the right to that idea during development and is asking the production house to fill in the skeletal image with personality and character structure"—Palmer, 1987,

p. 87.) Next, the production house fills out the idea with story boards, character descriptions, and, most important, a series bible (a description of the characters, their personalities, and interrelationships as well as scenic descriptions of setting). Meanwhile, at the network level, research is conducted on character appeal and script/situation appeal; this research typically consists of focus group interviews with children in New York and Los Angeles. By March or April, or sometimes as late as May, the networks make a decision about programs they will buy, and then production starts. As in the 1960s, network programmers are in constant interaction with the producers and also, increasingly, the toy companies involved in marketing the toys related to the programs. According to Palmer (1987):

> During the development season, the network will have regular involvement with the process. The degree of involvement will depend on numerous factors, among them the track record of the production house, the networks, past experience with the producer, how controversial the program or its main character may be and how much feedback the production house may seek at different points in the process. The natural aim of both production house and network is to create a program that will be engaging to children and will sell. Selling in this instance means attracting children to that specific network for that given hour of Saturday morning programming. (p. 89)

Research is used throughout the process to look at the appeal of the characters, toys, and plots to children. Scripts are reviewed by network programmers as well as advisers/consultants to check for appropriateness and, during the 1980s, for prosocial messages. Time pressures make the production process a harrowing one, without enough time to actually test rough cuts of programs with children or others (Palmer, 1987).

This process of children's television program development and production is but a modification of that found by Cantor in her research in the 1960s: Networks still predominate and programs still air before—from their producers' perspective—enough research has been done to check programming. Thus the process now involves ways of knowing the audience—through the eyes of programmers, many of whom are steeped in developmental notions; through expert advisers who specialize in child development and children's needs; and through market research that aims at finding out what kids like (and Nickelodeon is the channel best known for massive amounts of focus group research). But the process itself is still inexact and uncertain. Consequently, producers and programmers tend to fall back on their own "rules of thumb" or "beliefs" about "what will children like, what will they watch, what will they buy." And these rules of thumb have been remarkably stable over the past 25 years.

For instance, Cantor (1974) reported, from interviews with 20 producers and programmers involved in children's television in the late 1960s, that several beliefs about children guided production: First, she noted ratings data suggested that older brothers and sisters had greater control over the set than younger children, and therefore producers believed that they needed to satisfy the interest of older (presumably elementary school-aged) children and then younger children would follow along. Second, producers and writers believed that children have short attention spans and therefore fast-paced and noisy programs are needed to keep the children's attention. And, of course, they viewed their job as one of entertaining children—as did networks.

THE USES OF RESEARCH

Two studies in the late 1980s also examined producers' views of child audiences. First, Palmer (1987) pointed out that, while network programmers by the late 1980s did indeed have backgrounds in child development and expressed an understanding of developmental differences in child viewers' responses to television, the producers he interviewed almost uniformly dismissed a need for any understanding of child psychology. He noted that, to these producers, understanding children required "a feel for what kids like—a natural, gut instinct. This instinct is clearly seen as being 'born, not made' and in that context there is little, if anything, the child development background can add" (Palmer, 1987, p. 100). In short, Palmer found producers relying on their knowledge of how to tell a good story and how to entertain and on their technical knowledge about animation to make television programming attractive to their child viewers.

About the same time as Palmer's research, between 1985 and 1987, I conducted interviews with a dozen commercial children's television producers and programmers in New York and Hollywood. The open-ended interviews focused on the producers' understanding of "what children like to watch" and "what the child audience's" needs and interests in television are as well as the producers' experience in children's television. The intent of the interviews was to gain an understanding of how the children's television producer perceived his or her audience and the implicit "rules of thumb" used to develop programming for children.

A clear distinction emerged between those who were younger and had more recently entered the children's television field and the veteran producers. The most marked difference was found in the experts interviewed at Nickelodeon. For the younger producers and programmers, market research holds the key to what children like and do. For instance, Linda Kahn, vice president for production at Nickelodeon (personal communication, 1986), noted:

> We don't buy the series unless we go out and test it with kids. . . . We talk about them on a lot of levels, just on the shows themselves, on the characters, on what happened, on what they think might happen in other episodes, on things they might like to see happen. . . . And being in touch with the constituency is the key in anything that we do.

Another programmer, Steve Seidelman (personal communication, 1986), noted:

> We'll test ideas, and we'll test concepts, We'll test the developmental stage of a project. We'll talk to kids about what they like and don't like about an idea. And we'll try as best we can to avoid the classic stereotypes that they're conditioned to compare our programming to, or our ideas to, which is Saturday morning and prime time television.

Linda Kahn again:

> You keep going back to what do kids really want, what are their perceptions. I might think a show, or our staff—it's certainly not just me—might think a show is terrific for x, y, or z reasons. But what are kids thinking and what's their reaction and is it fresh and is it something that's a little different, is it something that's going to touch them, whether it's in a funny way or a serious way?

On the other hand, more senior children's television producers such as Lou Scheimer, who headed up the production of *HeMan Masters of the Universe,* among others, was quite blunt in his disdain for market research with children (personal communication, 1986): "If you have to go to research to find out what children like, then there is something wrong with you. You shouldn't be in the job."

The argument is one Muriel Cantor heard 20 years previously, that television production is a creative process, that children's producers "revert to being children" and so know how to please children, that producers have children of their own or know children and thus can appeal to them. Both older, more established producers and the younger ones as well reverted to rules of thumb or assumptions about what pleases children.

The increased use of research in commercial television production for children appears to parallel that in the production of children's educational television, which has, at least since the development of *Sesame Street* in the late 1960s, been identified with extensive use of research in the production of the educational curriculum and programming format (see Johnston & Ettema, 1982; Lesser, 1974; Palmer, 1987). But there is a major difference between the commercial model and the educational or public broadcasting model of producing educational television both in what research is used and in how it is used. What the Children's Television Workshop organization refers to as the CTW model is an approach to television production that brings together ongoing formative research, educational content specialists, and television production specialists who collaboratively produce television series.

In the CTW model, two kinds of research are used. Formative research involves studies of children's understanding of and reactions to programming elements and educational content. The studies are conducted before and during the production of a television series. Second, after the program airs (typically after the first season), summative research is conducted to ascertain the effects of the program on child audiences and whether or not the educational goals of the program were met. With some variation (such as the use of ongoing formative research throughout the production of an educational television series), the CTW model and its variants have become standard operating procedure for public broadcasting-based educational programs. For instance, according to the call for applications by the National Endowment for Children's Educational Television, applicants must describe how they will assess the impact of the programs on child audiences. Some programs as well have advisers or consultants who comment on the educational and programming appropriateness for the target age group of children (e.g., *Behind the Scenes, Mister Rogers' Neighborhood*).

One crucial distinction in the use of research in educational versus commercial children's programming is that much of the research for educational programming is directed at understanding what children are learning and can make sense of, as well as what they attend to and like about the program. That is, the impact of the program on children's knowledge and understanding of the world is assessed: Are children learning from the show and, if not, why not? What children take away from a commercial program not only is not assessed but is not of interest, it would appear. The major, and indeed perhaps sole, goal of commercial television research is to assess what children will watch, what they enjoy, what will sell to them. Thus, while both educational and commercial children's television increasingly use consultants, advisers, and research to create programs, the research is directed at different goals and different sets of needs. However, even in educational programming and even at the Children's Television Workshop, producers over time develop a set of beliefs about what children do and do not like to watch at different ages and what is appropriate programming for children. Johnston and Ettema (1992), for instance, describe the case of the former *Sesame Street* producer who insisted that even older 8- to 12-year-old children would best be served by a magazine format educational show intended to teach older children about career opportunities, despite the advice of child development specialists who insisted that older children would be more attracted to narrative plot lines. Only after pilots were tested using both formats and the child development experts were proven right did the producer agree that perhaps the successful *Sesame Street* format wouldn't work for all children of all ages and all educational programs. In short, there is some evidence that, even with educational programming, which is heavily subjected to testing as in the CTW model, producers develop their own images of what children like, what we call the rules of thumb for children's television production.

IMPLICIT VIEWS OF CHILD AUDIENCES

What we call rules of thumb, or implicit assumptions about what children like to watch and what pleases them, are for commercial producers and programmers the guidelines by which programming ideas are formulated and against which market research is pitted. (And, for the educational producers, they are the basis of their ongoing battles with researchers and content specialists; see, e.g., Broughton, 1986; Johnston & Ettema, 1982; Lesser, 1974.) That is, the commonsense view of the child audience over time may be informed by market research, audience ratings, programmers' experiences with their own or others' children, or some intuitive understanding of what pleases children. However the programmers and producers derive their commonsense views of the child audience, the important point is that the views they hold are important in the development of children's programs. Moreover, there has been considerable consistency over the years in terms of producers' notions of what children want in television. The following summary rules of thumb have been derived both from my interviews and from various others' interviews with children's producers (see, e.g., Broughton, 1986) as well as previous research by Cantor and Palmer:

(1) Children like comedy. In a variety of ways and over and over again, producers argue that children like funny characters and funny situations. Comedy is said to be the key to entertaining children. Cantor found this out in the 1960s as did Palmer and I in the 1980s. Humor of all sorts appears to be much of the basis of children's television, both educational and commercial.

Emily Squires, a director of *Sesame Street* in the 1980s, noted:

> The other thing—when you said that the show (*Sesame Street*) seemed geared to kids—it's true it is a children's show, but I believe there's a universal standard when it comes to entertainment, and I think the Muppets have proved that better than anyone. And we've discovered that adults who watch the show like it just as much as the kids do. For one thing, *Sesame Street* doesn't talk down to the kids, and it's genuinely funny. Children are surprisingly sophisticated in their sense of humor. I mean they really pick up the jokes; nothing goes by them. You can't just let something go by carelessly, you can't just say, "Oh, this is a kid's show. No one will get this. We'll just let it pass." (Broughton, 1986, p. 138)

(2) Repetition is a key to both educating and entertaining children. For instance, Lou Scheimer (personal communication, 1986) noted that much of *HeMan Masters of the Universe* was repeat material, "About a third of every picture is repeat material . . . what we are going to do are cycles . . . eyes in the same way all the time, fights the same way all the time, the moves are stock moves, the show has been set up in advance." Similarly, *Sesame Street* also uses Muppet inserts and other educational materials over and over again; only the "street pieces" or about 25 minutes of each hour-long show are shot anew each season. As described by Emily Squires:

> As I told you before, during the course of a season, when they are available, we will do certain Muppet inserts and other material, but after 20 years in production, we have a huge library of live action films, animated bits, cast inserts, Muppet inserts, none of which have aged, all of which we still use

occasionally in one show or another. We have it all computerized, so that we can program the various pieces, rotate them, use them again and again, without repeating ourselves. (Broughton, 1986, p. 139)

Of course, repetition works on children's shows because the audiences grow older and change over the years but also because of the nature of children. Fred Rogers of *Mister Rogers' Neighborhood* notes, "Yes, I think that children are comfortable with things that are repeated. It's just like children like to know where they're going to sit at the dining room table and when they're going to go to bed and who's going to tuck them in. You know, we all like to know what's in store for us" (Broughton, 1986, p. 56). But repetition works best for animation, not live action, according to several of the producers. As Jeff Heller, producer of *In the News,* noted: "You cannot run live programming over as many times as you can animated." Indeed, one of the attractions of animation is that, more than live action, it does not get dated as quickly and can be shown over and over again to new generations of children as well as to the same children. The likely success of the Cartoon Network on cable television is a testament to this.

(3) Children want recognizable characters and stories. Recognizability is a key to the production of children's programs. Producers talk over and over again about a "hot product." Eleanor Richmond, a longtime producer of Saturday morning children's television, was most succinct in noting this: "What producers look for is a recognizability factor, therefore certain books that have become fixed in the public minds but at least have sold well . . . certain ideas, toys of course with some prior success, some recognizability factor" (personal communication, 1986).

Why recognizability? Richmond recounts, "Again, children like the familiar, like to see stories they've read. They want to be able to play with the characters they see on television."

Indeed, as Engelhart (1986) notes, the creation of children's toy-related programming is an elaborated manifestation of the recognizability factor. But here the simultaneous production of the children's television show and its toy-related character is supported and reinforced via traditional product licensing such as for backpacks, sheets, towels, clothing, lunch boxes, and cereal products (e.g., *Mario Brothers, The Addams Family, Ghostbusters*); character appearances at shopping malls and holiday events; movie appearances (e.g., the current *Batman: The Animated Movie* is based on the Fox Network's children's television show, which in turn was issued after the success of the live action Batman films); and, of course, a host of new technology toys including arcade and home video games, story tapes, and home computer software. As described by Engelhart (1986):

> For the first time on such a massive scale, a "character" has been born free of its specific structure in a myth, fairy tale, story or even cartoon, and instead embedded from the beginning in a consortium of busy manufacturers whose goals are purely and simply to profit by multiplying the image itself in any way that will conceivably make money. (p. 93)

(4) Children watch up. According to commercial producers in particular, younger children like to watch what their older siblings are watching. Therefore, if you attract older children, you will carry along the young ones. According to Jeff Heller (personal communication, 1986): "The question was then why are you doing a program for teenagers if they're not watching. I said because young children will watch a program for teenagers and we can teach them something. Children tend to look up at the older peers. They don't look backwards."

The belief that children do indeed watch up—that is, watch what the older kids are attracted to—is one way of ignoring the preschool audience on commercial television. Producers effectively make their target age group more elastic by aiming at, say, 7- to 12-year-olds but drawing in the younger children as well.

For educational television producers, a variant of this theme is the need for polysemic television, that is, television that entertains the adults who will then make their children watch the educational fare. As Emily Squires noted, adult jokes and character turns, such as the current H. Ross Parrot, are clearly intended to engage the adults on *Sesame Street* to, among other things, encourage them to watch the television program with their children.

(5) There are gender differences in what children like about television. Boys like action-adventure and superheroes, a fast pace, and much action. Girls like fantasy and soft cuddly characters as well as more prosocial, slower paced television fare. As far back as the 1960s, Cantor (1974) found that shortened attention spans and boys' rough-and-tumble playing styles were assumed by producers to translate into the need for high action, fast-paced children's fare. More recently, Engelhart (1986) described in detail the "universe of the action-figure superhero" aimed at

boys and assumed to interest only boys as compared with the television of "managed emotion" or the happy realm of girls' television. The former is marked by "the introduction of new characters with their accompanying weapons, castles and other accoutrements; the necessity for teamwork and the displaying of the show's techno-weaponry through special effects" (p. 89). Action, and often violence, good versus evil, heroic feats, technical wizardry, and male-dominated characters are all marks of the boys' shows best typified by *HeMan, Thundercats, Ghostbusters, Teenage Mutant Ninja Turtles,* and so on. In contrast, children's programs for girls are dominated by sugary sweet programs about typically cute, doll-like characters (e.g., *Care Bears* and *Cabbage Patch Kids*) who demonstrate prosocial qualities of caring and helpfulness. As in boys' television, however, teamwork and the introduction of new characters, all of which can be sold as toys, are important as well. Engelhart argues, and more recent children's seasons also suggest, that boys' television tends to dominate girls' programs on Saturday morning and weekday afternoons. Part of this is the expectation that girls will watch boys' TV but not vice versa (see Cantor, 1974).

CONCLUSION

Children's television producers' notions of their audiences, as we have seen, originate from various sources. These notions are informed by the producers' practical experiences with making television, but some ideas, for some producers, are also informed by various sorts of research—even though the research itself is shaped by either commercial or educational imperatives.

By its insistence that television is obliged to serve child audiences and its requirement that broadcasters justify their programming choices and demonstrate that they have met their obligations, the 1990 Children's Television Act foregrounds the importance of how the child audience is conceived of. "Rules of thumb," which have to date served as producers' prime ways of seeing the audience, are insufficient, it may be argued, to this task.

One area of particular importance is the development of standards to determine whether television has met children's educational and informational needs. Debate over this part of the 1990 legislation lays bare the deficiencies in how programmers and producers understand their audiences and how they will meet this goal.

REFERENCES

Broadcasting and Cable. (1993, July 26). Newsnote.

Broughton, I. (1986). *Producers on producing: The making of film and television.* Jefferson, NC: McFarland.

Cantor, M. (1974). Producing television for children. In G. Tuchman (Ed.), *The TV establishment: Programming for power and profit* (pp. 103-118). Englewood, NJ: Prentice Hall.

Center for Media Education. (1992). *A report on station compliance with the Children's Television Act.* Washington, DC: Author.

Engelhart, T. (1986). Children's television: The Strawberry Shortcake strategy. In T. Gitlin (Ed.), *Watching television* (pp. 68-110). New York: Pantheon.

Ettema, J., & Whitney, D. C. (Eds.). (1982). *Individuals in mass media organizations: Creativity and constraint.* Beverly Hills, CA: Sage.

Federal Communications Commission. (1991). Policies and rules concerning children's television programming. *Federal Communications Commission Record, 6,* 2111-2127.

Johnston, J., & Ettema, J. S. (1982). *Positive images: Breaking stereotypes with children's television.* Beverly Hills, CA: Sage.

Kunkel, D. (1991). Crafting media policy. *American Behavioral Scientist, 35*(2), 181-202.

Kunkel, D., & Gantz, W. (1991). *Television advertising to children: Message content in 1990* (Report to the Children's Advertising Review unit, Council of Better Business Bureaus). Bloomington: Indiana University, Institute for Communication Research.

Lesser, G. S. (1974). *Children and television: Lessons from Sesame Street.* New York: Vintage.

McAvoy, K. (1993, July 26). FCC gets into the children's act. *Broadcasting and Cable, 123*(30), 42-43.

McNeal, J. (1987). *Children as consumers.* Lexington, MA: D. C. Heath.

Melody, W. (1973). *Children's television: The economics of exploitation.* New Haven, CT: Yale University Press.

National Association of Broadcasters. (1993, May 7). *In the matter of policies and rules concerning children's television programming.* MM Docket No. 93-48 before the Federal Communications Commission, Washington, DC.

Palmer, E. (1987). *Children in the cradle of television.* Lexington, MA: Lexington.

Turow, J. (1984). *Media industries: The production of news and entertainment.* White Plains, NY: Longman.

Wartella, E. (1988). The public context of debates about TV and children. In S. Oskamp (Ed.), *Television as a social issue* (Applied Social Psychology Annual, pp. 59-68). Newbury Park, CA: Sage.

Wartella, E., Heintz, K., Aidman, A., & Mazzarella, S. (1990). Television and beyond: Children's video media in one community. *Communication Research, 17*(1), 45-64.

Chapter 4

MADE-TO-ORDER AND STANDARDIZED AUDIENCES: FORMS OF REALITY IN AUDIENCE MEASUREMENT

Peter V. Miller

It is now almost impossible to find an intellectual who will use the word "reality" without quotation marks.

Jackson Lears (1993, p. 13)

IN THE WORLD OF publishing and broadcasting, it is still possible, even ordinary, to find people talking about "real" media audiences. The notion that the aim of audience measurement is to picture accurately the authentic audiences for media offerings is rarely questioned. For most media workers, "socially constructed reality" is not a description of what audience measurement can be at best but is a sad acknowledgment or winking recognition that human interests, greed, failings, and collusion pollute what ought to be an objective, empirical project. Philosophical sophistication, postmodern sensibilities, and postpositivist perspectives on social measurement do not complicate media workers' judgments about audience truth.

AUTHOR'S NOTE: I am grateful to many people in various advertising, media, and research companies who have spent time with me over the past several years. I wish to express particular thanks to Pam Baxter, Alice Sylvester, Bob Warrens, Ed Schillmoeller, and Gale Metzger for their help in my research. I alone am responsible for the opinions (and any errors) expressed here.

This chapter looks at the constraints and relationships that *necessarily* shape the "reality" of the media audience as it is known through commercial audience measurement. It examines how audience estimates emerge from the actions and interplay of several groups: the measurement companies, their clients, and their respondents. In contrast to the view that human interference confounds "real" audience measurement, I seek here to illustrate the intrinsic role of social forces in fabricating the audience realities found in commercial reports.[1]

The familiar trademark names associated with audience measurement reports—Nielsen, Arbitron, Simmons, and the like—give the impression that the information contained in the reports is the sole product of those firms. In fact, audience statistics could not be produced, and would not look they way they do, were it not for the influences of measurement service clients—media companies and advertisers—and those whose media behavior is assessed. Obviously, but nonetheless significantly, measurement firms need someone to buy their services and need people to agree to participate in media consumption measurement. The power of clients and respondents is not limited to these enabling roles, however; each of these groups forcefully shapes the information that measurement firms put forth as their own product. This chapter examines the audience images that emerge from this interplay of interests.

"MADE-TO-ORDER" AND "STANDARDIZED" AUDIENCES

How are audiences constituted in commercial measurement? The manifest process, of course, is the manner in which observations of actual viewers and readers are conducted. There is an abundant literature on the methods used by firms for this purpose, including descriptions and evaluations of various techniques of measurement: questionnaires, diaries, electronic devices, and so on. Useful methodological references include Beville (1985), Webster and Lichty (1991), and Wimmer and Dominick (1991). But the particulars of the audience measurement business change rapidly. At this writing, for example, Arbitron had recently announced that it would no longer provide local television audience reports. Rather than devote much space to describing data collection methods or major industry players, therefore, I want to describe the audience measurement process at a more abstract level.

More basic than the choice of methods are decisions on such questions as what sphere of human activity will be measured and how often it will be measured, what "standard package" of information will be supplied to clients, and how much control over the information will be relinquished to those who pay for it. Though these questions are often ignored or taken as given in discussions of audience measurement methodology, they are fundamental to the establishment and survival of a measurement service. The answers to these questions form the foundation upon which audience reality is built. Here I want to focus on the most basic question: What will be measured?

There are two facets to the question of media audience measurement: Which media content is to be assessed and what audience behaviors are to be recorded? Those who wish to conduct audience measurement must decide which publications, which radio or television channels, which portions of content carried in those vehicles (articles, programs, advertisements, quarter hours) will be examined for audience response. They also must decide how "response" will be defined and assessed—what will constitute evidence for the existence and duration of reading, listening, or watching. Ancillary audience characteristics such as purchasing power and social influence also are often of interest.

Decisions on measuring content offered, audience responses, and audience characteristics involve financial and logistical trade-offs. Because of cost and time limitations, the more media offerings assessed, the less extensive the response measurement that can be done and the fewer the audience characteristics that can be documented. Similarly, the more publications or broadcast channels measured, the less intensively individual articles or programs can be examined. Finally, the more information gathered during any one survey measurement, the less frequently such measurements can be taken. All audience surveys, no matter how costly, limit to some degree the scope and detail of measurement of media content, audience response, and audience characteristics measurement. The nature and extent of the limitations are determined in the marketplace, where client demands for information confront the realities of what can be done in a survey and at what cost. In general, there are two kinds of financial arrangements between research clients and measurement firms through which the trade-offs intrinsic to audience measurement are negotiated: custom ("made-to-order") and syndicated research contracts.

CUSTOM STUDIES

> In the beginning when the world was young there were a great many thoughts
> but no such thing as truth.
>
> Sherwood Anderson ("The Book of the Grotesque," *Winesburg, Ohio,* 1966)

Custom audience research is specially tailored inquiry, usually commissioned by one media client to focus on its own audience. Such research is common in the commercial media world but it does not receive the same attention as do syndicated studies, such as the celebrated Nielsen ratings, which measure the audiences of multiple media outlets. Custom studies are the media client's weapon in the struggle to document an economically meaningful audience. They are used to find a heretofore unmeasured audience, to correct a damaging impression of an audience, or to highlight flattering new details about an audience. Custom studies also are used to show just how loyal or attentive the audience is to the client's media content offerings. Information of this kind is used to insinuate that an advertiser's messages will receive similar notice. In short, custom studies often are used to document audiences that, at least to the client's way of thinking, have been overlooked or undervalued. The "real" audience picture somehow hasn't emerged from the data in earlier studies. Or, things have changed sufficiently to lead to the belief that audiences "really" aren't behaving like they used to. Such thinking about a natural audience reality that has not been documented impels a media client to invest in a measurement process whose outcome, as we shall see, is not judged automatically to be "real" by all who are led to it.

In custom studies, the survey design trade-offs inherent in all audience measurement are often negotiated by focusing only on the client's media vehicle and gathering considerable detail about its audience characteristics and experience. The necessary design compromise is constructed so as to limit the number of media offerings in order to examine them in greater detail. The advantage to the client in this approach is that the extensive information about the audience permits selling it in multiple ways. One strategy might be to focus on the demographic characteristics of the audience, another to advertise lifestyle or purchasing patterns, and another to show how involved the audience seems to be with the medium's content. Such unique detail from a custom study is used to distinguish the media vehicle from its competitors for the advertiser's dollar, to go beyond the crude criterion of audience size.

The custom study's information richness advantage is balanced by two disadvantages: Its unique information cannot be compared directly with that produced by other studies and its sponsorship by one client threatens its claim to objectivity. As Mayer (1958) pointed out long ago, there is no aspect of the advertising business so glutted with statistics as is the media buying function. The advertising agency's media planners and buyers are buried in studies on the merits of different media vehicles, many of them custom studies sponsored by the media vehicles themselves. "The problem," as Mayer (1958, p. 138) points out, "is that all media purchases represent a choice of alternatives, and only rarely are the alternatives really comparable." A custom study may show that one magazine's readers score high on some measure of purchasing power, but the media planner— who must choose from a number of publications (and other media, for that matter)—is apt to say, "Well, that's interesting, but what about the nine other custom studies I have that use different measures and contradict your claim?" In such instances, there are a great many thoughts, but no such thing as truth. The advertiser may not know what to do with the information; it may complicate, rather than simplify, an already complex decision on which media vehicles to choose.

Custom studies are most effective when they are introduced in an information void—that is, when a new target audience whose habits are little known becomes of interest to advertisers and the mountain of audience data on hand is not helpful. The growth of the personal computer market has spurred many such studies by different publications in recent years. Similarly, custom studies are useful and needed when new media vehicles are introduced and, having no audience track record in syndicated studies, must demonstrate audience drawing power. Audience *simulation* services for yet-to-be-published magazines constitute one example of such custom research.[2] Audience numbers for publications that have yet to offer one issue are, naturally, viewed by advertisers with some suspicion (just as television audience estimates for new programs in the "up-front" buying season need to be supported by "make good" guarantees). The fact that such estimates are produced and used at all is a testament to the powerfully soothing role that audience numbers play in justifying media buys. But all custom research—whether it involves simulation or not, and notwithstanding a client's sincere intent merely to document current facts—faces an issue of credibility, of whether the audiences turned up are "real" or not. In addition to being seen as idiosyncratic or not comparable to other research or out of step with previously established truth, custom research may be perceived as "bought and paid for."

To serve their persuasive purpose with skeptical advertisers, custom studies must appear to separate the client from the research process and the framing of lessons from the study itself. The more the findings of the research can be said to rest on the independent judgment, expertise, and rigor of the measurement firm, the greater the study's believability. The more money the client spends on the project, thereby allowing the research firm to spare no expense in search of the truth, the more persuasive the findings. The more experienced and reputed the measurement firm and the more careful and conservative its approach, the more advertisers are likely to find credence in its research.

For example, Alfred Politz's expensive and complex custom magazine readership studies, as reviewed below, became the "gold standard" for such investigations and served as the model for a syndicated magazine measurement service (Hardy, 1990). Similarly, Statistical Research Incorporated's (SRI) custom telephone coincidental studies of television viewing became the arbiter of truth in assessing syndicated television audience measurement methods such as the diary and the people meter (Beville, 1985). The coincidental method requires calling households and asking phone answerers to report whether television sets are on and, if so, to what channels they are tuned. This approach ostensibly eliminates recall error and permits accurate reporting of ongoing behavior. The SRI version of the technique is particularly rigorous in terms of its pursuit of respondents with answering machines and those whose telephones were initially unanswered. The Politz readership studies and the SRI telephone coincidentals demonstrate the sort of credibility that custom studies can achieve if conducted by careful, experienced researchers working with considerable independence. They provide models toward which custom research projects can strive so as to be believable.

Custom audience research illustrates the important collaboration of media clients and measurement firms in the creation of audience images. Clients enable research but constrain its possibilities. Research firms not only perform measurements to the client's specifications but also offer a scientific "cover," playing an intermediary role between the client and *its* clients. The interests and resources of clients and measurement companies shape the audience found in the custom study, no matter how disinterested they try to be. For the audience to seem "real" to prospective customers, however, the conjunction of interests that permits it to emerge must be visible only in the background, if at all. The new audience image proposed by the custom study may achieve the social status of "reality" only if the financial stakes that shaped it are obscured and the study can be depicted as a search for a truth unsullied by base motives. The unique, made-to-order nature of the custom study is both its chief benefit and its major cost. Because of its focus on one or a few media outlets, custom research can offer more careful documentation of audiences, their characteristics, and their experience. Such information can distinguish the outlets from their competitors or can prove the existence of an audience if no other proof exists. In fact, custom studies were once the only way for advertisers to learn about the audiences for media outlets. But custom studies then created a cacophony of incomparable audience claims, and advertisers demanded a different form of trade-off in survey design: studies that would measure *more* outlets with *less* detail but with the *same level* of detail. This demand resulted in what has become a common template for assessing audiences: the syndicated study.

SYNDICATED STUDIES

> Little pyramids of truth he erected and after erecting knocked them down again
> that he might have the truths to erect other pyramids.
>
> Sherwood Anderson ("Paper Pills," *Winesburg, Ohio,* 1966)

Syndicated studies are usually what we think of when we think of commercial audience measurement: television audience ratings by Nielsen, radio audience ratings by Arbitron, magazine readership estimates by Simmons Market Research Bureau (SMRB) or Mediamark Research Incorporated (MRI). These efforts involve substantially more complicated trade-offs than custom studies because they seek to describe audiences for a number of media products at the same time, and they are offered for sale to a number of clients. Developing a viable syndicated study plan depends on the willingness of clients to buy a standard package of information resulting from the multivehicle measurement and on the ability to solve the financial and logistical problems inherent in designing a standard format for measuring more than one media offering.

The syndicated study offers comparative, longitudinal information about audiences that can be used to sell advertising space or time. Unlike the custom study, the syndicated effort provides advertisers with a standard way to judge alternative vehicles for their messages. It offers an "apples-to-apples" sense of the audience value of alternative media offerings. It does not suffer from the same kinds of credibility problems as the custom study because competing interests serve as sponsors and because the same measurement regimen is applied to all. Thus a syndicated study is apt to be a more routine and important sales tool for media firms. At a minimum, it can produce information that the media company should know about whether favorable to a sales case or not (and, because it offers comparative information not under the individual client's control, the information often is not the most favorable).

While the custom study is the creature of an individual media client, the syndicated study is the conception of a measurement company. In establishing a syndicated study, the measurement firm counts on the value of standardized comparative audience information to advertisers, and the concomitant willingness of media companies to pay for it so as to build advertising sales arguments. A measurement firm often pitches a new syndicated study idea to large advertisers and their agencies early in the development process because the measurement firm hopes to so excite advertisers and agencies with the idea that they will demand that media firms provide them with the information to be produced by the study. For example, Television Audience Assessment, an unusual venture funded in the early 1980s by the Markle Foundation to provide an alternative television rating service, attempted to convince advertising agency personnel that its qualitative information about viewer reactions to television programs would help them to choose programs in which to place their commercials. (As it happened, these appeals were not convincing and the enterprise failed after the foundation's funding ran out.) Measurement firms also give substantial discounts to advertisers and agencies to subscribe to the service so that media sales people are forced to use the information too. Thus media research personnel in advertiser firms and agencies are important gatekeepers who determine whether a service will be adopted first by the advertisers and consequently by media companies.

Choosing to measure the audience for a number of media offerings across time provides other advantages over selling custom studies to one client at a time. The syndicated strategy holds out the promise of a steady income stream through long-term contracts with multiple clients. For survey firms, whose financial fortunes can be quite variable, the assurance of more consistent income is a significant incentive to initiate a syndicated measurement service.[3]

There are still other benefits to the syndicated research approach. It allows the measurement firm to routinize data collection, processing, and reporting rather than setting up procedures for these activities *de novo,* as in custom studies. Anticipating workload and making personnel and facilities decisions becomes easier for firms offering syndicated products.

Custom studies require more of a "craft" form of administration in which the organization needed to conduct the work is rapidly assembled and disassembled. Syndicated research, on the other hand, lends itself to a "bureaucratic" administrative framework because the reduced variability in the flow of work means more constant staffing, less reconfiguration of activities, and the development of a layer of administrative supervision responsible for policies and methods. (See Stinchcombe, 1959, for a discussion of the craft and bureaucratic forms of administration.)

A final advantage for the measurement firm in choosing the syndicated approach is the "public good" nature of the product. Once the measurement process has been completed and the report produced—the "first copy" cost—the report can be sold to additional clients at minimal expense. (See Rosse, Dertouzos, Robinson, & Wildman, 1978, and Wildman's chapter in this volume, for a discussion of public goods in media industries.) Further, the same information can be repackaged and sold as special reports to all clients or on a custom basis to individual customers. Customized analyses of the standard database can contribute a substantial amount to the measurement firm's revenue. And because the standard report issued to clients may contain bad news for individual clients, they may decide to pay for supplementary studies to check the findings or develop another angle for selling their audiences. These custom studies offer yet another spinoff source of revenue for the measurement firm. Finally, the firm can offer use of the standard data to clients along with software and consulting services, each of which adds revenue.

Altogether, through sales of the standard report, special analyses and repackaging, spinoff custom studies, and software and consulting support, the syndicated service offers the measurement firm multiple ways to tap into clients' money.[4] The syndicated study offers its clients both official truth and tailored reality. Pyramids of truth can be erected and knocked down so as to create others.

CREATING A CONVENTION

The choice for measurement firms between the custom and syndicated approaches seems clear. So, why don't all measurement firms set up syndicated studies so as to reap these, their many rewards? The answer is that founding and maintaining a syndicated measurement service is an extraordinarily difficult and costly affair. The value of syndicated studies lies in their general recognition as "official"—as the common basis for judgments made by parties with disparate interests. Because few measurement firms can achieve the status of providing this official reality, the competition for the position is a very high stakes game. Persuading important publics, media firms, and their advertiser clients that a particular view of audience reality is among the few that should serve as the basis for their costly transactions involves the measurement firm in an elaborate ritual of testing and "validating" the new measurement system and in a prolonged period during which the system can be examined by potential users. Substantial investment capital is needed to sustain the system until it is adopted by a sufficient number of clients. Audits of Great Britain (AGB), for example, spent tens of millions of dollars in its ultimately unsuccessful effort to unseat Nielsen as the purveyor of the U.S. national television audience reality. Nielsen, sustained by the deep pockets of Dun and Bradstreet and its base of preexisting clients, could afford to introduce and maintain its new people meter service until AGB gave up.

What a syndicated audience measurement service seeks to establish is a social *convention*. Lewis (1968) argues that a convention arises when all parties have a common interest in a coordination rule, none has a conflicting interest, and none will deviate lest the coordination is lost. The measurement firm wants its information to become an integral part of a coordinated system of judgment and exchange—the rule that all use to understand media audiences. The argument employed to achieve this status must proceed along two tracks to be successful. There must be an appeal, on the one hand, to the inherent correctness of the measurement process for revealing the audience in question, and there must be a demonstration that the information that emerges from the measurement process is eminently practical for day-to-day activities, easy to understand and manipulate, and not disruptive to entrenched routines.

The first line of argument—that the service is based on the most "valid" measurement process—is an appeal that seeks to ground the process in nature, in a reality that is *really* real. "A convention is institutionalized," as Douglas (1986) notes, "when, in reply to the question, 'Why do you do it like this?' . . . the final answer refers to the way the planets are fixed in the sky or the way that plants or humans or animals naturally behave" (pp. 46-47). No syndicated audience measurement service can make the claim that its way of doing things is somehow ordained by universal law, and none meets Douglas's definition of an institution, but all do seek to some degree to show that their process best captures the real audience experience. It would be fine for the service's commercial purposes if all potential users would simply agree to employ its information without such a demonstration. But because such agreements are not easily negotiated and because there are apt to be competing services that have the same commercial purposes and the same hopes, a measurement service's approach cannot seem merely arbitrary. An appeal to a higher order of things is necessary for a socially constructed common ground to emerge.

There are many criteria for judging the validity of measurement, too many to consider here. Successful arguments for syndicated services, however, seem to include the claim that the service has balanced two criteria commonly evoked in courts of law: "the whole truth" and "nothing but the truth." A service's case for becoming a convention is heightened to the extent that it can claim to capture *all* of those viewing, reading, or listening—every audience member for every program or article, at all times. This criteria is particularly important to media clients who will pay the most toward the service's existence. The service's bid to offer the official reality will also benefit from a demonstration that its method detects *only* real viewing, reading, or listening and not false or misleading impressions. This criterion is particularly important to advertisers on whom the media clients rely for income. Getting both media and advertisers to treat the service as a convention means both creating a sense that the service provides richly textured pictures of minds and bodies engaged with media content and finding a practical measurement approach that is an acceptable compromise between the partially conflicting goals of these two client groups.

As noted before, there is a trade-off between, among other things, the number of media offerings for which audiences can be assessed and the care and detail with which those audiences can be documented. Measurement resources are finite, and resources spent ensuring that all media offerings are covered by the system cannot be used to check the observations or provide detailed descriptions of the audience. The more quality controls built into the system, the more the operations will be found to need repair and thus not operate smoothly or on time. The more effort respondents are asked to put into measuring themselves, the less accurately they will do so over time and the more likely it is that their measurement obligations will affect their behavior. These facts of life in survey research make achieving a compromise between "all the truth" and "only the truth" difficult.

The history of syndicated audience measurement suggests that successful services have tipped the balance between the two objectives toward the first, compromising care in measurement of each media offering so that a minimally acceptable number of offerings receive *some* assessment. The definition of "minimally acceptable number" varies by medium and has evolved over time within media. Syndicated services featuring various measurement technologies, embodying different compromises between coverage and detail, have flourished and died in these changing circumstances.

The most notoriously successful service, the Nielsen television rating service, has survived for decades through a survey design trade-off that, while irritating to many clients as well as to advocates for better television fare, has provided a superficial, but generally reliable and comprehensive, measurement of the entire broadcast day. The compromise Nielsen has struck is based on its use of electronic meters to capture information from television sets. This technology permits assessment of all televised offerings that can be received by the sets; it does not tire no matter how long the sets are on; and it counts reception time continuously. The measurement trade-off therefore is clearly in favor of a wider coverage of televised offerings.

In comparison with other methods for capturing data about television offerings, the meter has obvious advantages. Telephone coincidental measurements are limited to telephone households and to those hours when telephone calls are socially acceptable. Recall questionnaires are hampered by the ability of people to remember and their willingness to report the totality of television contact, much of which may be experienced as Don DeLillo's "white noise." Viewing diaries, which come closest to meters in their ability to capture total television contact, are circumscribed by diary keepers' industry, forthrightness, and stamina. In short, meters are superior for assessing all television offerings—"all the truth"—because they do not rely upon the disruptive involvement of human beings.

Syndicated services based on telephone coincidentals, recall questionnaires, and, increasingly today, diaries, have been displaced by the meter-based system (even though they offered the potential to provide more detail about the viewing experience) because they all embodied design trade-offs that sacrificed too much in coverage. The irritating aspect of the meter compromise for many is that television *viewing* is not measured: The meters capture what television sets, not people, do. Advertisers long have figured that meter-based audience estimates were larger than the actual audience, particularly the audience for commercials. Television critics and academics often have complained that the meter-based numbers said nothing about audience appreciation or involvement. Even shows receiving high numbers might not really be popular, but just what most people could tolerate in view of the alternatives. This assumption was the basis for the Markle Foundation's funding of Television Audience Assessment, a qualitative diary-based measurement service, as an alternative to Nielsen. The notion was that, if high-quality programs with low meter-based ratings could be shown to have an avid and attentive audience, their commercial value to advertisers and their likelihood of survival might increase. But, despite its test demonstrations that television programs differed in audience involvement, Television Audience Assessment failed. Like its predecessors, it could not match the continuous coverage of all television offerings provided by the meter.

The fact that the television industry has consistently accepted the meter-based trade-off—coverage over actual viewing—is an eloquent illustration of the way compromises have generally been struck in the syndicated measurement business. A few additional examples will suffice to exemplify the priority placed on wider coverage over detailed images in audience survey design. In radio audience measurement, Hooper's telephone coincidental syndicated service, introduced in the mid-1930s, was seen as an improvement over Crossley's (CAB) 24-hour recall telephone method not only because it obtained reports about radio listening immediately (rather than trusting respondents' recall) but also because it offered a formula for imputing listening behavior to households whose telephones were busy or who refused to participate (Beville, 1985). This ability to cover households missed by the CAB approach heightened the advantage provided by the coincidental method.

But the coincidental method had coverage weaknesses, as we have seen above: It was limited to measurement of listening in households with telephones and was limited to those hours when telephone calls could acceptably be made. Hooper introduced a mixed methodology involving both coincidental calls and diary reporting when faced with competition from the Nielsen audimeter, a device not dependent on telephones or restricted to certain day parts. Eventually, Nielsen's electronic device attached to radio receivers supplanted the coincidental method, removing human beings from the measurement process and setting the stage for meter-based television ratings. Then the diffusion of transistor radios caused the household-based meter itself to have a coverage problem: It could not measure listening to portable or car radios. It was replaced by a personal diary, the method used by Arbitron today.[5]

In magazine readership measurement, the coverage issue led to the development of two successful and competing syndicated services. Simmons Market Research Bureau (SMRB) offered the "through-the-book" measurement approach based on a technique developed by Alfred Politz, a legendary market researcher who had done custom readership studies for a number of publications. The through-the-book approach is a complex, time-consuming personal interview in which respondents must complete a card sort of magazine logos and then peruse specially prepared issues of the magazines identified in the card sort as those read within the previous 6 months. Interviewers carry more than 100 magazines and 20 decks of cards with the magazine logos arranged in various orders to control for order effects in the screening phase. The specially prepared magazines are "aged" so that the respondents could have read them, but the magazines are not supposed to be so old that they might have been forgotten. Readership is determined by presenting respondents with the prepared ("stripped") magazine issues, guiding them through the issues, asking if they see anything "interesting," and finally asking if they have seen the issue before. Those reporting having seen the issue are counted as part of the average audience for the magazine and are asked follow-up questions about their reading of that publication.

This elaborate procedure was designed by Politz to avoid the overreporting of readership that might result from asking respondents to report their reading based on free recall. Counting as readers only those respondents who recognized the issue prepared for the interview offers conservative, tangible evidence of readership. The Politz method is an example of custom research that goes to extraordinary lengths to achieve credibility among advertisers who are, as noted above, likely to view custom research with a jaundiced eye. Custom readership studies conducted in this fashion by Politz for *Life* and *Look* magazines established the through-the-book approach as the "gold standard" of readership measurement (Hardy, 1990; Mayer, 1958). The approach was adopted by William Simmons some years later, this time as the basis for a syndicated service.

The obvious difficulty with the through-the-book approach in the syndicated setting is that its elaborate detail constrains the number of magazines that can be measured. If the list of measured publications was significantly lengthened, respondents would report a greater number of publications seen in the previous 6 months. And if, in turn, respondents were required to peruse stripped versions of all of the publications that they had seen, the interview would be intolerably lengthy. The through-the-book method was developed in custom research to address readership of a few publications. Its use in a syndicated research setting presents a significant trade-off between care in measurement and coverage of media content. Simmons's coverage problem opened the door for a competing measurement service. Mediamark Research Incorporated (MRI) addressed the problem by introducing a competing readership service based on the "recent reading" approach. Rather than having respondents look at prepared issues of magazines, this technique asks them to report which magazines they have read recently. This significantly abbreviated approach allowed MRI to measure the readership of considerably more publications. Because of its significant coverage advantage, MRI was able to establish itself as a source of official audience reality despite the fact that its measure of readership did not have the Politz reputation for care and conservatism. (To be sure, not all media clients appreciate conservatism in audience estimates even if their advertising clients do; MRI's generally more liberal estimates are appreciated by many simply because they are higher.)[6] Thus, for more than a decade, there have been two versions of magazine audience truth on the market in the United States. For the magazines measured by both services, the general approach to interpretation is that the through-the-book estimates are too low and the recent reading estimates are too high. The two services can be seen as providing alternative realities that offer checks and balances on each other.

The evolution of magazine and radio audience measurement illustrates the importance of coverage of media offerings in a measurement service's bid to become a social convention. Care and detail in measurement do matter, of course, but when these goals conflict with coverage, they are likely to be subjugated. This observation is reinforced when we consider the fate of services that never achieved conventional status, even though they provided careful measurement detail that all could acknowledge. Consider, for example, R. D. Percy's passive people meter operation, one of the casualties of the upheaval in television ratings in the 1980s. Percy offered a finely detailed, second-by-second examination of television viewing behavior using very expensive electronic monitoring and videotaping equipment. Unlike Nielsen's successful people meter system, the Percy approach provided more minute observations and did so without involving humans in measuring themselves. The investment in producing this level of detail meant that only limited coverage—the New York market—could be achieved with the funding from early sponsors. Percy (1993) has noted that sponsors underestimated by a factor of 10 what the

service would have cost to cover the national television audience. When assessing a syndicated service's claim to validity in practical terms, sponsors sign up for proposals that ensure "all the truth" more readily than those that emphasize "only the truth."

CONCLUSION:
THE SYNDICATED/CUSTOM BALANCE

The demise of the R. D. Percy system and Television Audience Assessment illustrates how difficult it is to establish a syndicated service. Though both offered interesting perspectives on television audiences, their truths were too precious and special to serve as conventions. Both could, however, serve as the basis for custom studies where the unusual, fine-grained approaches could draw attention despite single-client sponsorship. Of interest, subsequent to its demise as a syndicated service, a version of the Percy system was used in a custom effort measuring exposure to Whittle Communication's Channel One, a narrowcast news program for schools.

The strength of syndicated studies is in measuring "all the truth," while the advantage of custom studies is in assessing "only the truth." These complementary advantages suggest why the two approaches to building audience reality are still in regular use. While clients desire to be measured as part of the official truth provided by syndicated services, they rankle at the price of standardization. Cable television interests have complained for years about not being included in Nielsen's regular ratings reports. (The national sample is too small even today to reliably estimate the audience for such well-known offerings as CNN and MTV alone; and so the current Nielsen "Pocketpiece" includes audience estimates for all cable-originated national offerings grouped together.) CBS, on the other hand, has complained regularly in recent years that the standard Nielsen report does not present sufficient detail about its audience (because it focuses on viewers' demographic characteristics and not on their purchasing behavior). The custom study provides a means to document those audience images that are traded away in the syndicated study design. Thus custom studies provide not merely supplementary, but often oppositional, data to contrast with the syndicated mainstream orthodoxy. The two major forms of audience research play off against one another in the continuing social construction of audience reality, each in its own way claiming to reveal the audience that is really out there.

NOTES

1. The views expressed in this chapter are based on interviews with advertising, media, and research company personnel; my participation in activities of the Advertising Research Foundation; and my observations at media industry conferences and workshops.

2. Audience simulation involves entering information such as publishing philosophy and target audience into a computer program that weights these factors and produces, using information in its database on the audience drawing power of similar established magazines, estimates of the audience for the nascent publication. The service is essentially the same as ones that simulate the sales and market share of new consumer goods, and has been offered by BASES, a privately held marketing simulation firm.

3. The revenues of even very well established custom research firms are subject to substantial variability. Two diversified firms that gained considerable reputations through political polling and were associated with the Reagan and Bush administrations—The Wirthlin Group and Market Opinion Research—had revenues in the late 1980s that varied as much as 25% from year to year (Miller, in press).

4. Webster and Lichty (1991) provide a number of examples of supplementary products offered by audience measurement services as offspring of the standard database.

5. As media technologies and their uses evolve, methods suitable for assessing all of their offerings can run into increasing trouble and may be replaced by others. Just as the audimeter was replaced in the case of radio by the personal diary when radio listening outside the home became a prominent use of the medium, so too the household-based television meter has come under increasing criticism for not covering television use outside the home. Depending on the diffusion of miniaturized televisions and the popularity of sports bars, one may see household meter-based audience measurement supplanted or supplemented by other methods (probably personal diaries).

6. A comparison of the fall 1993 SMRB and MRI reports reveals that the MRI approach yields magazine audience figures that are 32% higher, on the average, than the Simmons numbers for the same publications. Illustrating the positive reaction that many media clients have to higher numbers for their offerings, Norman Hecht, former head of the Arbitron television audience measurement operation, is reputed to have had a sign on his desk to greet complaining clients, sardonically, with the phrase, "Up Is Right."

REFERENCES

Anderson, S. (1966). *Winesburg, Ohio*. New York: Viking.

Beville, H., Jr. (1985). *Audience ratings: Radio, television, cable*. Hillsdale, NJ: Lawrence Erlbaum.

Douglas, M. (1986). *How institutions think.* Syracuse, NY: Syracuse University Press.

Hardy, H. (Ed.). (1990). *The Politz papers: Science and truth in marketing research*. Chicago: American Marketing Association.

Jackson Lears, T. J. (1993). Sherwood Anderson: Looking for the white spot. In R. Fox & T. J. Jackson Lears (Eds.), *The power of culture* (pp. 13-37). Chicago: University of Chicago Press.

Lewis, D. (1968). *Convention: A philosophical study.* Cambridge, MA: Harvard University Press.

Mayer, M. (1958). *Madison Avenue, U.S.A.* New York: Harper.

Miller, P. (in press). The public opinion industry. In C. Salmon & T. Glasser (Eds.), *Public opinion and the communication of consent.* New York: Guilford.

Percy, R. (1993). If they come we will build it. *MRCC Review, 4*(6), 1.

Rosse, J., Dertouzos, J., Robinson, M., & Wildman, S. (1978). Economic issues in mass communication industries. In Federal Trade Commission, *Proceedings of the Symposium on Media Concentration* (pp. 46-47). Washington, DC: Government Printing Office.

Stinchcombe, A. (1959). Bureaucratic and craft administration of production. *Administrative Science Quarterly, 4,* 168-187.

Webster, J., & Lichty, L. (1991). *Ratings analysis: Theory and practice.* Hillsdale, NJ: Lawrence Erlbaum.

Wimmer, R., & Dominick, J. (1991). *Mass media research: An introduction* (3rd ed.). Belmont, CA: Wadsworth.

Chapter 5

POWER TO THE PEOPLE (METER):
AUDIENCE MEASUREMENT TECHNOLOGY
AND MEDIA SPECIALIZATION

Beth E. Barnes and Lynne M. Thomson

PICK UP ANY MEDIA industry trade journal today and you're likely to find at least one article referring to tumultuous changes in the television industry. Broadcast network audiences continue to shrink and cable channels continue to proliferate while advertising dollars continue to shift out of broadcast television. And, you'll probably also find some advertising agency's or television network's latest attempt to explain the fragmentation of the television audience and to project the future of the television industry. The last truly mass medium in the United States seems to be losing its grip on the masses.

Media diversification and specialization, while relatively new and urgent concerns for television industry insiders, are not new issues for media industry scholars. More than two decades ago, for example, Richard Maisel (1973) argued that, much as the socioeconomic change from preindustrial to industrial society had been marked by the development of mass media, so the change from industrial to postindustrial society was being marked by the development of "specialized communication designed for homogeneous audiences" (p. 161). And, indeed, his analysis of U.S. media growth rates between 1950 and 1970 showed greater growth in specialized media than mass media across a number of media industries including newspapers, books, and magazines. Maisel concluded that

AUTHORS' NOTE: We thank James Ettema for his guidance from the earliest beginnings of this chapter through to its present form.

75

communication scholars should "abandon the outmoded view of the individual as simply the recipient of standardized messages emanating from the mass media" and should broaden their "present preoccupation with the mass media to a full examination of all major media and communication systems" (p. 169).

A decade later, in another landmark analysis, Ithiel de Sola Pool (1983b) surveyed the technological innovations that were rapidly reorganizing all major media and communication systems in the 1980s. From his position of "soft" technological determinism, Pool saw, in these newly emerging communication and information technologies, the possibility of enhanced political freedom. "Freedom is fostered when the means of communication are dispersed, decentralized, and easily available, as are printing presses or microcomputers," he wrote (p. 5). "Central control is more likely when the means of communication are concentrated, monopolized, and scarce, as are great networks." Pool's primary concern was that the "era of giant media may nonetheless leave a set of permanent regulatory practices implanted on a system that is coming to have technical characteristics that would otherwise be conducive to freedom."

To be sure, socioeconomic change and technological innovation drive the process of media specialization and diversification. To understand the process itself, however, we must look at how media industries actually work—in particular, we must look at the relationship between media organizations and advertisers. Wilson and Gutiérrez (1985) adopted this premise in their own case for the likely "end of mass media" (p. 217). Like Maisel and Pool, they cite social and technological forces behind the move toward media specialization. Racial diversity creates significant new audiences, they argued, and developments in communication technology make new media forms and new media delivery systems possible. However, these observers emphasized the role of advertising in media specialization:

> More than population growth and technological advances, it is the economic mechanisms of support that control the development of media in the United States. . . . When advertising is increased for a particular segment of the population, the media that reach and influence that segment gain increased advertising dollars. These dollars also make it more profitable for managers of existing media to consider changing formats and content to try to attract that segment and the advertising dollars that will follow. (Wilson & Gutiérrez, 1985, p. 223)

As Wilson and Gutiérrez (1985) understood, the commodity that the media sell to advertisers is "not the amount of space or time for the advertising message, but the size and composition of the audience that will be exposed to the advertising message" (p. 225). They also recognized that advertisers were increasingly interested in more precisely segmented markets that could be reached through more precisely targeted advertising vehicles. Thus the logic of media specialization, according to Wilson and Gutiérrez (1985), was that media content producers would no longer look for "commonalities among diverse groups in the mass audiences" but would "look for differences and ways to capitalize on those differences through content and advertising" (p. 234).

A FIELD OF DREAMS

The logic of media specialization, as presented in these analyses, is that, under conditions of social differentiation and sufficient channel capacity, specialized media formats will be created to meet the needs and interests of specialized audiences because advertisers wish to reach those audiences. While this analysis of the role of advertising in "demassifying the media" is essentially correct, it contains a rather simplistic, *Field of Dreams* assumption: "If you build it [specialized content], they [specialized audiences and, in turn, advertisers] will come." The actual process through which audience needs and interests can be met by more specialized media offering greater content diversity is, as we shall argue here, far from technologically and organizationally simple. In addition to content delivery technologies such as cable television, there is another critical technology at play on this field of dreams: the technology for measurement of audiences and the accompanying conceptions of the audience held by those who employ these technologies.

In the United States, media content producers and advertising agencies (on behalf of their clients) subscribe to the reports produced by various audience measurement services. Producers use these reports to make decisions about programming and editorial content and to set advertising prices. Advertising agencies and their clients use them to make decisions about where to advertise and how much to pay for a given audience. Advertisers insist on documentation of the existence and composition of the audience before making any advertising expenditures. Thus, without audience measurement technology, any specialization among media audiences would go unrecognized—and unrewarded—by advertisers. Measurement services purport to reflect audience preferences. The audience is said to "vote with its eyes" and thereby establish relative popularity levels for electronic media programming and print media titles. That vote, however, is effective only once it is "tallied" and made public by the measurement services. The implication for media specialization is that, while societal forces may lead to changes in media consumption behavior such as increased popularity of specialized media vehicles, documentation of that changed behavior is necessary before the specialized vehicles can attract the economic support they need to survive in the media marketplace. In that sense, the *measurement* of audience behavior, not audience behavior per se, changes the media.

In *Forecasting the Telephone: A Retrospective Technology Assessment* (1983a), Pool argued that the most accurate projections of the social impact of new technologies are based on an examination of both technical capabilities and market realities. Any understanding of the changes in advertiser-supported media requires an understanding of the capabilities not only of content delivery technology but also of audience measurement technology. And it requires an understanding not only of the market for content but also the market for advertising. In this chapter, we pursue these issues in an attempt not merely to understand the changes under way in the television industry but to understand, more generally, the process of media specialization.

We begin our analysis with the process of specialization in magazine publishing during the 1960s. This provides a useful starting point for two reasons. One is that the changes in magazine publishing helped to lay the technical and conceptual groundwork for the changes in television two decades later. The other reason is that magazines provide a comparative case study that helps to illuminate the current state—and, perhaps, the future—of television. As we shall show, the history of both eras of increased media specialization turns on the replacement of an existing form of audience measurement with a newer, more technically advanced form.

MAGAZINES IN THE 1960s

The history of magazine publishing in the 1960s is often recounted as simply a story of changing content delivery systems in which one mass medium—general interest magazines—gave way to another—television. Conventional wisdom has long held that the lingering "deaths" of two well-known mass circulation publications, *Look* and *Life,* were the result of competition from television for advertising dollars. *"Look* suffered from the same disease that killed such magazines as the *Saturday Evening Post* and *Colliers* before it," *The Economist* reported (*"Look* Lost," 1971, p. 56). "The steady loss of advertising revenue to television was the worst drain." Reporting on the end of *Life* the next year, the same publication concluded that "television also drew the advertisers away; it offered them a larger audience at a comparatively low price" (*"Life* Bows," 1972, p. 54).

While the focus on advertising is correct, the conventional account is too simple. The story must include not only a change in content delivery technology but also a change in audience measurement technology; and it must include a change in the advertising industry's conception of the audience. In 1965 *Time* magazine commissioned a study that sparked considerable interest in the concept of market segmentation. In that study, the readerships of various magazines were characterized in terms of some basic demographic factors (education, occupation, and income); and, in turn, those demographic characteristics were matched with information about the use of 86 different products and services. The combination provided advertisers with new information on which publications were likely to do the best job of delivering audiences made up of the users of particular products. A report on the study in *Printer's Ink* noted the importance of such an analysis: "Data of this sort gives today's marketers the insight into markets so necessary to make effective decisions" ("New Focus," 1965, p. 34). Technical know-how and industry interest were coming together to rethink the role of magazines in the advertising media mix.

In one of the leading marketing texts of the time, Kotler (1967) described segmentation as an attempt to divide the broad market of the general public into meaningful groups and to focus marketing activities against those groups that are most likely to buy the product. In an advertising media selection context, an emphasis on segmentation would lead to the selection of media vehicles (television programs, magazine titles, and so on) on the basis of their ability to deliver members of the desired target audience rather than the selection of those vehicles that merely deliver the largest number of people overall.

Attention to segmentation in the academic literature and customized studies like that conducted by *Time* suggest that advertisers were beginning to see the importance of dealing with something other than a vaguely conceptualized mass market or mass audience. As their interest in audience segments grew, however, so did the need to measure and analyze media delivery of those segments. Another critical conceptual development of the 1960s, media reach and frequency, addressed those needs. Media reach and frequency involve looking at an entire media schedule for a particular product and estimating the total number of people exposed to the advertising (the reach), and the number of times each is exposed (the frequency). These ideas promoted further refinement in advertisers' images of media audiences. Rather than focusing on the consumer market as a whole, advertisers came to focus on that portion or segment of the market (e.g., women aged 25-44) that could be reached via a particular media vehicle or combination of vehicles. So, for the advertiser of the 1960s—and today—media exist to provide *reach,* at a desired *frequency* level, against a portion of the desired *market segment.*

To effectively estimate reach and frequency, however, advertisers needed much more sophisticated data about media audiences, and in the 1960s the availability of that data was facilitated through technological advances not in data collection but in data analysis. While some market researchers had experimented with the reach and frequency ideas as early as 1948, the industry as a whole did not make use of them until the 1960s. In a 1987 interview with the authors, longtime market researcher Seymour Banks of the Leo Burnett advertising agency in Chicago argued that the delay may have been due, in part, to "the great intellectual inertia in any industry." However, the complexity of the data necessary to calculate reach and frequency was another inhibiting factor. The necessary computing power to calculate national reach and frequency estimates was simply not available to advertising agencies until the 1960s.

The information on consumer magazine readership and product usage included in the *Time* magazine study was similar to that collected by the W. R. Simmons Company and other research firms at the time. During the mid-1960s, Banks, who was then director of media research for Leo Burnett, obtained original survey results from one of the magazine audience measurement services and loaded that data into Burnett's own computers. There, according to Banks, programmers were able to devise ways of recombining the data in custom formats not available in the published results provided by the measurement services. The availability of computers allowed advertising agencies to cope with massive quantities of media audience and product purchasing information and promised, according to *Advertising Age* ("Computers Open," 1964), a media selection tool that heretofore had been unavailable—indeed impossible.

Initially, the necessary computing capability was available only to a few of the largest advertising agencies, and so most advertising media plans continued to rely on the old mass audience/mass media concepts. This situation changed in 1969 when two companies were formed to provide more advertisers and agencies with access to sufficient computing power. Integrated Marketing Systems (IMS) and Telemar both offered clients on-line access to the Simmons's product and media audience data through terminals in the clients' own offices. Individual publications also subscribed to these services, enabling them to provide customized analyses to smaller clients who might not be subscribers themselves. The information provided through IMS and Telemar allowed publications to sell themselves on the basis of audience segmentation. "Print [media] could justify targeting because now they had the information," recalled Sue Hodson, midwest research manager for *Time* during the late 1960s (personal communication, 1987). "Print delivered specific target audiences."

The demise of *Look* and *Life* soon followed the widespread availability of this more detailed audience information. While some observers facilely laid all the blame on television, others saw that more specialized magazines were also to blame for the loss of advertising dollars suffered by those less specialized publications. A 1972 postmortem of *Life* in *Advertising Age* featured interviews with representatives of companies who had been heavy advertisers in *Life* ("*Life* Expires," 1972, p. 1). Perhaps the most telling comment came from a company that had decided to pull its advertising dollars from *Life* in the upcoming year. American Motors reported that it had used a computer program to select its magazine list for 1973 based on effective reach for the company's desired target audience. "Although it was an extensive list, including the auto buff books," *Advertising Age* noted, "three magazines were notable by their absence— *Life, Reader's Digest,* and *TV Guide*" ("*Life* Ad Dollars," 1972, p. 89). While *Life* and other mass circulation magazines could provide advertisers with a large audience at a relatively low cost for each audience member, the cost to reach specific audience segments could be quite high (compared with the cost of advertising in a more targeted publication). Thus American Motors chose magazines with more specialized audiences to achieve its print media objectives.

Other advertisers offered similar explanations for their decisions to move their companies' advertising dollars from mass circulation publications like *Life* to more targeted magazines. Representatives from Seagram's noted that "the demographics of *Life* had become 'less and less attractive' " and said that they would shift their dollars to *Playboy, Time,* and *Newsweek* (quoted in *"Life* Ad Dollars," 1972, p. 89). Similarly, the manager of advertising and sales promotion for Mazda Motors said that " 'the book' no longer fitted the needs of enough auto marketers" and that "the publications targeted on specialty areas are the ones 'growing by leaps and bounds' " (p. 89).

The proportion of total spending allocated to magazines by these and other advertisers did not decrease greatly following the demise of the mass circulation magazines (Barnes & Thomson, 1988a). Rather, the spending shifted to more specialized publications. As *The Economist* pointed out in its report, "The specialist magazines are the dream of the marketing men and advertisers who can be sure that they are reaching potential customers" (*"Life* Bows," 1972, p. 54). Altogether, this evidence strongly suggests that television has been overrated as a cause of the mass circulation publications' downfall. Instead, the technological advancements in audience information availability coupled with the market's increased emphasis on audience segmentation paved the way for the growth of more specialized magazines with more narrowly defined audiences.

Content specialization is now the norm in the magazine industry, and audience measurement continues to play a critical role in any publication's success or failure. Writing in 1981, Rosse noted that "magazines tend to seek a well-defined demographic profile in their readership so as to attract an advertising clientele interested in marketing to a particular age-income-education-sex-race-occupation group" (p. 43). Today, the Standard Rate and Data Service (SRDS) (1992) lists magazine titles under approximately 70 different subject classifications, many of which have been added over the last two decades, such as "Computers," "Fitness," and "Mature Market."

In today's advertising marketplace, however, a narrowly targeted publication still cannot get the attention of advertisers unless it can provide third-party documentation of its audience delivery. In a 1989 presentation to a symposium of advertising agency media planners, Debbie Solomon, then a media supervisor with the J. Walter Thompson advertising agency, noted that magazines not measured by the various syndicated audience research services were at a tremendous disadvantage to their measured competitors. While many unmeasured publications might offer very selective, highly interested audiences, those publications would not show up on standard media planning computer runs; and if they did not show up there, they would not attract advertiser support. Thus the lack of generally accepted audience data robs a publication of an image of its audience to sell to advertisers. For example, a highly specialized publication such as *Vegetarian Times* has not been listed because of its small circulation while *Entertainment Weekly,* a larger circulation publication, was not listed for several cycles after its introduction simply because of its newness. Both publications had problems gaining advertiser support.

TELEVISION IN THE 1980s

The history of television in the 1980s, much like that of magazines in the 1960s, is often recounted as a story of changing content delivery technology. As recently as 1983, the typical U.S. household received 14.6 television channels (Seagren, 1988) but by 1989 it received 30.5 channels (Nielsen Media Research, 1989). The increase was due in large part, of course, to the expansion of cable television. In a 1982 guide to incorporating cable television into advertising media planning, Kaatz provided programming summaries for 16 cable networks, but by 1990 27 national networks were broadcasting 24 hours a day (McManus, 1990).

The increase in the number of cable networks was likely fueled in part by cable's penetration gains throughout the 1980s. Basic cable television was found in 24% of U.S. television households in 1980, 42% in 1985 (Kaatz, 1982), and 61% by the third quarter of 1992 ("Summary," 1992). While the impressive growth of cable television penetration across the 1980s provided would-be cable programmers with larger potential audiences, a change in audience measurement technology provided another strong impetus for the viability of cable network television as an advertising medium. In fall 1987, A. C. Nielsen Company introduced the "people meter" technology that could collect data on the viewing behavior of individual audience members. This technology was heralded as an improvement over the previous "audimeter" technology that could only capture viewing data at the household level. The audimeter was a passive monitoring device attached to the television set in participating homes that recorded when a television set was turned on and to which channel it was tuned; the meter could not record which members of the household were actually watching the program. With the people meter, however, each household member is assigned an identification number. When a television set is turned on, the meter records the channel to which the set is tuned and presents a message on the television screen prompting each viewer to enter his or her identification number using a keypad that resembles a television remote control device. In this way, the people meter collects data on viewing behavior for each household member.

Nielsen's decision to make the change from audimeters to people meters was primarily a competitive marketing decision. While Nielsen has long been the dominant force in national television audience measurement in the United States, other firms provide similar services in other countries. One of those companies, Audits of Great Britain (AGB), attempted to break into the U.S. market by introducing the people meter technology. When AGB began a field test of people meters in the Boston market, Nielsen responded to the competitive threat by announcing that it would convert its measurement system to people meters as well. When it became clear that the advertising and media industries would not support two national people meter systems, AGB withdrew from the United States (Webster & Lichty, 1991). The genesis of people meter measurement underscores the fact that audience measurement is, itself, a media industry in which decisions are made based on market factors rather than social scientific measurement ideals. These events echo one of Pool's (1983a) observations on the development of telephony: "What actually emerged was determined by what could be effectively marketed . . . in short, by economic considerations" (p. 155).

Before the introduction of people meters, Nielsen estimated the demographic composition of the network television audience by combining household viewing data from audimeters in 1,400 U.S. households with audience composition data from a similar number of paper-and-pencil diaries distributed to other households (Beville, 1985). While this method and sample size provided adequate audience measurement for the broadcast television networks (CONTAM, 1989), the sample was too small to produce reliable audience composition estimates for the lower penetration cable television networks. To measure cable television audiences, Nielsen combined the household tuning information from the national audimeter sample with audience composition estimates from 100,000 local market diaries distributed quarterly during rating sweeps months ("Highs and Lows," 1985; Katz & Lancaster, 1989). This form of audience measurement put the cable networks on an unequal footing with the broadcast networks because the information on cable television viewing for different demographic groups, so vital for audience segmentation strategies, was only made available several months after the end of the sweeps month rather than overnight as was the case with the broadcast television networks.

In addition to data availability problems, many people in the advertising industry felt that the diary form of audience measurement (in which the respondents were asked to keep records of their television viewing over the course of a week) was not appropriate for cable television networks. Kaatz (1982) summarized the problems with the use of diaries to measure cable television viewing:

- By and large there is not adequate space for listing all of cable's multiple channels.
- There is a general confusion on the part of the viewer as to identification of the different cable channels.
- Just as it has long been felt that diaries tend to penalize the lower-rated, occasionally viewed broadcast programs, there would be an even greater problem with cable's small audience levels. (p. 126)

The lack of acceptable audience measurement data kept many advertising agencies from recommending cable to their clients. As Anne Benvenuto (1987), vice president of planning and media resources, Time Buying Services, Inc., wrote 7 months before Nielsen made the switch to people meters: "For cable to achieve its potential as an advertising medium, it must move swiftly to establish more credible and accurate reporting of audience measurement" (p. 72). All in all, the cable networks had a very difficult time constructing a description of the audience that they had available to sell to advertisers, a situation similar to that faced by unmeasured magazines.

At the time of its introduction, the people meter audience measurement technology was expected to benefit cable in two ways. First, audience measurement at the individual (rather than household) level would help many of the cable networks support their contention that they were delivering audiences that were more demographically attractive than those delivered by the broadcast networks. The cable networks believed that they had the audience segments advertisers wanted to reach, but they did not have acceptable data to support that belief. When comparisons were made on the basis of aggregate (household) level data, the cable networks' audiences were so small compared with those of the broadcast networks that there was little to attract advertisers' attention. Once the cable networks had data available that showed that their small audiences were also demographically selective, the small size could be downplayed in favor of the ability to reach attractive market segments.

Second, and perhaps more important, to implement the people meter system successfully, Nielsen had to increase the size of its metered sample from 1,400 households to 4,000 households. This increased sample size meant that ratings for the cable networks would be more statistically reliable and available overnight (Barnes & Thomson, 1988b; Thomson, 1990). Dan Fisher, director of research at the Discovery Channel cable network (quoted in "Television," 1987), commented on the twin benefits of increased sample size and individual level measurement: "The real benefit of people meters for cable will come with the daily demographic data that will come from a larger sample base, making it easier to sell advertising for cable's narrowly targeted programming" (p. 38). Nielsen's people meter sample reached the 4,000 household level by the fourth quarter of 1988, and by the spring of 1990 a leading advertising industry trade publication was able to report that "cable executives say they're finally on a level playing field with broadcast" (Barrett, 1990, p. 32).

With the new audience measurement technology, advertising agencies finally had access to the kinds of audience measurement numbers that they needed to include cable in clients' media schedules, and cable advertising revenues began to increase steadily (McManus, 1990). While advertising industry sources cited a variety of reasons for the growth in cable revenues, including increased penetration levels and improved programming (McManus, 1990), Thomson (1990) provides evidence that the introduction of people meters had an impact on the revenues of cable networks— particularly the more specialized networks. An interrupted time-series analysis of the advertising revenues for the six largest cable networks— CNN, MTV, and ESPN, which concentrate on particular audience segments, as well as CBN (now The Family Channel), WTBS, and USA, which try to attract much broader audiences—found that the introduction of people meters had a positive effect on the amount CNN and ESPN were able to charge advertisers for each viewing household. At the same time, the prices the three less targeted networks (CBN, WTBS, and USA) were able to charge advertisers decreased. The pattern for MTV was different in that the impact of people meters on revenue occurred much more quickly than for the other networks. However, MTV's per-household revenue also increased following the introduction of people meters.

Thomson's conclusions were based on an analysis of revenues across 23 broadcast quarters beginning with the first quarter of 1985 and ending with the third quarter of 1990. Each cable network's revenue-per-household rating point was adjusted to remove the effects of inflation and the overall increase in advertisers' demand for national television audiences. After detrending, the data indicated that, during the quarter when people meter data were first available, the less targeted networks' revenues declined by 4% from the previous quarter while the more specialized networks' revenues increased 22%. And, over the four quarters following the introduction of people meters, the less targeted networks saw a 3% net decline in advertising revenues compared with an 18% net increase for the more specialized networks (Thomson, 1990).

While these results suggest that the new measurement technology facilitates specialization, our interpretation of the results has not met with universal agreement among industry insiders. In interviews conducted in 1990, some advertising media professionals agreed that people meter data provide the greatest benefit to the more targeted cable networks: "The theory is right," said Jon Mandel, senior vice president and director of national broadcasting, Grey Advertising. "The more targeted people [networks] were helped." Others, however, felt that all measured cable networks would benefit equally from the new technology because they could, at last, document audience size. Kevin Killion, then director of media research at DDB Needham Worldwide advertising agency, noted that with the old technology "there was a tremendous amount of fear [among media planners] in using cable TV because the cable networks couldn't prove it [size of audience delivered]." Thus some advertising professionals continued to emphasize audience size over specialization. As expressed by Wes Dubin, senior vice president, DDB Needham Worldwide (who was director of national broadcasting when interviewed in 1987): "Now that the group [cable networks] can give some semblance of mass, they can go for targeting; but the horse is size, the cart is targeted audiences."

Despite this enduring tendency to view television as the last bastion of mass appeal, some industry analysts thought they had spotted the trend toward greater segmentation in the medium. Jon Steinlauf, executive vice president of Sports News Network, noted, "All of the successful networks [launched] over the past five years have been vertically programmed" (quoted in Keefer, 1990, p. 26). And at the same time, analysts saw advertisers becoming increasingly dissatisfied with the "waste" inherent in broadcast media vehicles (Button, 1988). That is, advertisers were increasingly unwilling to pay to reach people who were not prospective purchasers of their product or service. As Wilson and Gutiérrez (1985) noted, "Rather than wanting to address an undefined mass audience, advertisers prefer to target their messages to specific audiences whose demographic profiles are known to them" (p. 225). A 1992 survey of advertising agency media directors revealed that "76.6% of respondents are defining target audiences more narrowly than they were just three years ago" (Loro, 1992, p. S-18). A media manager at Grey Advertising said, for instance, "Budgets from clients are under pressure; we can't afford waste" (quoted in Loro, 1992, p. S-34).

In response to the pressure to reduce waste in advertising schedules, the more detailed audience data available from people meters should direct media planners' attention toward more specialized, and therefore more efficient, media. And these data show that the cable networks do, indeed, offer more homogeneous audiences—a reality that not all industry insiders accepted before the technology was implemented. As people meters were being introduced in fall 1987, Barry Cook, then vice president of media research for the NBC television network, told the authors that "cable promised narrow-casting but all they ended up with is a small-casting." However, Barnes (1990) provides evidence that many of the cable networks now in operation do provide far more homogeneous audiences (defined in terms of the basic demographic factors of age and sex) than do the broadcast networks. Using published ratings reports, audience homogeneity values (as shown in Table 5.1) were calculated for the combined audience of the three broadcast networks and for the audiences of 21 cable networks regularly measured by people meters. The demographic profile of the actual audience for each network during the first quarter of 1989 was compared with the potential audience, where potential audience was defined as the demographic profile of the entire people meter sample. The lower the audience homogeneity value, the closer the composition of the actual audience to the potential audience. In other words, lower values indicate less homogeneous demographic profiles. Only two cable networks (USA and WTBS) deliver audiences as heterogeneous as those of the broadcast networks. Nickelodeon, Financial News Network, and MTV are among the most targeted cable networks.

Further evidence comes from a comparison of people meter data on national cable television network audience composition with data on local radio and television station audience composition in three markets (Los Angeles, New York, and Denver). The results of the comparison show that radio delivers the most targeted audiences, followed by cable networks and then over-the-air television networks. These findings further support our contention that cable is leading the way in demassifying the last mass medium. The people meter measurement system has provided cable networks with a means to document their delivery of specific audience

TABLE 5.1. Demographic Audience Homogeneity Values, First Quarter, 1989

Network	Audience Homogeneity
National Broadcast Networks	
(ABC, CBS, NBC)	13.2
Cable Television Networks:	
Nickelodeon	94.1
Financial News Network	79.8
MTV	67.6
Cable News Network	65.0
The Discovery Channel	50.9
The Nashville Network	50.8
Headline News Network	49.9
The Weather Channel	48.8
Arts & Entertainment Nighttime	46.1
ESPN	42.4
VH-1	42.2
Black Entertainment Television	38.2
Nick at Nite	37.4
Showtime	36.7
Arts & Entertainment Daytime	36.7
The Family Channel	33.6
Turner Network Television	32.6
Lifetime	30.1
Home Box Office	27.6
WTBS	12.0
USA Network	11.6
Cable Network Average	44.5

NOTE: The audience homogeneity index is based on data from the *Nielsen Homevideo Index: Cable Network Audience Composition Report* (first quarter 1989), which divides the audience into 11 age/sex categories (i.e., children 2-5, children 6-11, teens 12-17, men 18-34, women 18-34, men 35-49, women 35-49, men 50-64, women 50-64, men 65+, women 65+). The index was computed following these steps: (a) The number of persons in each of these categories who viewed each of the networks was converted into a percentage; (b) the number of persons in each of these categories included in the total people meter sample was converted into a percentage; (c) for each category, the percentage of persons who viewed the network was subtracted from the percentage in the total sample; (d) the absolute value of these differences were summed for each network to yield the index for that network.

segments, although it should be noted that the various audience measurement services continue to wrestle with the problem of underrepresentation of minority audiences in their samples. While Wilson and Gutierrez (1985) emphasize the growing importance of those audiences to advertisers, minority media consumption is still not well documented.

TELEVISION AT A TURNING POINT

The early 1990s saw no "deaths" among broadcast television networks corresponding to those among mass circulation magazines in the early 1970s. However, in a development highly reminiscent of the last days at *Life,* a major advertiser announced in 1992 a plan to shift significant portions of its media budget out of broadcast network television. That advertiser was Chrysler Corporation—the firm that had absorbed American Motors some years before. "We have a better understanding of who the buyer is," said John Damoose, Chrysler's vice president of marketing, explaining his firm's plan to move dollars to "more targeted media" (quoted in Serafin, 1992, p. 44). "If you're building products that are clearly targeted, then the mathematics [of media efficiency] brings you to the media that go right to your prospects." Part of Chrysler's former broadcast network advertising budget was allocated to cable television.

Into the 1990s, the broadcast networks' share of the television audience continued to shrink, forcing them to scramble to maintain their advertising revenues. From the fourth quarter of 1989 to the third quarter of 1990, for example, the three major networks' share decreased from 58% to 52% while the basic cable networks' share increased from 16% to 20% during those same months (Saldivar, 1991).

The introduction of people meters provided the measurement technology that could make these changes real to the television industry. Into the 1990s, media content producers, advertising agencies, and their clients were still trying to construct images of audience behavior that they could all believe. *Adweek* noted in 1990 that Nielsen had "been slow in delivering computer software that cable networks and advertising agencies need to fully understand the ratings and to manipulate the numbers into effective sales tools" (Barrett, 1990, p. 32). And so industry observers expected the cable networks to be the beneficiaries of further refinements in the technology. At the same time, advertisers were increasingly budget conscious. "Clients have been paying more attention to their media in the last several years than they did before," said a senior media professional (quoted in Lafayette, 1991, p. 12). Thus increasing pressure on agency media departments to eliminate waste in advertising schedules, along with the availability of more detailed audience data through the people meter measurement system, were expected to make targeted cable television channels a still more attractive option for advertisers.

While the economic picture for cable appeared favorable, conceptual issues related to market and audience segmentation remained problematic.

The logic of media specialization requires an emphasis on advertising vehicles that deliver more homogeneous (and therefore smaller) audiences over vehicles that deliver larger (and therefore more heterogeneous) audiences. Cable audiences were more homogeneous (and smaller), as documented here, but the advertising industry had yet to fully relinquish its emphasis on audience size. To interest national advertisers, cable networks had to balance the demand for homogeneity with sufficient audience size. "Critical mass [for a new cable service to attract national advertisers] is probably 20 to 25 million homes," said Larry Gerbrandt, analyst with Paul Kagan Associates. "A network has got to see its way to that level within three years" (quoted in Keefer, 1990, p. 27).

Thus, in the early 1990s, television was poised at a turning point. While media history suggested that segmentation would win out over sheer size, advertising agencies were slow to relinquish the cherished image of television as the last great mass medium.

THE LOGIC OF SPECIALIZATION

Our look back has been an attempt to show, first, how magazines "have become so specialized in targeting homogeneous segments of the population," according to Hirsch (1981, p. 198), "that they may no longer even fit the traditional definitional requirement that mass-media channels appeal to a heterogeneous mass audience." We have argued that the received history of specialization in magazine publishing is, at best, incomplete. The demise of large circulation magazines is the history of innovation in not only content delivery technology but also in audience measurement technology—a story not only about the incursion of television but also about computer analysis of survey data. Further, it is the history of changes not only in audience behavior but in advertisers' conceptions of audiences—a story not only about what audiences wanted but about how to segment and reach those audiences. We have also argued that an understanding of how audience measurement technologies affected magazines can help us understand the more recent changes in television.

The socioeconomic and technological developments described by Maisel, Pool, and others are certainly among the fundamental causes for media specialization. However, the logic of the specialization process— that smaller, more homogeneous audiences offer advertisers more value per person than larger, more heterogeneous audiences—requires acceptable audience data to operate. Without that data, the audience has no reality for advertisers and, consequently, no value (or, at least, greatly reduced value relative to a "known" audience). And, if the audience has no value, the medium will not attract advertiser support. Thus audience measurement technologies play a vital role in sustaining the media whose audiences they measure. And as the measurement technologies have changed over time to adapt to their own markets, they have facilitated the specialization of the mass media.

Great changes such as postindustrialism are only realized through many smaller changes in the specific practices of particular organizations. Our examination of one characteristic feature of postindustrialism—media specialization—makes these changes seem somewhat less necessary and inevitable; or, at least, our examination makes the presumed death of the mass media seem somewhat less peaceful. Increased social diversity or increased channel capacity do not somehow *naturally* give us the blessings of more specialized media formats and more diverse media content. As we have shown, the relationship between the fundamental causes and ultimate effects is mediated by the specific practices of audience measurement.

But now that facilitative measurement technologies are in place, will the process of diversification in advertiser-supported media continue to some logical and inevitable conclusion? Decreases in sheer audience size caused by specialization must be balanced by advertisers' willingness to pay for those specialized segments. That willingness to pay, along with the ability of audience measurement services to keep up with the need for increasingly precise measures, will determine the ultimate degree of diversification. Thus the history of the media will continue to be the story of audience images and of the measurement technologies that generate those images.

REFERENCES

Barnes, B. E. (1990). *Electronic media audience behavior in the multi-channel environment: Patterns of demographic homogeneity and time spent viewing.* Unpublished doctoral dissertation, Northwestern University.

Barnes, B. E., & Thomson, L. M. (1988a, May). *How will networks respond to the advent of peoplemeters?* Paper presented at the meeting of the International Communication Association, New Orleans, LA.

Barnes, B. E., & Thomson, L. M. (1988b). The impact of audience information sources on media evolution. *Journal of Advertising Research, 28*(5), RC-9 to RC-14.

Barrett, S. (1990, April 2). The power of the people. *Adweek,* p. 32.

Benvenuto, A. (1987, February 16). More clients will use cable TV when cable fills its data vacuum. *TV/Radio Age,* p. 72.

Beville, H. M., Jr. (1985). *Audience ratings: Radio, television and cable.* Hillsdale, NJ: Lawrence Erlbaum.

Button, G. (1988, May 16). The big picture. *View,* p. 22.

Computers open new vistas in pinpointing audiences, seminar told. (1964, June 1). *Advertising Age,* pp. 3, 98.

CONTAM (Committee of National Television Audience Measurement). (1989). *Methodological research on television audiences.* Westfield, NJ: Statistical Research, Inc.

Highs and lows of Nielsen Homevideo Index. (1985, November). *Marketing and Media Decisions,* pp. 84-85, 134.

Hirsch, P. M. (1981). Institutional functions of elite and mass media. In E. Katz & T. Szecsko (Eds.), *Mass media and social change* (pp. 187-200). London: Sage.

Kaatz, R. B. (1982). *Cable: An advertiser's guide to the new electronic media.* Chicago: Crain.

Katz, H. E., & Lancaster, K. M. (1989). How leading advertisers and agencies use cable television. *Journal of Advertising Research, 29*(1), 30-38.

Keefer, D. (1990, April 2). It's a small world after all. *Adweek's Spring Television Report,* pp. 26-27.

Kotler, P. (1967). Market segmentation. In *Marketing management: Analysis, planning, and control* (pp. 43-65). Englewood Cliffs, NJ: Prentice Hall.

Lafayette, J. (1991, March 4). Agency media staffs gain clout. *Advertising Age,* p. 12.

Life ad dollars will remain in print. (1972, December 11). *Advertising Age,* pp. 1, 89.

Life bows out. (1972, December 16). *The Economist,* p. 54.

Life expires after absorbing loss of $30,000,000 in last four years. (1972, December 1). *Advertising Age,* pp. 1, 8.

Look lost. (1971, September 25). *The Economist,* p. 56.

Loro, L. (1992, July 20). Media planners zoom in for a consumer close-up. *Advertising Age,* pp. S-18, S-34.

Maisel, R. (1973). The decline of mass media. *Public Opinion Quarterly, 37,* 159-170.

McManus, J. (1990, April 2). Growing pains. *Adweek,* pp. 24-25.

New focus on potential markets. (1965, March 12). *Printer's Ink,* pp. 33-34.

Nielsen Media Research. (1989). *The television audience: 1989.* New York: Author.

Pool, I. S., de. (1983a). *Forecasting the telephone: A retrospective technology assessment.* Norwood, NJ: Ablex.

Pool, I. S., de. (1983b). *Technologies of freedom.* Cambridge, MA: Belknap.

Rosse, J. N. (1981). Mass media: The economic setting. In E. Abel (Ed.), *What's news* (pp. 33-53). San Francisco: Institute for Contemporary Studies.

Saldivar, L. (1991, January 23). *Cable TV performance and viewing distribution report.* New York: Saatchi & Saatchi Advertising.

Seagren, S. (1988). Station and channels: Receivable vs. actually viewed. In *Television audience 1988* (pp. 55-62). New York: Nielsen Media Research.

Serafin, R. (1992, March 23). Chrysler may switch off prime time ads. *Advertising Age,* pp. 1, 44.

Solomon, D. (1989, June). Romancing the data: Justice for unmeasured magazines. In J. Z. Sissors (Chair), Media Planning Symposium. Evanston, IL: Northwestern University.

Standard Rate & Data Service. (1992, May). *Consumer magazine and agri-media rates and data.* Wilmette, IL: Author.

Summary of broadcasting and cable. (1992, September 21). *Broadcasting,* p. 77.

Television in the peoplemeter age. (1987, September 7). *Broadcasting,* pp. 35-40.

Thomson, L. M. (1990). *The impact of audience information sources on media evolution.* Unpublished doctoral dissertation, Northwestern University.

Webster, J. G., & Lichty, L. W. (1991). *Ratings analysis: Theory and practice.* Hillsdale, NJ: Lawrence Erlbaum.

Wilson, C., II, & Gutiérrez, F. (1985). *Minorities and media: Diversity and the end of mass communication.* Beverly Hills, CA: Sage.

Chapter 6

THE CHANGING INFRASTRUCTURE
OF PUBLIC OPINION

Susan Herbst and James R. Beniger

IN EVERY POLITY there exist distinctive relationships among conceptions of "the public," the dominant techniques for assessing "public opinion," and the media through which members of the public may express their desires. At any given historical moment, the nexus of these relationships can be viewed as an *infrastructure of public opinion*—a patterned, orderly arrangement that dictates the form and content of public sentiment. This infrastructure legitimates particular means of opinion expression and devalues others. It includes some social groups in the political process and excludes others. And it enables political leaders to maintain social control.

In contemporary American politics, for example, the public is often conceptualized as a highly fragmented, if not entirely atomized, entity that the mass media, nonetheless, try to characterize as cohesive. While public opinion polling now may be the principal means of opinion assessment, voting remains the most highly valued form of opinion expression. In any case, both polling and voting embrace a conception of public opinion as the aggregation of individual opinions and both provide means for elite management of those opinions.

One useful way to gain perspective on the contemporary infrastructure of public opinion is to examine the patterns of expression found in previous eras. Thinking about the structural components of public expression and how they fit together forces the analyst to ask a series of critical questions: What has constituted "the public" at pivotal moments in political history? How have connotations of "public opinion" changed over time? In what ways do innovations in communication technology affect prevailing ideas of public opinion? How does change in one component of the infrastructure affect the other components? By delineating historical trends in communication technologies, in techniques of opinion expression and measurement, and in conceptions of the public, the unique—and contingent—nature of contemporary expression becomes apparent.

In this chapter, we outline three idealized infrastructures of public opinion based on brief sketches of three interesting moments in political history. Because ideal types are abstract, they facilitate the identification and comparison of key aspects of a phenomenon and thus facilitate the building of theory. Most difficult in analyzing public opinion infrastructures is the identification of prevailing conceptions of the public. For most historical periods, we are forced to rely on the writings of intellectuals who were interested in assessing the publics of their own periods and who attempted to provide realistic portraits of a public's nature and behavior.

For example, James Bryce, the nineteenth-century British statesman, wrote extensively about the public behavior he saw on his several visits to America. Bryce's observations, though empirical, were nevertheless colored by his own grand theoretical assumptions about the public. Even though most of those who have written about public opinion have similarly chosen to ignore or distort phenomena inconsistent with their own theories, we cannot afford to dismiss their work. The writings of Bryce, Tocqueville, and Rousseau, among others, contain much unique, and therefore invaluable, data about the societies in which they lived. While such work confronts us with epistemological problems—ones that deserve far more attention than we can give them here—we acknowledge such problems by attempting to reconcile intellectual and social historical evidence from a wide variety of sources.

TECHNOLOGIES AND PUBLICS

Although scholars from history, political science, sociology, and other fields have long studied the history of public opinion (Noelle-Neumann, 1984; Palmer, 1964; Speier, 1950; Tilly, 1983), few have scrutinized the role of technology in shaping notions of the public. With the significant exceptions of Wilhelm Bauer (1930) and Jürgen Habermas (1989), theorists have usually opted to gather definitions of "public opinion" from different eras without attending to changes in communication technologies (e.g., Childs, 1965; Noelle-Neumann, 1984).

To the extent that publics might be viewed as bodies formed through communication, inattention to technology becomes problematic. As Gabriel Tarde (1901/1969) argued almost a century ago, it is communication or "the transportation of thought across distance" that distinguishes a public from a crowd (p. 279). Because crowds must occupy physical space, Tarde reminds us, an individual can be part of only one crowd at a time. Publics, by contrast, bind people only by virtue of their shared interests and ideas; any one individual might belong simultaneously to a variety of publics. Communication technologies provide the means by which interests and ideas are shared, especially as societies grow larger and more complex; hence such technologies are necessary to form and sustain publics.

Because printed materials facilitate the exchange of ideas across vast geographic areas, some scholars argue that the sixteenth-century adoption of printing in the West enabled the eventual emergence of publics. Eisenstein (1979) notes that, although printing weakened patterns of oral communication, it created modern publics by strengthening other types of interaction and expression:

> By its very nature, a reading public was not only more dispersed; it was also more atomistic and individualistic than a hearing one. Insofar as a traditional sense of community entailed frequent gathering together to receive a given message, this sense was probably weakened by the duplication of identical messages which brought the solitary reader to the fore. . . . But even while communal solidarity was diminished, vicarious participation in more distant events was also enhanced; and even while local ties were loosened, links to larger collective units were being forged. Printed materials encouraged silent adherence to causes whose advocates could not be found in any one parish and who addressed an invisible public from afar. (p. 132)

Whatever the merits of Eisenstein's argument, a problem remains: Definitions of the public and public opinion did not assume an atomized, mass public in the sixteenth, the seventeenth, or even the eighteenth century. Such connotations did not appear until the late nineteenth and early twentieth centuries, three centuries later than Eisenstein's study would suggest (Herbst, 1993). Although modern notions of the public may have existed in the sixteenth century and even much earlier, they did not become commonplace, we shall argue, until the diffusion of the straw poll in the mid-nineteenth century.

Because there are several periods in Western European history in which the meaning of public opinion is fairly clear, these might serve as case studies to inform theories about changing concepts of the public and about the changing roles of public opinion. Particularly useful to social theorists searching for ideal typical public opinion infrastructures are three of these historical periods: mid-eighteenth-century France, late nineteenth-century America, and the United States from 1936 to the present. Even though our analysis must blithely leap over many other critical times and places, regrettably limitations of space confine us to these three historical case studies in the remainder of this chapter.

MID-EIGHTEENTH CENTURY: THE ELITE PUBLIC

With the exception of Jürgen Habermas (1989), few scholars have recognized the political, literary, and religious discussions of the French *salons* as critical to the development of public opinion. Habermas argues that the salons heralded the emergence of a middle class that stood apart from the State by engaging in the critical analysis of governmental affairs. Although salons might be seen as vehicles for the development of the bourgeoisie, they might also be viewed as a critical part of the public opinion infrastructure of mid-eighteenth-century France.

Despite voluminous research on salons (Clergue, 1971; Coser, 1970; Lougee, 1976; Tinker, 1915), scholars have paid relatively little attention to this institution as a means of communicating public opinion. This oversight is particularly striking considering that when Jacques Necker, finance minister to Louis XVI, coined the phrase *public opinion,* he is generally held to have had salons in mind (Palmer, 1964).

Salons were gatherings of statesmen, business leaders, and intellectuals held in Parisian sitting rooms. Although such meetings took place from the late seventeenth century well into the nineteenth century, some of the more interesting and influential salons were established during the years immediately before the French Revolution. Many of the eighteenth-century *philosophes,* including Rousseau, Montesquieu, Diderot, and Voltaire, not only frequented the salons but often used them as forums to elaborate their ideas (Coser, 1970; Roustan, 1926; Tinker, 1915).

Many of the most famous eighteenth-century salons were organized and maintained by women, some wives of political elites and others of more independent status. As Roustan (1926) notes of the period's intellectuals:

"Were he even a Montesquieu or a Voltaire, it was indispensable to have the support of women. That is how things were done from the beginning of the century, and d'Argenson declares that Madame de Lambert [a well-known salon keeper] created half the academicians of that day" (p. 178).

For our purposes here, salons might be seen as but one component of an opinion infrastructure. Although the books published by active salon members could be influential (e.g., Rousseau's *Social Contract,* published in 1762), salon discussions themselves often had immediate impact. Ideas born in these elite circles were thoroughly discussed there and eventually disseminated through the writings of the philosophes. As historian Paul Palmer (1964) notes, the French king frequently sent emissaries to the salons to achieve an understanding of public opinion. According to Jacques Necker, "During the reigns of Louis XV and Louis XVI the courtiers and even the ministers would have risked displeasing the royal family in preference to exposing themselves to an unwelcome reception in the leading salons of Paris" (Palmer, 1964, p. 238).

The fact that kings monitored the talk of the salons indicates just how central they were to opinion expression and assessment. Any intelligent leader, whether he has read Machiavelli or not, keeps abreast of public opinion because it might turn against him at any time. Public opinion was manifested not only in salon talk but also in the books and essays generated by these gatherings.

It might at first seem odd that the free-flowing, widely varied discourse of the salons could be considered public opinion. Is not the public much larger and more diverse than these exclusive cliques gathered in bourgeois living rooms? In eighteenth-century France, the public was thought to consist exclusively of this intelligentsia, with public opinion the convergence of the views of the statesmen, authors, and critics who debated the political and literary issues of the day. Certainly public opinion was not—in sharp contrast to today—the aggregate distribution of opinions held by all citizens of France.

Although we still have salons (groups of insiders trading gossip and insights at Washington dinner parties, for example), we do not think of these gatherings as *public opinion.* On the contrary, the entire population is thought to constitute the contemporary public, for which public opinion is merely the aggregation of individual opinions (Ginsberg, 1986; Herbst, 1991).

Despite the arguments of Rousseau (1762/1950) that a "general will" served as the basis of a just society, public opinion in the mid-eighteenth century was not generally equated with any such will. On the contrary, the public was an educated elite with the time, ability, and inclination to debate policy and artistic issues, an elite conception of the public that one might argue did not begin to change until the coming of the American and French revolutions.

Perhaps these new democratic movements did forge the way for broader conceptions of the public. By any reasonable reading of the intellectual history of eighteenth-century France, however, commoners of that era were not thought to be members of the public. Intellectuals believed the public to be the bourgeoisie, and they were correct to some extent for widespread participation did not characterize French political life until the days preceding the revolution. Although we may never know just how much attention peasants or workmen paid to state activity before the pre-revolutionary period, it seems safe to say that there was considerable lack of interest among these parties until the latter years of the ancient régime.

During the era of the great salons, public opinion—including its communication and assessment—was much less routinized than it is today. Salon conversation in the eighteenth century was, by most published accounts, unstructured and unconstrained (Coser, 1970). Certain artistic, religious, and political ideas were pursued at length simply out of curiosity and not out of a desire to resolve policy debates.

The specific content of salon discourse is not well recorded because most of the participants chose to write about the forum itself instead of providing detailed accounts of conversations. Several of the philosophes did, however, describe how the salons changed (or failed to change) their thinking (Martin, 1954; Roustan, 1926; Tallentyre, 1901; Tinker, 1915). Even though many of these intellectuals attended salons regularly, the composition of the groups continually changed, and with these changes the form and content of the discourse changed as well.

We identify mid-eighteenth-century France with what we call the *elite model* of public opinion infrastructure. The public in this model is composed of only the most highly educated and influential members of society, while the bulk of the people are purposely excluded because their opinions are thought to be uninformed, and are in any case irrelevant—most people have no political power. Central technologies for the expression and assessment of public opinion in the elite model—namely, salons, books, and essays—are distinguished by unstructured discourse created and exploited exclusively by the elites themselves. The form of opinion expression is critique and the content of public opinion is often oriented to the appraisal of state action.

Although there is no question that many individuals outside of the French salons discussed politics, and that a variety of opinion assessment techniques existed during this period, the model—an elite ideal type— captures well the dominant public opinion infrastructure of the era.

LATE NINETEENTH CENTURY: A PUBLIC OF GROUPS

Much of the Colonial American dialogue about publics and public opinion had begun centuries earlier in Western Europe. Principles set forth in America's Declaration of Independence, for example, echo the seventeenth-century Putney Debates in which Oliver Cromwell's New Model Army openly discussed the problems of majority rule. Various factions of Cromwell's Roundheads, including the Puritans, Pilgrims, and Quakers, took their opinions to North America after the restoration of the British monarchy in 1660. A century later, their descendants carried on the discussion in debates over *The Federalist Papers* (Madison, 1787/ 1961; Wilson, 1942).

American discourse about the nature of publics and public opinion grew throughout the nineteenth century as the new republic industrialized and urbanized. Much of this interest, especially following the Civil War and the rise of a mass press, derived from the writings of two foreign visitors, Alexis de Tocqueville and James Bryce. Their own accounts of their visits, separated by more than half a century, neatly delineate the dramatic changes in political power and public opinion in the United States during the 1800s.

Tocqueville, a French aristocrat who traveled extensively in America in 1831, explicated the mechanics of participation in a democracy in his *Democracy in America,* first published in French in 1835. He is perhaps best known for his theorizing about what he called the "tyranny of the majority" and about the difficulty of challenging popular norms (Tocqueville, 1835/1969). Based on his many critical firsthand observations of life in the new democracy, Tocqueville remained skeptical if not pessimistic about the role of the public in the democratic process.

A half century passed before the arrival of James Bryce, a British jurist and statesman. During the intervening decades, from the democratic reforms of Andrew Jackson through the Emancipation Proclamation to the end of Reconstruction, the right of suffrage had expanded from white property-holding males to all adult males. Not a surprise, Bryce's 1888 work, *The American Commonwealth,* is more optimistic than is Tocqueville's *Democracy in America* about the potential role of the public in government (Bryce, 1894, pp. 354-364). Less interested than Tocqueville in the social psychology of political participation, Bryce focused instead on public opinion, which he termed "omnipotent yet indeterminate," and on the role of the press in influencing and reflecting such opinion.

In the half century since Tocqueville's visit, the American press had begun to develop as a truly mass public institution. The first penny newspaper, the New York *Sun,* opened the way for a mass press in 1833 (2 years after Tocqueville's visit); and in 1883 (5 years before the publication of Bryce's book), Joseph Pulitzer took over the New York *World* and made it into America's first modern mass circulation daily (Beniger, 1986, pp. 264-278). As Bryce observed in 1888, "Newspapers are powerful in three ways—as narrators, as advocates, and as weathercocks. They report events, they advance arguments, they indicate by their attitude what those who conduct them and are interested in their circulation take to be the prevailing opinion of their readers" (Bryce, 1894, p. 263).

Bryce found that political parties and associations, working at times through the press, also influenced the nature of opinion in America. Closely aligned with these parties were newspapers, Bryce argued, that could serve as powerful "advocates of political doctrines" (p. 264). Later scholars (Emery & Emery, 1987; Mott, 1968; Schudson, 1978) have found just such partisanship to be typical of most mid-nineteenth-century newspapers.

One might argue that, at least for the period from the mid-nineteenth century into the early twentieth century, the American public was—and was seen to be—a conglomeration of many diverse groups, political parties being only the most vocal. As these parties and their urban party bosses extended their influence by welcoming immigrants, granting patronage jobs to loyalists, and taking leadership roles in local government, they also became purveyors of public opinion. Not only did they heed public opinion, they also claimed to represent it. Parties almost always took clear positions on issues such as slavery and tariffs, positions that they claimed represented the views of most citizens. According to Hays (1975):

> Political parties, in contrast with other systems of decision-making, were
> uniquely capable of expressing community impulses. Since the party's roots
> lay in geographically organized wards and precincts, in which it had to
> contend for majority support, it reflected closely the character of community

life. . . . If the community sustained a leadership of its more affluent families, so did the party; if it gathered around such local functionaries as the real estate developer, the saloonkeeper, or the grocer, so did the party. (p. 157)

In concert with the newspapers that shared their ideologies, political parties were a critical component of the late nineteenth-century American infrastructure of public opinion expression and assessment.

Other organized groups were part of this same infrastructure. James Q. Wilson (1973) notes that the first "wave" of interest group formation in American politics occurred in the mid-nineteenth century with the founding of various abolitionist groups, the National Grange, Elks, Knights of Pythias, college fraternities, craft unions, and other groups. He argues that new developments in transportation and communication during these years made it easier for groups to organize and to express themselves.

In fact, increased mobility of Americans accelerated the development of groups as key components of the opinion expression process. Local groups became national groups with conventions and newsletters. The notion that one's group was affiliated with other groups was attractive because it legitimated the local group. Affiliations enabled even small local groups to think of themselves as large and influential at the national level.

Political activity of the period remained grounded mostly in local communities. Party candidates and bosses developed and nurtured personal relationships with voters to secure their loyalty to the party. Maintenance of strong and active political parties and interest groups was the major means by which public opinion was expressed and assessed. Although such groups were able to educate and persuade members, they usually merely represented members' needs and opinions. Constant surveillance of public opinion was critical to this task.

Activist politicians knew that they must constantly measure and persuade. When Samuel J. Tilden ran for governor of New York in 1874, for example, he

directed a tightly knit organization that used circular letters to reach down to loyal personal representatives in each township across New York. Through polls of the entire electorate, these men identified the undecided and independent. To capture their votes, the organization tried to cultivate a sense of personal contact with the candidate. Party workers visited each wavering voter and left behind pamphlets about Tilden, copies of his speeches, and issues of Democratic newspapers. (McGerr, 1986, p. 71)

.Although straw polls were used throughout the nineteenth century, they were not the dominant means by which journalists and politicians assessed public opinion. The idea of counting individual opinions to determine public opinion was antithetical to the operations of parties and interest groups that rarely believed public opinion to be volatile enough to require assessment by polling. Party bosses took pride in the fact that they understood the nature of public opinion in their own precincts and communities without resorting to polls.

Throughout the nineteenth century, public opinion was held to be the domain of competitive groups vying for members and offices. We might think of this public opinion infrastructure as a second ideal type, what we shall call the *group-based model.* Although Arthur Bentley wrote as late as 1908, his definition of public opinion seems more accurately to describe the public of the previous century:

> There is no use attempting to handle public opinion except in terms of the groups that hold it and that it represents. Public opinion is an expression of, by, or for a group of people. . . . When we examine this public opinion with its onward tendencies, we find that, besides being borne in a group, or given differentiated expression for a group, it always is directed against some activities of groups of men. (Bentley, 1908/1967, pp. 236-237)

Communication technologies were crucial to this group-based model of public opinion infrastructure. Newspapers, often affiliated with major parties, solidified publics by editorializing (Mott, 1968). The content of the typical nineteenth-century urban newspaper reflected the strong influence of groups because party activity was always news. The combined force of highly organized parties and partisan mass media created a new system for the expression of public opinion. Parties consistently used newspapers, among other media, to persuade and mobilize constituents and potential members. Several scholars (Dinkin, 1989; Jensen, 1971; McGerr, 1986) have documented the extent of such systematic organizing by the parties during this period.

By the turn of the century, parties had begun to lose both their influence and their ability to speak for the public (Burnham, 1975; McGerr, 1986; Sundquist, 1983). Keller (1977) notes that the economic disruptions of the 1890s (agricultural pricing problems, depression in industry, massive unemployment) strained social cleavages and served as a catalyst for change. The structures and values of the old partisan politics were the first victims of reform-seeking activists.

Other changes in social life also made partisanship less popular. McGerr (1986) argues that the idea of leisure, born in the late nineteenth century, was responsible for steadily decreasing enthusiasm for party activities as amusement parks, boxing, football, and bicycling displaced the parades and demonstrations of party politics (p. 148). Ever-expanding transportation and communication systems forced everyone to confront new people, groups, and ideas often more stimulating than those found in their own local neighborhoods. Above all other factors, it was the shift away from community-based activities that weakened local parties.

Few reformers in the progressive movements of the decades between 1890 and 1920 could resist attacking political parties and their influence in local government. The Mugwumps, for example, argued that parties ought to be temporary and formed around current issues. As one Mugwump reasoned, "We should not go on stupidly transmitting from sire to son the antipathy begotten by obsolete party differences which have been outlasted by party names" (Keller, 1977, p. 551).

The progressive movement changed the nature of both political discourse and political institutions. Old-style local political bosses and personal politics were weakened by the new national politics. Technologies like direct primary elections and the civil service system developed to rationalize traditional politics. By the turn of the century, Americans' ideas of public opinion began to assume characteristics of the new mass society.

THE TWENTIETH CENTURY: PUBLICS AS AUDIENCES

With the increasing popularity of film in the early twentieth century and the rapid diffusion of radio in the 1920s and 1930s, the composition of the public shifted dramatically. As the new media captured the public imagination, community-based groups—like the nineteenth-century political parties—faded further. Advertisers and politicians started to exploit new communication technologies to influence buying and voting decisions while broadcasters developed new means to study their audiences.

The new radio networks, the newly formed National Association of Broadcasters, and the new quantitative social science all began in the 1930s to study radio audiences in earnest (Beniger, 1986, chap. 8; Hurwitz, 1983). Audimeter-based "Nielsen ratings" of radio programming, introduced in 1935, enabled broadcasters and advertisers for the first time to evaluate the detailed composition of audiences.

These ratings also served to atomize the broadcast audience by grouping listeners into a large, anonymous mass. According to Hurwitz (1983), "By cutting across virtually all groups of society with its programming appeal and statistical apparatus, broadcasting depersonalized audiences and allowed them to reconstruct their identities in its own, more individualistic image" (p. 18).

As the broadcasting media developed more scientific approaches to audience and opinion assessment, those interested in politics began to adopt many of the same measurement activities. George Gallup's success in predicting the outcome of the 1936 presidential election proved a turning point in the conceptualization of public opinion. Since the late 1930s, survey researchers have worked to perfect large-scale sampling procedures and questionnaire design (Beniger, 1986, chap. 8; Converse, 1987).

As polling and survey research became increasingly attractive to politicians, journalists, and market researchers (Sabato, 1981), these techniques began to reinforce the image of the public as an aggregation of individuals rather than a conglomeration of groups (Ginsberg, 1986; Herbst, 1993). This image of the public as an aggregation of individuals dates back at least to the Greek democracies, where each man had one vote and votes were totaled so as to make policy. Not until the twentieth century, however, did a variety of parties begin to see how more sophisticated opinion assessment techniques might provide deeper insights into individual voting intentions and behavior.

Two relatively minor events in the history of public opinion—separated by 80 years—illustrate the shift from publics to audiences during the intervening period. In 1856 Norfolk, Virginia, theater managers refused to let journalists take a straw poll in their theater because the managers did not want to demean the play by talk of electoral politics. Apparently in 1856, politics constituted one realm, theater quite another.

In 1936, by contrast, Charles Pettijohn, counsel for the Motion Picture Producers and Distributors Association, announced the results of straw polls, conducted in 900 theaters throughout the United States, in which observers judged the enthusiasm of audiences for screen images of President Roosevelt and his Republican opponent, Alf Landon. Evidently, polls of theater audiences had become commonplace between 1856 and 1936.

Buried deep in one newspaper report of these polls was this qualification: "While White House attachés attributed considerable importance to the Pettijohn report, movie audience reaction has yet to be accepted as an entirely reliable means of judging public sentiment" ("Roosevelt Aids," 1936, p. 9). Because modern sampling methods are supposed to allow us to capture the public mood in a "scientific" manner, we rarely see such qualifications today. Even though today's polls and surveys may be more accurate than those of the past, the value of their data as indicators of public opinion is still challenged by scholars (Blumer, 1948; Bourdieu, 1979).

With the expansion of broadcast media and the introduction of sample surveys and audience ratings, publics and audiences began to seem interchangeable: Politicians used these media to persuade us even as advertisers used them to sell us consumer goods. The difference between audiences and publics remains important, however, because "public" implies political participation while "audience" has a more passive, reactive connotation (Fiske, 1987).

We identify the third of our three ideal types, the *audience model* of public opinion infrastructure, as based on a mass public composed of individuals linked mostly by communication media, if at all, and described "objectively" by market researchers and public opinion pollsters. In sharp contrast to the elite and group models, the *audience model* is associated with a variety of highly organized communication technologies including mass media, sample surveys, and broadcast ratings. Although the idea that individuals—when aggregated—might constitute a public has a long history, this notion did not became hegemonic until the twentieth century.

In contemporary social life, the content of public opinion is discerned through polls of an atomized mass. In its ideal type, the public of this model is an audience that watches but is also watched, thereby yielding greater control over these preferences (Beniger, 1983, 1986). In fact, an infrastructure of public opinion that boasts an atomized public is more readily manipulated from above, as so many mass society theorists have argued (Beniger, 1987). This group of theorists, which includes members of the Frankfurt School, were intensely interested in public opinion infrastructure but chose to write about components and not patterns— about *gesellschaft* in the absence of an elaborated structure of *gemeinschaft.*

INFRASTRUCTURE, RATIONALITY, AND SOCIAL CONTROL

Historical changes in public opinion infrastructure follow a predictable pattern of increasing rationalization. Compared with the free-flowing and loose opinion communication among the elites of the salons, opinion communication in our time is highly constrained by pollsters. Opinions are embodied in numbers and not in conversation. This is not to say that political conversation has disappeared but that public opinion is thought to be contained in the succinct statistics disseminated by the mass media. Thus we might view the group model of public opinion as a transitional stage, one in which patterns of expression are becoming more routinized but are not yet fully rationalized.

The theorist who wrote most eloquently about historical processes of rationalization was Max Weber (1920/1958, 1946, 1978). Weber believed that, as social and political systems evolve, the central institutions that compose these systems become increasingly structured, hierarchical, and organized. Efficiency and effectiveness become the key goals of such institutions, Weber argued, and bureaucracy is the ultimate exemplar of a highly rationalized system. In fact, bureaucratic organization based on standard operating procedures and regulations was for Weber the quintessential model of rationality. As with all ideal types, however, no empirical bureaucracy approaches the ideal, although some are much more rationalized than others (Albrow, 1990).

This Weberian conception of rationality must not be confused with other more commonplace uses of the term *rationality*. Because Weber found that rational means might be used to achieve irrational ends, he did not consider more rational systems necessarily superior to less rational ones. On the contrary, he believed that increasing rationalization would most likely have detrimental consequences, including the suppression of spirituality, brotherly love, and emotion-based action (Bendix, 1962; Brubaker, 1984; Weber, 1920/1958).

Although communication scholars rarely apply Weber's insights, concepts like rationalization can be useful in the study of infrastructures and systems. Like organizational systems, systems of public expression might be similarly classified according to how rational they are. In our three-model historical analysis, it is clear that the public opinion infrastructure of the mid-eighteenth century was comparatively less rational. Discussions in the salons proceeded in a disorderly fashion and debates remained unresolved—more questions were asked than were answered. Occasionally salon conversation may have inspired themes for books and essays, but generally this was not the case.

Although the king's emissaries to the salons were an occasional presence, there is no evidence that these men systematically visited a sample of salons to get a representation of general public opinion. Because most French citizens were excluded from the public opinion expression and assessment process, the system was not as efficient as it might have been. A more rationalized system might have included at least the peasant and working classes. The result—the French Revolution—provides evidence enough that the public opinion infrastructure lacked sufficient means for efficient societal control short of brute force.

In nineteenth-century America, the infrastructure of public opinion began to take on more rational, modern characteristics. Newspapers affiliated with parties and groups worked hard to organize their constituents. Because the notion that organized groups could express opinions and thereby influence government became more deeply ingrained in the political culture, political parties could develop more highly routinized procedures of opinion assessment and expression. One element of irrationality remaining in this group-based infrastructure, however, was a deficiency in technologies for the precise measurement of public opinion. Although legislators and party bosses kept an ear to the ground, they were often surprised by the behavior of voters (McGerr, 1986).

The contemporary American infrastructure of public opinion is much more rationalized than those of previous eras. Mass media now transmit much of the information needed to formulate opinions; survey researchers now poll the populace overnight on any issue; and political elites now predict election outcomes with considerable confidence. On the surface, at least, this would appear to be an effective system of social control, certainly a highly rationalized one. And yet Weber worried—nearly a century ago—about the tendency of advanced rationalization to produce a growing "disenchantment" with life. Post-cold war students of public opinion would do well to reexamine such concerns, which seem more pressing today than they did in Weber's lifetime.

One reason rationalized systems usually work well is that they are specifically oriented to social control. Bureaucracies, for example, can be extremely efficient, yet they are also easily manipulated by those who hold high positions within them. Similarly, highly rationalized public opinion infrastructures are also amenable to control by elites. Media executives and pollsters can decide what issues the public will be queried about; presidents can usually monopolize the nation's attention through their access to centralized media; and public opinion data enable political candidates to structure persuasive rhetoric.

In the age of salons, comparable dominance by a few was much more difficult to obtain. The French monarch was much less able to control his subjects except through the use of force. By the nineteenth century, real competition among political parties had emerged because control of the public remained difficult to obtain. When a Republican newspaper attempted to shape reality according to its views, a Democratic newspaper would construct a competing, alternative reality. Lacking centralized media, how could a class of elites possibly control such systems? If they usually managed to do so, they rarely did so efficiently or without protracted conflict.

Rationalization, which works best for those at the top of a given system, works best today. Weber, who thought long and hard about the implications of this tendency, could find no way to escape it. There are always trade-offs, he argued, among the effectiveness of a given system, the amount of social control exerted by its elites, and the equality of its citizens. These trade-offs remain today, still largely unaddressed and certainly unresolved.

TOWARD A THEORY OF
PUBLIC OPINION INFRASTRUCTURE

The content of public opinion usually changes with developments in opinion infrastructure. As one of us has argued elsewhere (Herbst, 1993), the dominance of polling as a means of opinion communication produces a public sentiment that is wide but not deep. Random sampling enables the efficient representation of American public opinion by a few thousand respondents, yet the opinions expressed are reactive and brief. In contemporary politics, the audience model honors succinct numerical portrayals of public opinion over "messier," less structured ones. Poll data are often pitted against less rationalized forms of opinion data (e.g., speeches, demonstrations, letter-writing campaigns) and are usually seen as more legitimate (Ginsberg, 1986). In many issue debates, polling numbers are viewed as data about public opinion, while statements about the issue by organized groups (like labor, environmentalists, or women's groups) are explicitly labeled as "special interest" opinion.

A public opinion infrastructure necessarily includes a shared definition of who "the public" is, various dominant opinion expression and measurement technologies, and a centralized means for disseminating these opinions. Although opinion infrastructures therefore change with developments in technology, they cannot be abstracted from political structure and culture. Particular opinion infrastructures develop simultaneously with emerging political systems in a mutually reinforcing fashion. At times a new development in technology might accelerate a change in infrastructure, but this must be accompanied by a strong desire to use the technology if it is to become part of the opinion communication system.

One example of a technological breakthrough that accelerated a change in opinion infrastructure is the sample survey. With Gallup's successful use of random sampling in the 1936 election, elites and citizens began to realize that public opinion might be expressed and measured more "scientifically." It was apparent that the straw poll, exemplified by the disastrous 1936 *Literary Digest* survey, could not compete with more rigorous, accurate assessment techniques.

Scientific polling techniques would not have developed, much less gained widespread attention, however, if an aggregation-oriented model of the public had not already existed. But this model did exist in 1936, and grew in the popular imagination as polling became more refined and more accurate. Today the mass media not only communicate poll data to the public but also have begun to develop their own survey capabilities (Beniger & Herbst, 1990).

The question of causality—of whether the development of public opinion technologies precedes or follows conceptions of the public—is not central to a theory of public opinion infrastructure. As in much historical research, specifying the precise dates for the emergence of an idea or a technology is extremely difficult. Such difficulties in mapping causal relationships ought not to detract from the analysis of infrastructures and the construction of ideal types. Theorists of public opinion might simply take the long view of the chronicle of public opinion, much as Weber, Marx, Durkheim, and the other grand social theorists of the nineteenth century did in their own historical analyses.

If we are to expand on the usefulness of the idea of public opinion infrastructure, an enormous amount of archival research must be completed. Certainly this will require sources spanning broad periods as well as considerable expertise in textual analysis. Much of this work would be labor intensive, to be sure, but it would nonetheless seem worth the effort. Without it, we cannot know the extent to which we have allowed our technologies to determine the nature of our public discourse and affairs rather than shaping our technologies to serve the kind of civil society in which we would most like to live.

REFERENCES

Albrow, M. (1990). *Max Weber's construction of social theory.* New York: St. Martin's.

Bauer, W. (1930). Public opinion. In E. Seligman (Ed.), *Encyclopedia of the social sciences* (pp. 669-674). New York: Macmillan.

Bendix, R. (1962). *Max Weber: An intellectual portrait.* New York: Anchor.

Beniger, J. R. (1983). The popular symbolic repertoire and mass communication. *Public Opinion Quarterly, 47,* 479-484.

Beniger, J. R. (1986). *The control revolution: Technological and economic origins of the information society.* Cambridge, MA: Harvard University Press.

Beniger, J. R. (1987). The flirtation with mass society. *Public Opinion Quarterly, 51,* S46-S66.

Beniger, J. R., & Herbst, S. (1990). Mass media and public opinion: Emergence of an institution. In M. Hallinan, D. Klein, & J. Glass (Eds.), *Change in societal institutions* (pp. 211-238). New York: Plenum.

Bentley, A. (1967). *The process of government.* Cambridge, MA: Harvard. (Original work published 1908)

Blumer, H. (1948). Public opinion and public opinion polling. *American Sociological Review, 13,* 242-249.

Bourdieu, P. (1979). Public opinion does not exist. In A. Mattelart & S. Siegelaub (Eds.), *Communication and class struggle* (pp. 124-130). New York: International General.

Brubaker, R. (1984). *The limits of rationality: An essay on the social and moral thought of Max Weber.* London: George Allen & Unwin.

Bryce, J. (1894). *The American commonwealth.* New York: Macmillan.

Burnham, W. D. (1975). American politics in the 1970's: Beyond party? In W. N. Chambers & W. D. Burnham (Eds.), *The American party systems: Stages of political development* (2nd ed., pp. 277-357). New York: Oxford University Press.

Childs, H. (1965). *Public opinion: Nature, formation, and role.* Princeton, NJ: Van Nostrand.

Clergue, H. (1971). *The salon: A study of French society and personalities in the eighteenth century.* New York: Burt Franklin.

Converse, J. (1987). *Survey research in the United States: Roots and emergence 1890-1960.* Berkeley: University of California Press.

Coser, L. (1970). *Men of ideas.* New York: Free Press.

Dinkin, R. (1989). *Campaigning in America: A history of election practices.* Westport, CT: Greenwood.

Eisenstein, E. (1979). *The printing press as an agent of change: Communications and cultural transformations in early-modern Europe.* Cambridge: Cambridge University Press.

Emery, E., & Emery, M. (1984). *The press and America: An interpretive history of the mass media.* Englewood Cliffs, NJ: Prentice Hall.

Fiske, J. (1987). *Television culture.* New York: Methuen.

Ginsberg, B. (1986). *The captive public: How mass opinion promotes state power.* New York: Basic Books.

Habermas, J. (1989). *The structural transformation of the public sphere: An inquiry into a category of bourgeois society.* Cambridge: MIT Press.

Hays, S. (1975). Political parties and the community-society continuum. In W. Chambers & W. Burnham (Eds.), *The American party systems* (pp. 152-181). New York: Oxford University Press.

Herbst, S. (1991). Classical democracy, polls, and public opinion: Theoretical frameworks for studying the development of public sentiment. *Communication Theory, 1,* 225-238.

Herbst, S. (1993). *Numbered voices: How opinion polling has shaped American politics.* Chicago: University of Chicago.

Hurwitz, D. L. (1983). *Broadcast "ratings": The rise and development of commercial audience research and measurement in American broadcasting.* Unpublished doctoral dissertation, University of Illinois, Champagne-Urbana.

Jensen, R. (1971). *The winning of the Midwest: Social and political conflict, 1888-96.* Chicago: University of Chicago Press.

Keller, M. (1977). *Affairs of state: Public life in late nineteenth century America.* Cambridge, MA: Harvard University Press.

Lougee, C. (1976). *La paridis des femmes: Women, salons and stratification in 17th century France.* Princeton, NJ: Princeton University Press.

Madison, J. (1961). Paper No. 10. In C. Rossiter (Ed.), *The Federalist papers.* New York: New American Library. (Original work published 1787)

Martin, K. (1954). *The rise of French liberal thought: A study of political ideas from Bayle to Condorcet.* New York: New York University Press.

McGerr, M. (1986). *The decline of popular politics: The American North, 1865-1928.* New York: Oxford University Press.

Mott, F. (1968). *American journalism, a history: 1690-1960.* New York: Macmillan.

Noelle-Neumann, E. (1984). *The spiral of silence: Public opinion—Our social skin.* Chicago: University of Chicago.

Palmer, P. (1964). The concept of public opinion in political theory. In *Essays in history and political theory in honor of Charles Howard McIlwain* (pp. 230-257). New York: Russell and Russell.

Roosevelt aids stirred by movie audience reaction. (1936, August 19). *Chicago Tribune,* p. 9.

Rousseau, J. J. (1950). *The social contract and the discourses* (G. D. Cole, Ed. and Trans.). New York: E. P. Dutton. (Original work published 1762)

Roustan, M. (1926). *The pioneers of the French revolution.* Boston: Little, Brown.

Sabato, L. (1981). *The rise of political consultants.* New York: Basic Books.

Schudson, M. (1978). *Discovering the news: A social history of American newspapers.* New York: Basic Books.

Speier, H. (1950). Historical development of public opinion. *American Journal of Sociology, 55,* 376-388.

Sundquist, J. (1983). *Dynamics of the party system: Alignment and realignment of political parties in the United States.* Washington, DC: Brookings Institution.

Tallentyre, S. (1901). *The women of the salons and other French portraits.* New York: Longman, Green.

Tarde, G. (1969). The public and the crowd. In T. Clark (Ed.), *On communication and social influence* (pp. 277-294). Chicago: University of Chicago. (Original work published 1901)

Tilly, C. (1983). Speaking your mind without elections, surveys, or social movements. *Public Opinion Quarterly, 47,* 461-478.

Tinker, C. (1915). *The salon and English letters.* New York: Macmillan.

Tocqueville, A. de. (1969). *Democracy in America* (J. P. Mayer, Ed.). New York: Anchor. (Original work published 1835)

Weber, M. (1946). Science as a vocation. In H. H. Gerth & C. W. Mills (Eds.), *From Max Weber: Essays in sociology* (pp. 129-156). New York: Oxford University Press.

Weber, M. (1958). *The Protestant ethic and the spirit of capitalism* (T. Parsons, Trans.). New York: Scribner. (Original work published 1920)

Weber, M. (1978). *Economy and society: An outline of interpretive sociology* (G. Roth & C. Wittich, Eds.). Berkeley: University of California Press.

Wilson, F. G. (1942). The Federalist on public opinion. *Public Opinion Quarterly, 6,* 563-575.

Wilson, J. Q. (1973). *Political organizations.* New York: Basic Books.

Chapter 7

ONE-WAY FLOWS AND THE
ECONOMICS OF AUDIENCEMAKING

Steven S. Wildman

THE FILMS AND TELEVISION programs produced and distributed by the major U.S.-based studios dominate the international trade in video entertainment and have for decades (Guback, 1969). For example, in 1992 the United States realized export revenues of $3.7 billion on sales of audiovisual products to Europe while spending just $288 million importing audiovisual products from Europe (Waxman, 1993). The European situation is not atypical. If anything, Europeans supply more of their own video entertainment than most market-oriented nations.[1] U.S. films and television programs dominate the video imports of most nations and they are a conspicuous, and often a dominating, presence in the cinema and on television almost everywhere.[2] By contrast, foreign producers, especially those from countries in which English is not a native language, have had little success cracking the American market.

The dominant position of the United States in the international trade in films and television programs has been a prominent topic and the source of considerable controversy in the communication literature. While foreign audiences have been enthusiastic consumers of U.S. films and programs, policymakers and film and television producers in these countries, and academics almost everywhere, have been much more critical—seeing American video exports as threats to domestic cultures and cultural industries. A number of theories have been advanced to explain the success of U.S. video exports. The economic model of commercial responses to audience heterogeneity set out in this chapter is a fairly recent addition to the list. Both commercial and political motives have been implicated in the earlier work on this topic. Schiller (1969) is probably most closely identified with the argument that intensive exposure of audiences in other countries to U.S. films and programs is "part of a general effort of the American military industrial complex to subject the world to military control, electronic surveillance and homogenized American commercial culture" (p. 89).[3] According to this scenario, first American films, and later American television programs, were seen by powerful members of the U.S. government as valuable instruments for demonstrating to the world the superiority of American values and the American lifestyle. Of course, exports of American goods would follow the export of American ideals. Thus U.S. government efforts to open foreign markets to U.S. films and programs served the dual goals of promoting U.S. foreign policy aims and the sales of U.S. industries.

Other theorists have seen U.S. dominance of video trade flows more simply as a consequence of commercial strategies employed by the major U.S. studios. Guback (1969, 1977) has pointed to the U.S. major studios' control of the primary distribution channels in most countries as an important factor contributing to American dominance of the film trades in these countries. According to this argument, control of distribution channels is used to keep competitors' films from exhibitors. Related arguments have pointed to allegedly anticompetitive practices such as block booking as contributing to American dominance[4] (Pruvot, 1983). More benign in terms of the motives of the parties involved are arguments that U.S. producers have found a large international audience because the products they offer are intentionally crafted to appeal to such an audience (Biltereyst, 1992). Whereas films and programs produced in most other countries deal with themes and issues that appeal to domestic tastes and interests, U.S. producers have chosen to produce films and programs attractive to a broader international audience.

More recently, several authors have argued for a microeconomic model in which one-way geographic flows emerge as natural consequences of firm and industry responses to the commercial incentives created by the divisions within a heterogeneous world audience for films and programs (Frank, 1992; Hoskins & Mirus, 1988; Owen & Wildman, 1992, chap. 2; Waterman, 1988, 1993; Wildman & Siwek, 1987, 1988, 1993). A basic premise of the explanation for one-way flows based on this model is that the worldwide audience for films and programs is divided by political boundaries and linguistic and cultural differences into numerous smaller audience segments that differ dramatically in population and how much they spend, or cause to be spent,[5] on video entertainment.

The model predicts that profit-maximizing producers will spend more to produce films and programs targeted (by language or content) to the linguistically and culturally defined audience segments that generate substantial film and television revenues than they will spend on films and programs targeted to smaller audiences with less commercial potential.[6] More is spent on films and programs produced for the high-revenue linguistic and/or cultural audiences because viewers value the greater production value purchased with larger production budgets, and the extra share points of high-revenue audiences won with increased production expenditures are worth more to commercial producers and distributors than equivalent share increases for low-revenue audiences. The extra audience appeal purchased with a larger budget also makes a film or program more attractive to viewers with different languages and cultures, which are generally located in other countries. So higher budget films and programs from large markets have an advantage in international competition over lower budget productions from small markets. The microeconomic model thus explains one-way flows of films and programs as by-products of media firms' attempts to create actual audiences from the potential audiences represented by the populations of diverse linguistic and cultural groups residing in different countries.

A GENERAL MODEL OF MEDIA FLOWS

At the heart of the microeconomic analysis of trade in films and programs is a more general model of how audiences are produced in time and space that has applications to other media and to nongeographic flows such as the flows of media products among distribution channels over time. While we tend not to think of them as similar in kind, one-way flows are also prominent structural features in media markets other than those governing international trade in films and television programs. Daily newspapers provide an example of one-way flows in a print medium that are primarily regional in character. Rosse's influential umbrella model of competition in the newspaper industry (Rosse, 1975; Rosse & Dertouzos, 1978) describes a pattern of newspaper distribution in major metropolitan areas that is strikingly similar to the global pattern of video trade flows.[7] Newspapers originating in the major city at the heart of a large metropolitan area typically circulate throughout the region while papers produced in the smaller suburbs that surround it have much smaller circulation zones, in many cases restricted almost entirely to their own city limits. Here the unidirectional flow is newspapers shipped from the center city to the suburbs, with virtually no product moving in the reverse direction.

Cable superstations, such as Chicago's WGN and Atlanta's TBS, whose signals are distributed to cable subscribers across the United States, are another example of one-way flows, in this case flows of programming among local television markets within the United States. The superstations are all over-the-air broadcasters in major metropolitan areas whose signals are carried by satellite and microwave to television viewers in smaller communities and rural areas. But small market stations have never achieved any prominence as sources of the distant signals imported by cable systems. As with newspapers and video products, the flows are predominantly from large to small markets.

The flows of superstation programming and daily newspapers are just as much one-way geographic trade flows as is the international trade in films and programs. The fact that media products flow across national borders in one case but don't in the other two should not obscure the basic similarity of the phenomena observed. In each case, media products originating in one geographic region are transported to others, but the balancing reverse flows of goods and services that are required to sustain long-term trading relationships are not made up of similar media products.

In addition to the geographic flows described above, the mass media are characterized by important flows of product among distribution channels over time. For example, the feature film released in the cinema this summer is likely to be found in the late-night schedule of an independent, over-the-air television station 10 years from now. In the intervening years, it will have been released at different times on videocassettes, pay-per-view television, premium cable services such as HBO and Showtime, the over-the-air broadcast networks, and basic cable networks such as TNT and USA Network. As we shall see, a feature film's release into different media channels over time follows a relatively fixed sequence with most of these outlets being visited by a film only once. Furthermore, films and programs originating in the channels that follow the cinema in a feature film's release sequence tend to follow the film release sequence from that point on. Thus the flow of films and programs among distribution channels over time is also largely one way. There are similar intertemporal flows among distribution channels in print media. Intertemporal-intermedia (ITIM) flows are the subject of the third section of this chapter, where I will argue that economic forces similar to those shaping geographic flows of media products also explain certain features of ITIM flows.

The ITIM analysis feeds back into the analysis of geographic flows. Proliferating distribution technologies make it possible for producers and distributors to increase their earnings on sales to any given geographic audience by segmenting that audience into subgroups that are relatively homogeneous in terms of how much they are willing to pay or how much advertisers are willing to pay to reach them. Because producers respond to increases in earnings potential by increasing their production budgets to increase their audience appeal, programs produced for this audience should find a larger international audience as well. Advances in audience measurement technologies that make it easier to identify and target subgroups within audiences (such as those described by Barnes and Thomson in this volume) should have similar effects.

Of course, the microeconomic model presented here does not rule out the possibility that trade flows have been influenced by anticompetitive tactics and political machinations, but it does raise questions about the relative importance of these other influences. The one-way flow of internationally traded films and programs is not unique; the same basic pattern is evident in within-country flows of these products, in geographic flows of printed media,[8] and in the intertemporal flows of media products among distribution channels. But while the microeconomic model successfully explains the observed pattern in all cases, the political influence and anticompetitive tactics explanations depend on circumstances peculiar to a single industry.[9] The anticompetitive tactics and political influence arguments are just not credible when applied to within-country flows such as superstations and daily newspapers. No one would be taken seriously who attributed the *New York Times*'s success in selling its paper in large cities throughout the United States to pressure exerted by the city of New York on other cities' governments or newspapers or who claimed that the *Times*'s "export" success is due to its control of a nationwide newspaper distribution system to which other daily papers are denied access.

On the other hand, the cultural argument that U.S. film and television producers succeed internationally because they deliberately produce to the tastes of an international audience seems to be complementary to the microeconomic model. The relevant question here is which comes first: the large international demand for American films and programs (due to their larger budgets) or international themes? Here the evidence seems to favor the primacy of the large domestic market leading to large budget productions and international appeal argument. If U.S. films and programs are going to attract an international audience anyway, it would be financially foolish not to take its tastes into account so as to increase the yield from this part of the audience. To explain U.S. export success as due primarily to programs and films with broader thematic appeal, however, it is necessary at the same time to explain why profit-motivated producers from other countries (especially countries where English is not the native tongue) have not employed the same strategy to achieve international success and profits.[10]

GEOGRAPHIC FLOWS:
TRADE IN VIDEO PRODUCTS

Key to the microeconomic model of trade in films and programs is the distinction between what economists call "public goods" and "private goods." A public good is a product or service for which one individual's consumption does not reduce the amount available to others. Another way of stating this in the language of economics is that public goods are not "naturally excludable in consumption." The plays of Shakespeare, which exist independently of the media on which they are recorded, are examples of public goods. Their availability and value to current readers and theatergoers have not been diminished by the millions of people who have read and watched them in the past. By contrast, a private good, such as an apple, is excludable in consumption. What one person consumes, another cannot. Most media products, like most other products, have both public and private good elements. Recording media—film, tapes, CDs, paper, canvas, and so on—are private goods.[11] The content preserved with these media—ideas, words, images, performances, and so on—are public goods.[12] The demand for media products is determined largely by their public good elements and, not a surprise, expenditures on the public good elements of media products loom large in their total costs.

Unfortunately, the theories and models economists have traditionally employed to explain trading relationships are designed to explain trade in products that are pure private goods. Reliance on private good models, whether explicit or implicit, is one reason some people have argued that one-way international flows in television programs and films cannot be explained as natural outcomes of competitive free trade (Pruvot, 1983). For example, low-cost producers have a competitive advantage when private goods are traded, yet the most successful international films are produced in Hollywood, a location noted for high production costs. But what is natural for private goods is not natural for public goods and economists have been slow to wake up to the importance of this distinction for analyzing trade flows. In particular, domestic market size, which, in the absence of trade barriers, is not important in models explaining trade in private goods, is a critical determinant of public good flows.

While there is no special relationship between the cost of a private good and the size of the primary market for which it is produced, for public goods the situation is different. Profit maximization dictates larger expenditures on the content of films and programs originating in large markets than for films and programs produced for small markets, where size is measured in terms of the revenue potentially available to the suppliers of media products.[13] As long as the audience appeal of a film or program can be increased by spending more on creative and artistic inputs (such as actors, directors, writers, special effects, or editing), the (expected) payoff to these expenditures should be greater in large markets than in small markets. This is a direct consequence of the public good character of media content.

Consider, for example, a filmmaker deciding on the production budget for a feature film. To maximize profits, the filmmaker should increase expenditures on content-related inputs as long as a dollar spent is expected to generate more than a dollar of additional revenue from the film's audiences in the cinema and other distribution channels such as broadcast television, cable, and videocassettes. Expected revenue should increase as more is spent on inputs that add to a film's audience appeal for two reasons. First, holding price constant, a more appealing film or program will draw a larger audience, which means more people paying to see it and/or advertisers paying more for access to a larger audience. Second, individual audience members should be willing to pay more for the privilege of watching a more appealing program or film. Thus, for example, the amount a cable operator can charge subscribers for HBO (and thus the amount the cable operator is willing to pay HBO) is likely to reflect in some measure how much HBO spends on its programs.

Of course, increased expenditures on content cannot continue to generate more than commensurate increases in revenue indefinitely. The law of diminishing returns dictates that eventually the return on a dollar added to the production budget will begin to fall and at some point less than a dollar in additional revenue will come back. For example, car crashes may help draw audiences to action-adventure films, but at some point they start to become repetitive and lose their impact. The uncertainties inherent in film and program production also must be taken into account. Because it is not possible to predict with certainty how audiences will respond to new ideas (or old ones trotted out again), there is a high degree of risk associated with investments in most media products. But there is a reasonable expectation that a more expensive production will attract a larger audience than a less expensive one. Budgets should therefore be set on the basis of these expectations, recognizing the uncertainties and risks involved.

Maximization of (expected) profits requires that a production budget be increased up to the point at which spending more on content-related inputs no longer makes an at least equivalent contribution to expected revenue—where the revenue contribution of an increase in a production budget is the product of the amount a new viewer contributes to revenue and the number of new viewers added to the audience.[14] Increased production budgets can influence the viewing choices of more people in a more populous market (holding other things such as viewers' incomes constant). In addition, audience members with higher incomes generally both are willing to pay more for video entertainment and are themselves worth more to advertisers. Therefore an increase in the incomes, as well as the number, of potential audience members in a market should increase the expected returns to expenditures on production inputs and thus should increase the size of the production budget required to bring the net return to additional expenditures to zero. In other words, microeconomic theory tells us that larger budget films and programs should be produced for wealthier and more populous markets.[15]

To illustrate the basic logic of this analysis, consider the situations facing filmmakers in two hypothetical film markets, a "large" market with a $100 million annual box office and a "small" market with a $10 million annual box office. Suppose that $2 million spent on equipment and technical experts to improve visual quality would add 5% to a film's share of the box office in either market. Filmmakers in the large market, where 5% of the box office is worth $5 million, would spend the extra $2 million, while filmmakers in the smaller market would not because 5% of the smaller market amounts to only half a million dollars.

The same logic is reflected in the special effects expenditures for the 1993 hit film *Jurassic Park*. The film is reported to have cost upward of $60 million to produce. Of this, slightly over $15 million was used to create dinosaurs and another $22.5 million was spent on computer animation.[16] Spending millions of dollars on special effects makes financial sense when a film's primary audience is the large English language market dominated by the United States, because realistic dinosaurs can increase attendance by millions and increase the box office take by tens of millions of dollars (hundreds of millions in the case of a megahit). For a smaller linguistic market, say Italian, the upside potential is much less.[17]

Now compare the choices of viewers in a large linguistic market that produces large budget films and programs with those of viewers in a smaller linguistic market with smaller budget domestic films. Suppose both sets of viewers have access to the films originating in each market. Consider viewers in the smaller market first. Other things equal, viewers in the smaller market would prefer films and programs produced in their native language. While foreign language productions can be subtitled or dubbed, something is always lost in translation. Plus, differences in cultures reflected in the way films and programs are made also reduce the entertainment value of foreign films and programs to domestic audiences. But other things are not equal. The producers of films and programs from the larger market are willing to meet the salary demands of internationally recognized stars, spend more on writers and directors, use a wider variety of camera angles, have better lighting, commit more time and resources to editing and retakes, and employ equipment for special effects that is too expensive for domestic producers. These things also add value and are an advantage large market productions have over the lower budget domestic fare. Thus it is not surprising that viewers in the smaller market watch a mix of foreign and domestic programs and films, given that each has certain advantages over the other.

For the large market's audience, the advantages all lie with domestic films and programs. They are produced in the native tongue, show an appreciation for domestic tastes and preferences, and offer production values that only lavish budgets can buy. Thus it should not be surprising that films and programs from the large market find an audience in the smaller market while viewers in the large market are not drawn in large numbers to films and programs from the smaller market.

In explaining why films and television programs from the United States are dominant in the international video trade, proponents of the microeconomic trade model point to the size of the U.S. domestic audience and the fact that the spending power (aggregate income) of the much larger worldwide English-speaking audience dwarfs that of the world's other linguistic populations. Statistics on national incomes and populations reported by Wildman and Siwek (1987, 1988) and Siwek and Furchtgott-Roth (1993) showed the combined GNPs of English-speaking countries to be from approximately two-and-a-half times to nearly four times the national incomes of the world's Japanese- and German-speaking populations, which ranked second and third internationally on this measure.[18] Production budget data collected by Waterman (1988) for television programs and by Wildman and Siwek (1988) for films reveal U.S. production budgets to be several to many times larger than budgets for programs and films produced in non-English-speaking countries, which corresponds to the general relationship predicted by the model. The predicted positive correlation between linguistic market size and film budgets is also generally borne out in comparisons that do not involve the United States. For example, if measured by total spending power, the French and Italian film markets are much larger than the market for Arabic films, and the French and Italians produce much more expensive films than do Egyptians producing for the Arabic market (Wildman & Siwek, 1988).

While the microeconomic model of one-way flows was originally developed to explain international film and television program flows, the model itself does not depend on assumptions that distinguish film and television from other media. At the heart of the microeconomic explanation of film and program flows is a more general economic model of trade in media products that rests on these five assumptions:

1. a product (or service) for which demand is determined largely by content, which is a public good;
2. content that is costly to produce;
3. producers able to increase the value of their products to consumers by spending more on content elements[19] (although value to consumers increases at a diminishing rate at higher levels of content expenditure);
4. geographically distinct "home" markets that differ in size in which home market producers have an advantage over producers resident in other markets in attracting home market consumers;[20] and
5. the possibility of transporting different firms' versions of the product from one market to another.[21]

These five assumptions are descriptive of many, if not most, media products. For the video trade application developed above, "homeness" and domestic market boundaries are determined by linguistic and cultural differences. Because linguistically and culturally distinct audiences tend to be geographically concentrated and these geographic concentrations are closely correlated with national borders, film and program flows have been described primarily in terms of trade among nations. But, excepting the influence of nationhood on culture, the international character of these flows contributes nothing to their explanation. According to the microeconomic model, if nations merged or national boundaries were done away with entirely, the same geographic flows would still be observed.

Furthermore, similar geographic flows should be observed in any media industry in which the five assumptions of the general model are satisfied. U.S. superstations and regional flows of U.S. newspapers are examined below to illustrate generalizability of the model.

OTHER GEOGRAPHIC FLOWS: SUPERSTATIONS AND NEWSPAPERS

Under the compulsory license of U.S. cable copyright law, cable systems have the right to import the signals of television stations located in other markets (distant signals) without the explicit permission of the imported stations or the permission of the holders of copyrights to certain types of programs carried on these stations.[22] While cable systems import many stations as distant signals, a few of these stations have achieved such extensive national carriage on cable systems that they are commonly referred to as "superstations." Table 7.1 lists in descending order of cable subscribers reached the seven stations typically accorded superstation status, the metropolitan areas they are licensed to serve as over-the-air broadcasters, their subscriber counts, and the television households rankings of these metropolitan areas among the 200-plus U.S. television markets identified by Nielsen. Each of the superstations is an independent television station from one of the largest television markets.[23] (The reason superstations are independents is fairly obvious—for the most part the affiliates of a major broadcast network carry the same programs.)

The largely unidirectional pattern of program flows via satellite-carried superstations from large local television markets to smaller ones within the United States is just what the logic of the microeconomic trade model should lead us to expect. The fact that television signals fade with distance gives television stations licensed to serve a metropolitan area an advantage in reaching local viewers over stations assigned to other markets. Cable carriage of distant signals offsets this advantage only partially because a substantial portion of television households do not subscribe to cable (about 40% on average in the United States), and even for cable subscribers, the number of cable channels available and competition from cable networks limit the number of over-the-air signals imported from other markets.

Large market independent stations respond to larger local audiences by spending more to acquire more popular films and syndicated series, hiring better and more attractive on-air talent, spending more to equip their

TABLE 7.1. Origins of U.S. Superstations

Superstation	Home Market	No. Subscribers (millions)	TVHH Rank
WTBS	Atlanta	55.2	10
WGN	Chicago	34.4	3
WWOR	New York	14.0	1
WPIX	New York	9.2	1
KTLA	Los Angeles	4.9	2
KTVT	Dallas-Fort Worth	2.2	8
WSBK	Boston	2.0	6

SOURCE: Data compiled from *TV and Cable Factbook* (1993).

studios, and committing more resources to the selection and scheduling of programs than do their counterparts in smaller markets. The result is a more polished and more appealing program service that viewers in other markets find attractive, even though certain features such as local newscasts may have little innate appeal to audiences in the most distant markets.[24]

Circulation patterns for newspapers in major metropolitan areas are also strikingly similar to the patterns that characterize international trade in films and programs. Just as films and programs flow primarily from large countries to smaller ones (or from large linguistic markets to smaller ones), newspapers published in the major city at the heart of a metropolitan area attract substantial readership in the surrounding suburbs (and in some cases hundreds of miles beyond), while papers published in the smaller surrounding suburbs are rarely read by center city residents. Thus we observe largely one-way flows of papers from major cities to their suburbs and more distant small cities and towns.

This pattern was first described in terms of an umbrella model of competition by then Professor James Rosse of Stanford University (1975).[25] As described by Rosse, a dominant paper (or papers in a few cases) from the major city that is the commercial and population hub of a metropolitan area casts a circulation umbrella over the smaller cities and towns surrounding it. In some cases papers from the larger suburbs may cast more limited circulation umbrellas of their own covering the still smaller suburban communities that are their nearest neighbors, so that daily papers from smaller communities may constitute yet a third layer under the umbrella of a big city paper.[26] Below the dailies serving smaller communities is a fourth layer of weeklies and throwaways (papers with no subscription fees) that are targeted to even smaller geographic territories. The flow of papers within the umbrella structure is predominantly from larger to smaller urban communities.

Again, as with the international video trade and with superstations, the pattern is one we would expect to see if media firms in larger markets respond to the opportunities posed by a large local audience by spending more on content, which in turn makes their products attractive in smaller markets that are not their primary targets. Large city papers do spend much more on content-related inputs than do papers in smaller markets. They pay the higher salaries required to hire more skilled reporters, writers, editors, columnists, and other talent, presumably because the effect of the subsequent improvement in newspaper quality has a larger effect on circulation, subscription fees, and advertising revenues in a large city than in a small one. The same logic applies to expenditures on wire services, syndicated features, graphics capabilities, and so on. It is in the larger papers that a reader is most likely to find sophisticated graphics, color photographs, and nationally known syndicated columnists.

Quantity, as well as quality, of content also differentiates big city dailies from papers originating in smaller places.[27] Large city papers devote more pages to news events and offer their readers specialized feature sections that are not provided by their counterparts from smaller places. The comparison of the August 5, 1993, editions of the *Chicago Tribune* and the *Warsaw Times-Union* in Table 7.2 is illustrative. The 1990 U.S. Census recorded a population of 2,783,726 for Chicago, which is the commercial hub of a primary metropolitan statistical area (PMSA) with a census population of 6,069,974 people. Warsaw (the author's home town), which is on the fringe of the *Tribune*'s circulation umbrella, had 10,968 people according to the 1990 census. Warsaw is the county seat and commercial center of Kosciusko County, Indiana, which has a census population of 65,294.

The same economic logic that leads large city papers to invest more in the quality of their product also explains their larger size. With larger populations to draw from, added features and pages of news coverage attract more subscribers, and through them more advertisers, to large city papers than to small city papers. Thus, in determining whether the additional revenue generated by an extra page of international news or another feature section is sufficient to cover the first copy costs plus additional printing expenses that would be incurred, the answer is much more likely to be yes for papers serving large markets than for papers in small markets. The extra two pages of sports news that might increase readership for the *Chicago Tribune* by, say, 5,000 could at most boost circulation by a couple

TABLE 7.2. Quantitative Differences Between Two Representative
Newspapers

Newspaper	No. of Sections	No. of Pages
Chicago Tribune	7	114
Warsaw Times-Union	3	32

of hundred readers for a small city daily such as the *Warsaw Times-Union.*
So we see that basic economics-of-public-good considerations predict
larger and higher quality papers for large cities than for small ones, which
is just what we see.

Given their advantages in terms of quality and quantity of content, it is
easy to see why suburban readers subscribe to major metropolitan dailies.
But why do they also read the local paper? It is the local paper's advantage
in providing coverage of events of special interest to hometown readers—
city council meetings, elections of school boards and city officials, church
socials, local births, deaths, and weddings, high school graduations and
sporting events, and so on. Readers' interest in local news and the advantage of the local newspaper in responding to that interest is the source of
the "localness" of newspaper markets and the advantage of local papers.

In metropolitan newspaper markets, political boundaries and the local
interests they spawn play much the same role in producing unidirectional
flows as do linguistic and cultural differences in the international market
for films and television programs. Suburban readers buy suburban papers
for their coverage of local politics, schools, and social events and subscribe to a major metropolitan daily for more in-depth coverage of
regional, state, national, and international news. Residents of the center
city, on the other hand, have little interest in the majority of news stories
specific to any given suburb and so have no compelling reason to purchase
suburban papers.

INTERTEMPORAL-INTERMEDIA (ITIM) FLOWS

In addition to the geographic flows just discussed, the mass media are
characterized by largely unidirectional flows of product among distribution channels[28] over time. I will focus on two distinct but related features
of ITIM flows. The first is the practice of releasing a media product—such
as a book, a film, or a television program—in different distribution

channels at different times, often pulling the product from one channel before releasing it in another. These timed-release distribution strategies are known as sequential release strategies. The second feature is the nearly unidirectional flow of media products among distribution channels. For example, feature films are released first in the cinema and released later on videocassettes, but programs first released on video do not migrate to the cinema afterward. Similarly, many of the prime-time series broadcast by the major broadcast networks later are syndicated directly to stations who air them in other time periods. But programs produced for syndication aren't acquired by the networks after their syndication debuts. In what follows I will refer to a distribution channel that precedes another channel in a media product's temporal release sequence as the *upstream channel* and will refer to the channel that follows in the release sequence as the *downstream channel.*

The most studied of the sequential release strategies for media products is the practice known as "windowing" in the motion picture and television industries.[29] The typical feature film released in the United States by a major studio begins its commercial life with a short (usually less than 6-month) cinema run, followed in order by releases on videocassettes, a pay-per-view cable service, a premium (pay) cable network such as HBO, a major broadcast network, and then syndication to individual television stations and/or basic cable networks. Each of these venues for the film is in effect a different channel for retail distribution. The period during which a film is available for showing within one of these distribution channels is known as that channel's window. Six years or more may elapse between a film's initial release in the theatrical window and its eventual release to basic cable networks and/or individual television stations, where it may keep recycling virtually forever. With the exception of the videocassette window, which lasts indefinitely, the release in each window is generally exclusive to that window and, excepting the last window, of strictly limited duration.[30]

Films and programs are also produced for initial release in each of the channels that are "downstream" of the cinema (follow the cinema) in the feature film release sequence. For example, films and instructional programs are produced for initial release on videocassettes; sporting events (such as boxing matches) and concerts are sometimes carried first by pay-per-view networks; both premium and basic cable networks, like the broadcast networks, produce (or commission) some of their own series and made-for-TV movies; and series and "made-for" movies are also produced for first-run syndication to local television stations.

Like feature films, movies and programs produced for initial release in a distribution channel downstream of the cinema channel may later be rereleased in another channel; but flow of product among channels is almost always downstream in terms of the ordering of channels in the feature film release sequence. Thus, for example, prime-time series commissioned by the major broadcast networks may later be syndicated as off-network product to individual television stations and to basic cable networks, but series and movies produced for basic cable and first-run syndication to stations are not picked up by major broadcast networks following their syndication runs. Thus we have one-way flows of films and programs among video distribution channels that correspond to the windowing sequence employed by feature film distributors.

While less studied, one-way ITIM flows are also important in print media. When books are released in both hardcover and paperback, the hardcover edition is usually released first. Books by popular authors are sometimes serialized in magazines before their release to bookstores, but the reverse never happens. Although the newspaper and magazine columns of well-known feature writers are sometimes collected and published as books, books of essays are not turned into features for newspapers and periodicals. Novels optioned as the basis of scripts for motion pictures are an example of an intertemporal flow from a print medium to an electronic medium. While the scripts for popular motion pictures are sometimes rewritten and sold as novels (e.g., *Star Wars*), this is a relatively rare occurrence. As with geographic flows, intertemporal-intermedia flows are also explainable in terms of commercial responses to differences among audience members in their demands for (primarily) public goods.

ITIM FLOWS AS
AUDIENCEMAKING STRATEGY

The timing of a media product's releases into different distribution channels is an important component of the overall strategy employed to maximize the financial returns to a product whose content is not diminished by consumption. The analysis of the previous section showed that there are important advantages to building the audience for a media product by aggregating geographically dispersed viewers and/or readers. The logic of sequential release strategies is analogous. When audience members in a given locality differ in what they are willing to pay for a particular media product, or differ in their value to advertisers, sequential release strategies such as windowing are employed to build a media product's audience over time in a manner that maximizes the sum of profits realized from its audience as a whole.

From an economist's perspective, windowing is a form of price discrimination—the practice of charging different buyers different prices for the same product. If the buyers differ in their valuations of a product, price discrimination can be used to increase profits above what would be possible if both were charged the same price. Suppose, for example, that, for every serious fan of western movies, there are three other people for whom westerns are mildly entertaining but usually not their first choices among the films available in the theaters. While the avid western fan may be more than willing to pay the $7 theatrical admission fee to see a newly released western, for the other three people any price above $2 is too much. If constrained to charging a single price, the film's distributor's options would be a price of $7, which would limit the audience to serious western fans, or a price of $2, which could quadruple the size of the audience and increase total revenue by one seventh, but with a much lower profit margin per viewer. The option chosen would depend on the costs incurred in serving individual viewers and the per-viewer profits on sales of ancillary products such as popcorn and soft drinks. Whichever option is chosen, a considerable amount of potential revenue will be left on the table. If admission is priced at $7, for each ticket sold there is a sacrifice of $6 in potential sales to viewers willing to pay $2. If tickets are priced at $2, avid western fans get in for $5 less than they are willing to pay.

This trade-off between the price charged and the size of the audience can be reduced considerably if there is a mechanism for segregating true western fans from other viewers and charging each what they are willing to pay. A video release following the theatrical release might serve this function. The film could then be priced at $7 for western fans in the theater and rented for $2 to more casual consumers of westerns by video stores.[31] This would work as long as the true western fan was too impatient to wait for the video release. The contribution to total revenues of this type of discrimination among audience members can be huge. Suppose there were 10 million true western fans and 30 million more casual western viewers. Without the video window, the options would be a $70 million box office gross at a $7 theatrical price or a $80 million box office gross if $2 were charged for admission. But by charging hard-core western fans $7 to see the film at the cinema and later renting it to more casual consumers of westerns for $2 through video stores, the total take can be increased to $130 million.[32]

The advantage of selling to high-value audiences first should be quite clear in this example. If a western was released first on video at $2, western fans who had rented the video probably would not be willing to pay $7 to see the film in the theater, reducing the theatrical take considerably.[33] Windows for channels generating lower per-viewer earnings should therefore be scheduled later in the release sequence so that viewing a film on these channels does not reduce its audience in channels producing higher earnings per viewer.[34] Not a surprise, this is what film distributors do. Data reported by Waterman (1985) showed that the typical release sequence for U.S. feature films was a progression of releases to channels with smaller and smaller per-viewer earnings for the firms holding the primary distribution rights.

The preceding analysis of sequential release strategies tells us that channels with high earnings per audience member should precede those with lower earnings per audience member—hence the unidirectional nature of interchannel flows—but it does not tell us why some films and programs begin the process in downstream channels in the feature film release sequence and are never given the chance to build audience and revenues in the earlier channels with higher earnings per audience member. This question has been largely ignored in the small literature on sequential release strategies. The explanation for a variety of entry points in the unidirectional intertemporal flows of media products among distribution channels is similar to the explanation for native-language films being produced for sale in small linguistic markets and suburban dailies surviving in competition with major city papers. Films and programs produced for downstream channels also have certain "home market" advantages.

Films released in the cinema have the advantage of much bigger budgets and higher production values than films and programs produced for release into the distribution channels that provide subsequent release windows for feature films. In recent years U.S. feature film production budgets have averaged in the neighborhood of $30 million dollars, or approximately $15 million per hour for films that typically run about 2 hours. Budgets for movies and programs with initial releases in other distribution channels are much smaller. For example, single episodes for prime-time series on the major broadcast networks average about $1 million an hour. Made-for-TV movies and miniseries on the networks may have somewhat higher budgets, perhaps up to $3 million per hour if overseas syndication or repeat showings by the same network are anticipated. Movies made for release on premium cable networks and the top tier of basic cable networks such as USA Network and TNT may have budgets similar in size to those of the broadcast networks, although series programming on these channels is generally less expensive than that on the broadcast networks. Programs, such as game shows, produced for syndication to television stations that show them during low viewing hours may cost less than $100,000 an hour to produce.

Clearly, even the budgets of the most expensive television series and made-for-TV movies are dwarfed by the budgets for feature films. Feature film budgets are large because feature films can take advantage of all the windows to build large audiences and large aggregate revenues. Films and programs that start later in the feature film release sequence have smaller potential audiences and therefore smaller budgets. The extra production value purchased with larger budgets is an advantage for feature films over smaller budget productions in all of their subsequent release windows. But feature films also have the disadvantage in postcinema windows that some members of the audience will have seen them before and therefore will value them less as repeats. Furthermore, many of those who didn't see them in the cinema did not because they didn't find them appealing. Prior viewing and the fact that no film appeals to everyone makes it possible for lower budget new releases in postcinema distribution channels to be competitive with feature films in the same channel that have had one or more prior releases.

The lower budget films and programs produced for release in channels other than the cinema cannot compete with feature films in the cinema because, in addition to the disadvantage of having their audiences diminished by previous TV exposure, cinemagoers given the alternative of watching large budget feature films they haven't seen before will choose the feature films.

The analysis of windowing should also make clear why it is not possible to use simple measures of population or income as measures of market size in analyzing the geographic flows of media products. For video products in particular, differing national media policies have created vast differences among nations in the per-viewer revenues that the various television distribution channels contribute to the financing of films and programs. For example, restrictions on cable television and on television advertising generally have greatly reduced the revenue contributions of these media in most European countries. Until the late 1980s, broadcast television was largely a nonprofit service in most European countries to which advertisers had little access.[35] The combination of direct government support and receiver fees that were the primary sources of funds for most national broadcast services did not come close to matching the revenues generated by commercial systems in the United States (Commission of the European Communities, 1984; Wildman & Siwek, 1988). From the perspective of the media trade model developed in this chapter, the effect of restricted commercial opportunities was to reduce the effective size of the domestic markets for films and programs in most European languages relative to the video markets of their trading partners with fewer restrictions on media commercialization—the United States in particular. This no doubt contributed to the magnitude of the imbalance in European imports and exports of video products with the United States and English language countries generally.[36] Because ITIM flows enable media firms to more fully exploit the commercial potentials of the markets they serve, and thereby their relative sizes, they must be considered factors that influence geographic flows.

CONCLUDING OBSERVATIONS

The microeconomic model explains one-way geographic flows of films and programs as consumer responses to media industry responses to divisions in a heterogeneous audience that are largely coincident with political boundaries and geographic divisions. Regions with relatively homogeneous populations in terms of language, culture, and/or political interests are serviced by "domestic" media with products tailored to the preferences of the local audience. The producers of media products targeting larger audiences tend to spend more on content than is spent on media products produced for smaller audiences because it is profitable to do so. The added investments in content make large market media products attractive to the smaller audiences located elsewhere and this creates a demand for large market products in smaller markets that is not reciprocated by larger market audiences. The result is one-way geographic flows and umbrella structures.

In addition to international trade in films and television programs, flows of superstation programming within the U.S. and regional umbrella structures in newspaper markets were shown to exhibit the patterns predicted by the microeconomic model. The list of applications could easily be expanded.[37] The point is that the basic logic of the microeconomic model of trade in public goods can be usefully applied to a wide variety of media structures and practices. The breadth of its applications in its more general form is a distinct advantage of the microeconomic trade model over other explanations that have been offered for one-way flows of internationally traded films and programs. Government machinations and anticompetitive practices would not be taken seriously as explanations of unidirectional within-country flows such as those of newspapers and superstation programming explored in this chapter. To an even greater extent than are the foreign recipients of these video products, 48 U.S. states are inundated with films and programs produced in California and New York. (Complaints that Hollywood is subverting fundamental mid-American values are also reminiscent of the claims of intellectuals and officials in importing countries of cultural domination due to the pervasiveness of U.S. productions in domestic theaters and on television.) If each of the 48 states were suddenly declared separate countries, would the economic forces driving these flows be any different? For the most part, national boundaries have been a red herring to analyses of international media flows. This is not to say that sovereign states do not have legitimate policy interests in the political and cultural implications of imported media, only that it is not necessary to posit unfair advantages and agents working with harmful intent to explain U.S. dominance of these flows.

On the other hand, the microeconomic model of trade in public goods complements—to a degree—the cultural argument that the success of U.S. films and programs abroad is explained in part by their being "designed for a huge international audience" (Biltereyst, 1992, p. 518). Broader international appeal of U.S. films and programs is a crucial element in both explanations. However, from the perspective of the microeconomic model, while the selection of themes that appeal to an international audience contributes to U.S. films' and programs' international appeal, this strategy is also properly seen as another consequence of the factors that lead U.S. producers to create more expensive films and programs. The production values purchased with the enormous budgets required to be successful in the large and wealthy English language market—over half of which is accounted for by the United States—draw foreign audiences. But given the existence of a foreign demand for their output, it is hardly surprising that U.S. producers would modify their films and programs to increase the take from the foreign segment of their market. Thus emphasis on themes appealing to a broader audience should contribute to the international success of U.S. films and programs as cultural theorists have claimed, but this strategy is itself a product of the factors identified in the microeconomic model as producing unidirectional flows. We see the similar content strategies employed in metropolitan newspaper markets where center city papers add sections covering suburban news (often delivered only to suburban readers) to broaden their appeal and attract suburban readers whose natural affinities are for suburban papers.

The flows of product among media distribution channels over time also reflect the bidirectional influence of the audience on media structures and practices and of those structures and practices on the audience. Sequential release strategies are employed to induce audience members to self-select into smaller subaudiences whose members are similar in what they are willing to pay to mitigate the trade-off sellers face between price per audience member and audience size. Sequential release strategies can be used to discriminate among buyers (either audience members or advertisers paying for access to audiences) with different willingnesses to pay because distinct distribution channels employing different media have evolved to deliver products to audiences with different demand characteristics.

Audience measurement also plays a role in geographic and ITIM flows, although its role is less obvious. As Barnes and Thomson show in this volume, magazines targeted to smaller demographic audiences began to proliferate when new techniques for measuring audiences made it possible to "see" differences among members of the aggregate magazine audience and demonstrate to advertisers the advantages of specialized magazines that could reach well-defined audience subgroups. Because advertisers pay more for measured audiences than for unmeasured audiences, measurement of television audiences no doubt plays a similar role in determining the windowing contributions of the different distribution channels using cable and over-the-air television.[38] Thus, like windowing and other sequential release strategies, audience measurement technology increases the size of the effective market for media products, with its attendant effects on content expenditures and geographic flows.

Thus we see that one-way media flows both construct audiences and are constructions of the audience. Media flows construct audiences because they are used by media firms to build larger audiences from smaller, geographically dispersed ones and to disaggregate larger, heterogeneous audiences in a given location into smaller, more homogeneous ones, at least in terms of demand characteristics. Media flows are constructions of the audience in the sense that they mirror basic characteristics of the audience itself. If the composition of the audience were to change, the flows would too.

NOTES

1. Japan has been the biggest single-country importer of U.S. films in recent years. But dependence on films and programs from the United States is generally greatest for smaller countries (Biltereyst, 1992).

2. To turn again to the European situation, which tends to be best documented, *Newsweek* reported that 81% of films shown are U.S. made ("Here Comes," 1993). See Varis (1983), Varis and Nordenstreng (1974), Waterman (1988, 1993), and Wildman and Siwek (1987, 1988, 1993) for more extensive, earlier documentation of this general trend for films and television programs.

3. See also Guback (1969), especially chapter 7, where financial issues on which the Motion Picture Export Association of America (MPEAA) and U.S. occupation authorities in postwar Germany were not in agreement are also discussed.

4. Whereas, in an earlier era, economic scholars primarily viewed block booking as a mechanism for excluding competitors, more recent work reported in the economic literature has pointed out that it may promote economic efficiency by limiting what would otherwise be excessive prior search by exhibitors (Kenney & Klein, 1983).

5. While viewers do not pay for advertiser-supported television, advertisers pay stations and networks for access to the audiences attracted by the programs they supply for free. Advertisers pay more for access to larger and higher income audiences.

6. Audience size and wealth are obviously important determinants of an audience's commercial potential. In addition, the commercial potential of the audience for an individual country's mass media is affected by the extent to which the country restricts media commercialization.

7. For a concise summary of Rosse's model, see Owen (1975, chap. 2).

8. In addition to the newspaper and superstation examples discussed here, Wildman and Siwek (1993) provide data showing that international flows of recorded music are similar to those of films and television programs.

9. Even here there are important exceptions to the claimed patterns of abuses that the political influence and anticompetitive tactics models have a hard time dealing with. U.S. films dominated the international trade in films as early as the 1920s (Guback, 1969), but the evidence offered of government intent to use exports of U.S. cultural products to promote U.S. political and trade goals is taken largely from the red scare era of the early post-World War II period. The control of distribution channels argument cannot account for the fact that U.S. films have been extremely successful in countries in which U.S. distribution companies were not allowed to operate (Wildman & Siwek, 1988). Finally, while U.S. exports dominate the international flows of both films and television programs, and have for decades, until the recent (since the late 1980s) international movement to privatize public channels, government-controlled broadcasters have handled the acquisition and distribution of television programs in most countries.

10. The analogous question of why U.S. producers should be uniquely successful in employing anticompetitive tactics is also a problem for those favoring the anticompetitive tactics explanation for the U.S. dominance of the international video trade. Similarly, why should the U.S. government be uniquely successful and/or uniquely motivated to use its influence to open foreign markets for its films and programs?

11. A distribution medium may be either a public or a private good. Videotape is both a recording and a distribution medium and is a private good. The electromagnetic spectrum used for over-the-air broadcasting is a public good because the number of people watching or listening to a broadcast program is not a physical constraint on the number of people who may be added to the audience.

12. A live performance may be a pure public good.

13. A number of factors contribute to the earnings potential of a film or program in a particular market. The number of people in the market is obviously important. So is the amount of disposable income available to audience members, because this both affects how much they are willing to pay for the privilege of viewing and it also affects their value as an audience to advertisers.

14. Of course, this decision-making process is not as mechanical as this description makes it sound. These expected value calculations are often more implicit than explicit and based on intuition and "gut feeling."

15. If the number of competing video services increases as the size of the market increases, then increased competition will offset the positive influence of a larger market on budgets to some degree, because increased competition makes it harder to attract new viewers by increasing production budgets. In the more formal (mathematical) analyses by Wildman and Siwek (1988, App. B) and Frank (1992), the positive effect of a larger market dominates.

16. As reported in the Press Association Newsfile, July 15, 1993, dinosaurs constructed for the movie cost 10 million pounds and 15 million pounds was spent on computer graphics. The exchange rate at the time of the press report was 0.66511 pounds to the dollar.

17. Measured in terms of GNP, Wildman and Siwek (1988) estimated the Italian market to be about one eighth the size of the English language market.

18. Siwek and Furchtgott-Roth (1993) report the lower multiples. This reflects in part their attribution of West German per capita income levels to the East German population now incorporated in the unified Germany. Using this approach, Siwek and Furchtgott-Roth calculated a larger aggregate income for the German linguistic market than for the Japanese linguistic market, the opposite of the ordering reported by Wildman and Siwek. Changes in exchange rates underlying the calculations may also have contributed to the apparent growth of the German and Japanese linguistic markets relative to the English language market.

19. The fact that media firms producing similar products produce more expensive products in some markets than in others is strong evidence supporting this assumption. If the effect of increased expenditures on content did not increase either audience size or what audience members are willing to pay, or both, profit-maximizing media firms would always supply the least expensive version of the product.

20. The home market advantage of home market producers may be either distribution cost advantages or a predisposition of home market consumers to consume locally produced products. In the latter case, home market production refers to products designed primarily to appeal to the preferences of home market consumers, even if the producer does not reside in the home market.

21. This last assumption could be stated more generally to allow both media products and media consumers to move from market to market. Thus we could describe as "trade" a small town family's visit to a major city to see a baseball game or a concert. As people much less frequently travel from cities to small towns to attend these types of events, flows of consumers of these types of public goods also seem to be largely unidirectional.

22. This blanket right does not apply to syndicated television programs on imported stations that are also carried on television stations in the same market as the importing cable

system, when the local station has the exclusive right to the program in its own local market. In this case the cable system must (a) black out the offending program, (b) pay the local station for the right to import the duplicated program, or (c) negotiate with the program supplier to sell its program on a nonexclusive basis to stations in the cable system's markets. "Active" superstations, those that actively promote their superstation status, generally either negotiate nonexclusive contracts with suppliers of syndicated programs in their schedules or will arrange for their satellite carriers to substitute other programs for those that run into syndex difficulties in their national feeds.

23. The fact that the network-supplied portion of network affiliates' schedules (about two thirds of program time) is the same in all markets (excepting the few too small to have three stations) makes network affiliates less attractive as sources of imported signals.

24. Local news on superstations appears to appeal to cable viewers in the same region of the country as the superstation. For example, local news on the Chicago superstation WGN may appeal to viewers elsewhere in the Midwest but not in other parts of the country. The independent companies that provide satellite carriage of superstations sometimes substitute other programs for local newscasts and certain other superstation programs.

25. Rosse is currently president and CEO of Freedom Newspapers.

26. For example, the *San Francisco Examiner* and *Chronicle* (marketed through a joint operating arrangement) circulate throughout the San Francisco Bay area of Northern California, and for hundreds of miles both north and south along the coast. The cities of San Jose and Oakland are the two largest secondary centers of commerce and population in the Bay Area. The *San Jose Mercury* is sold throughout the south bay region while the *Oakland Tribune* has good sales in communities on the northwest side of the Bay.

27. The amount of time available in a broadcast day places a constraint on the quantity of content on single-channel broadcast vehicles such as radio and television stations for which there is no counterpart in print media. In this regard, multichannel electronic media such as cable television and direct broadcast satellite services are much more like magazines and newspapers than the single-channel electronic mass media.

28. *Distribution channels* refer to a well-defined set of organizations and practices for delivering media products to consumers using a given distribution medium. For example, pay-per-view services, pay cable networks such as HBO and Showtime, and basic cable networks such as CNN and USA Network are different types of distribution channels using cable television as a medium.

29. For other discussions and analyses of windowing, see Vogel (1986), Waterman (1985), and Owen and Wildman (1992).

30. Licensing contracts generally specify the number of months or years a film (often as part of a package of films) or program is available to a firm licensing it for exhibition in a given distribution channel and the maximum number of times it may be shown during this period.

31. For simplicity, I am ignoring the fact that for most films the big screen contributes a value of its own. With high-definition television and bigger television screens, the theaters' added value may decline.

32. I have vastly simplified the nature of the trade-offs that must be considered to make the basic point about the profitability of segregating audiences through windowing. The costs and distributor margins associated with distributing the film in the different distribution channels must also be considered along with the opportunity cost of postponing earnings in one channel to increase the take from a prior channel. See Owen and Wildman (1992, chap. 2) for an in-depth treatment of the factors considered in designing windowing strategies.

33. Of course, it is the distributor's margin after costs and payments to firms operating the channels, not price per audience member, that matters most; but the ordering of channels by price per audience member approximates the ordering according to margin per audience member.

34. Distributors' per-viewer margins are indirect reflections of viewer willingness to pay for media supported by viewer payments and reflect advertisers' valuations of audiences for ad-supported media.

35. Television policies varied considerably among European countries. In the United Kingdom, for example, a healthy private television system has coexisted with a relatively well-funded public television service. In most continental countries, however, television has until recently been dominated by public broadcasters. See Noam (1991) for an in-depth study of the economics and politics of European television systems.

36. While less market oriented than the United States, television in other English-speaking countries is generally more commercialized than it is in non-English-speaking nations.

37. For example, Wildman and Siwek (1993) have argued that the basic media trade model explains the observed pattern of international trade in recorded music, which is very much like that of films and television programs. The same basic considerations seem to explain the structure of professional team sports in the United States, with major league franchises located in the largest cities and minor league teams playing in smaller cities and towns. Major league sports are exported from large cities to smaller markets via radio and television, but minor league contests are not broadcast in major metropolitan areas. Putting major league baseball on television was apparently responsible for a significant decline in minor league attendance as television spread in the early postwar years.

38. Higher quality audience measurements (more frequent measurements with smaller confidence intervals) are probably one of the reasons for the premiums advertisers pay for access to broadcast network audiences over what they pay for access to audiences for syndicated programs. By contributing to the differential earning potential for programs released in the network and syndication channels, measurement technology influences their relative positions and importance in the windowing sequence.

REFERENCES

Bilatereyst, D. (1992). Language and culture as ultimate barriers? An analysis of the circulation, consumption and popularity of fiction in small European countries. *European Journal of Communication, 7,* 517-540.

Commission of the European Communities. (1984, June). *Television without frontiers: Green paper on the establishment of the common market for broadcasting, especially by satellite and cable* (COM [84] 300). Brussels: Author.

Frank, B. (1992). A note on the international dominance of the U.S. in the trade in movies and television fiction. *Journal of Media Economics, 5*(1), 31-38.

Guback, T. H. (1969). *The international film industry.* Bloomington: Indiana University Press.

Guback, T. H. (1977). The international film industry. In G. Gerbner (Ed.), *Mass media policies in changing cultures* (pp. 21-40). New York: John Wiley.

Here comes a new golden age—literally. (1993, August 23). *Newsweek,* pp. 50, 51.

Hoskins, C., & Mirus, R. (1988). Reasons for US dominance of the international trade in television programmes. *Media, Culture and Society, 10,* 499-515.

Kenney, R. W., & Klein, B. (1983). The economics of block booking. *Journal of Law and Economics, 26*(3), 491-540.

Noam, E. M. (1991). *Television in Europe.* Oxford: Oxford University Press.

Owen, B. M. (1975). *Economics and freedom of expression: Media structure and the First Amendment.* Cambridge, MA: Ballinger.

Owen, B. M., & Wildman, S. S. (1992). *Video economics.* Cambridge, MA: Harvard University Press.

Pruvot, M. (1983, July 15). *On the promotion of film making in the community* (Working document 1-504/83). Report to the European Parliament on behalf of the Committee on Youth, Culture, Education, Information, and Sport, Brussels.

Rosse, J. N. (1975). *Economic limits of press responsibility* (Studies in Industry Economics discussion paper no. 56). Stanford, CA: Stanford University.

Rosse, J. N., & Dertouzos, J. N. (1978, December 14-15). Economic issues in mass communication industries. In *Proceedings of the Symposium on Media Concentration* (Vol. 1, pp. 40-192). Washington, DC: Federal Trade Commission.

Schiller, H. I. (1969). *Mass communication and American empire.* New York: Kelley.

Siwek, S. E., & Furchtgott-Roth, H. W. (1993). *International trade in computer software.* Westport, CT: Quorum.

TV and cable factbook. (1993). Washington, DC: Warren.

Varis, T. (1983). The international flow of television programs. *Journal of Communication, 34*(1), 143-152.

Varis, T., & Nordenstreng, K. (1974). *Television traffic: A one-way street?* Paris: UNESCO.

Vogel, H. L. (1986). *Entertainment industry economics: A guide for financial analysis.* Cambridge: Cambridge University Press.

Waterman, D. (1985). Prerecorded home video and the distribution of theatrical feature films. In E. M. Noam (Ed.), *Video media competition: Regulation, economics, and technology* (pp. 221-243). New York: Columbia University Press.

Waterman, D. (1988, June). World television trade: The economic effects of privatization and new technology. *Telecommunications Policy,* pp. 141-151.

Waterman, D. (1993). World television trade: The economic effects of privatization and new technology. In E. M. Noam & J. C. Millonzi (Eds.), *The international market in film and television programs* (pp. 59-82). Norwood, NJ: Ablex.

Waxman, S. (1993, October 3). France fears U.S. will smother its cinema. *Chicago Tribune,* sec. 7, p. 2.

Wildman, S. S., & Siwek, S. E. (1987). The privatization of European television: Effects on international markets for programs. *Columbia Journal of World Business, 22*(3), 71-76.

Wildman, S. S., & Siwek, S. E. (1988). *International trade in films and television programs.* Cambridge, MA: Ballinger.

Wildman, S. S., & Siwek, S. E. (1993). The economics of trade in recorded media products in a multilingual world: Implications for national media policies. In E. M. Noam & J. C. Millonzi (Eds.), *The international market in film and television programs* (pp. 13-40). Norwood, NJ: Ablex.

Chapter 8

THE STOCK MARKET AS AUDIENCE: THE IMPACT OF PUBLIC OWNERSHIP ON NEWSPAPERS

Paul M. Hirsch and Tracy A. Thompson

NEWSPAPER EXECUTIVES, like managers in many other industries, have discovered that selling ownership shares to investors with no particular concern for their business means risking a loss of control over the definition of acceptable quality and profitability for their organizations. At best, the financial world of investors and analysts is indifferent to the traditional values and ideological underpinnings of the newspaper business and, at worst, it imposes an alternative and conflicting perspective on the mission and performance of the news media. Many news executives now must respond not only to the market for advertising space but also to the market for financial capital, and they must cater not only to the audience of news readers but also to the audience of securities analysts whose recommendations can either make or break a company on the stock market.

In this chapter, we argue that many of the curious and paradoxical recent developments in the newspaper industry result from a dependency on Wall Street that comes with public ownership. While the newspaper industry remains one of the most profitable, a cursory review of trade publications reveals widespread concern, even panic, about the prospects of the business. A popular consensus within the industry projects continuing declines in newspapers' two most important markets: advertising and circulation. Changing strategies among retail marketers, shifting work and leisure patterns of consumers, and increasing competition from other media are all seen as fundamental challenges for the newspaper industry to overcome. (For an interesting review, see Fitzgerald, 1991.) At the same time, trade publications present countless reports of drastic cost cutting and budget slashing as well as repeated calls for new and innovative strategies designed to attract readers. Knight Ridder's major reinvention of *The News* in Boca Raton and Gannett's *USA Today* and "News 2000" project are several well-known efforts to use a marketing approach to create a "user-friendly" newspaper that appeals to a generation raised on television.

Despite this great commotion in the industry, it may be argued that claims about the demise of the traditional newspaper reflect a shared psychology among managers more than the actual economic conditions of the industry. For example, Templeton's (1990) insightful analysis reveals that the decline in newspapers' household penetration rates has been due less to readers' disinterest than to publishers' deliberate decisions to let readers go. That is, when profits fall during a recession, the common reaction has been to cut costs by shrinking circulation operations. When better times return, newspapers regain circulation, but not enough to keep pace with the increase in new households.

In addition, one particular demographic trend, "the graying of America," may actually offer promising market opportunities despite the belief that the future of the newspaper is endangered because of low levels of readership among baby-boomers. A hectic suburban lifestyle combining dual career pressures and child rearing prevents many people from reading the paper on a daily basis. However, as this large demographic group moves toward the slowed-down pace of a retirement lifestyle, they may regain the time to read the paper and return to the readership fold. Given the attractiveness to advertisers of this wealthy segment of the population, the future may be quite bright for the traditional newspaper format.

Despite such arguments, however, many newspaper executives focus exclusively on other long-term demographic trends that make them anxious to attract a younger and increasingly diverse audience. They see their marketplace as fraught with threats that demand a drastic and immediate revamping of their organizations and products. These executives realize that many other American industries have encountered changing demographic situations, increasing competition, and new technologies. And they know that these industries have responded not only by downsizing and restructuring but also by developing new ways of doing business. Like these other industries, newspapers have discovered externally oriented ideologies (i.e., being "customer driven" and providing "added value") and have adopted new management techniques (i.e., "continuous quality improvement" or "total quality management"). In the newspaper industry, these ideologies and techniques have resulted in greater reliance on consultants' strategic and economic models as a rationale for action; they have produced changes in the traditional power structures within the organization as the news side loses power to advertising and marketing; they have spurred the development of "info-tainment" and other media formats; and, in general, they have resulted in hypersensitivity to the economic conditions of the moment.

Of course, this ideological shift runs the danger of alienating the journalistic profession. The traditional logic of news production is being reversed as external (i.e., economic, demographic, and competitive) pressures rather than internal editorial values and policies define the way newspapers identify and serve their markets. News as defined by customers and not by editors and reporters threatens journalistic control over the production of news and seems—to the profession, at least—to undermine the traditional concept of the newspaper as an independent voice providing reliable information to the community. It is hardly surprising, then, that some professional constituencies argue that newspapers are overreacting when they threaten to discard their historical franchise in favor of market-driven ideologies and televisionlike entertainment products (e.g., Squires, 1993).

In this chapter, we explain these contested developments by examining the organizational consequences of selling ownership stakes in newspaper companies to anonymous investors or traders who elect to purchase stock on the open market. In general, our argument is that the move to dispersed ownership through the offering of stock on a public exchange results in the emergence of a new market or "audience" of Wall Street investors and analysts. We explain how the demands of this audience, which have changed significantly since the turbulent decade of the 1980s, affect the goals and incentives of executives in publicly held newspaper companies; and we draw out some of the implications of these demands for the ideology and performance of publicly held newspapers. We begin by suggesting why two other factors commonly believed to influence the behaviors of the newspaper industry—shifts in the prevailing economic environment and chain ownership of newspapers—are inadequate explanations of the current behavior of the industry.

OWNERSHIP FORM AND
ORGANIZATIONAL BEHAVIOR

Organizational theory challenges the idea of a monolithic economic environment that singularly determines the behavior of newspapers or any other organization (Child, 1972; Weick, 1979). Instead, the environment is *interpreted* by managers who are influenced by a host of social and psychological factors, including those stemming from forms of organizational ownership. At least three different forms of ownership have evolved over the life cycle of the newspaper industry: the family owned, single newspaper; the privately owned group; and the publicly owned group. Through its effects on the goals, incentives, and pressures facing managers, the type and nature of ownership can explain many newspapers' reaction—indeed, *overreaction* from the point of view of journalism critics—to the economic doldrums of the 1990s.

Typical ownership explanations of how the news media interact with their markets generally contrast the first two types of ownership, that is, the independent paper with the group or chain (defined as a conglomerate consisting of two or more separate newspapers). Since the turn of the century, newspaper operations have expanded, and ownership in the industry has moved from being dispersed and fragmented to being significantly more concentrated. Once there were nearly as many papers as communities, and most papers were owned individually by single families. However, the expansionist post-World War II economy and tax disincentives for passing newspapers on to family members fostered the growth of large groups of newspapers owned by one company. Thus in 1920 31 groups accounted for only 8% of the total national circulation, but by 1986 127 groups accounted for over 70% of total newspaper circulation (Lacy, 1991). It is this concentration of ownership, by altering managerial perceptions and goals, that is usually said to adversely affect the way news organizations define and interact with their audiences and markets.

Business historians have long noted how the activities and goals of management change along with growth from small to large organizations (e.g., Chandler, 1977). In a small company, the owner-manager's responsibilities encompass both the management of long-term financial and strategic objectives as well as day-to-day business activities. As a small business evolves into a larger corporation, however, these functions become too much for a single person to manage. Owners, as top executives, become more concerned with running the corporation as a system.

Their activities revolve around issues of resource allocation among separate businesses and strategic direction of the corporation, leaving day-to-day business operations of individual corporate units in the hands of local managers who operate under the guidance and control of the parent corporation. Thus the original owner-manager is no longer directly involved with local markets and operations and relies increasingly on bureaucratic mechanisms of control to manage local units.

A consequence of this organizational process for the newspaper industry, according to critics, is deterioration in the ideal of journalistic service by the shifting of the goals of management toward maximization of profits across a number of newspaper organizations and away from maximization of service to the local readership (Bagdikian, 1990; Lacy, 1991; McManus, 1992). This effect of ownership form and associated increase in size and complexity of the newspaper operation is believed to operate through several mechanisms, especially the rules and methods for how resources are allocated and how work is distributed. Because allocation of resources is based more on considerations of profit and loss and less on the needs of the local community, group ownership might be expected to increase emphasis on profitability through cost cutting (Lacy, 1991) and decrease the resources for reporting the news (Compaigne, 1985; Roach, 1979).

Although the traditional emphasis on size and chain ownership appropriately focuses critical attention on the changing incentives of managers and the consequences for news content, it fails to adequately explain the behavior of newspapers today. Researchers have failed to find a consistent relationship between ownership concentration and content; for example, a recent study (Lacy, 1991) found group ownership has no relationship to the allocation of news space and only a limited effect on budgetary processes. Such findings suggest that the emphasis on size (i.e., group ownership) *per se* is incomplete and that closer attention to the meaning and nature of public ownership (especially its influence on managerial goals) offers a better explanation of the newspaper industry's behavior today.

The third stage in the newspaper industry's life cycle, the move toward public ownership, has been overlooked in most treatments of the newspaper business. As large chains grew and expanded in the post-World War II economy, and particularly in the 1960s and 1970s, the need for new capital propelled private owners in the direction of public ownership through stock offerings (Bogart, 1989; Meyer & Wearden, 1984). Furthermore, the bullish environment of the 1980s encouraged even more firms to go public. By 1990 one half of daily circulation was held by public corporations (Bogart, 1991).[1] At the same time that ownership in the newspaper industry was becoming increasingly concentrated, it was being even more fully transformed by this shift from private to public ownership. The potential influence of public ownership on the behavior of newspaper companies has been previously (albeit rarely) noted. Those noting this change (Bagdikian, 1980; Blankenburg & Ozanich, 1993; Bogart, 1989, 1991; Meyer & Wearden, 1984) argue that managers of publicly traded companies have different incentives and goals than managers of private companies. Managers of publicly owned newspapers are restricted in their ability to pursue goals and behaviors that conflict with, or do not clearly contribute to, maximizing the company's value to shareholders. In contrast, owners and managers of private newspapers enjoy a greater degree of freedom. They can choose among a number of options above and beyond money, for example, the pursuit of nonfinancial satisfactions such as increasing public awareness or pursuing political agendas.

These new realities reflect the demands of a new set of stakeholders in the newspaper organization. Ben Bagdikian predicted the power shifts that follow public ownership as far back as 1978 when he wrote:

> The impact of trading newspaper corporate stock on the stock market has meant that news companies must constantly expand in size and rate of profits in order to maintain their position on stock exchanges. This means that companies no longer reach a steady state of profits in real dollars; instead, the new ethic encourages them to squeeze the maximum from every newspaper unit in the corporation in order to buy ever more properties, not always in the news business, and to declare ever growing dividends. . . . This has introduced yet a third constituency for daily newspapers—stock market investors. Instead of the single master so celebrated in the rhetoric of the industry—the reader—there are in fact three masters—the reader, the advertiser, and the stock market. And with the increase of size of the corporation the emphasis shifts steadily toward the last two, in order for the large news corporations to maintain their economic position with other national and transnational corporations. (Bagdikian, 1980, pp. 63-64)

Thus, with public ownership, many of the activities of managers focus on the demands of financial markets. Managers of public newspapers spend a great deal of time justifying their operations and profit margins to an audience of financial analysts and investors. The rising importance of this powerful new audience is revealed, for example, by the attention it has received at the annual American Society of Newspaper Editors. In recent years the program has included sessions addressing the impact of public ownership on the newspaper industry with such titles as "Chief Executive Officers View the Impact of Public Ownership" (1989) and "1990 Issues and Trends in Newspaper Ownership" (1990).

Our general argument is that, by virtue of their exposure to, and dependence on, the judgment of the stock market, publicly owned newspapers should be expected to behave differently than privately held papers. However, the movement from private to public ownership, taken alone, does not fully account for the dramatic changes the newspaper business has undergone since the 1980s. Many papers have been publicly owned for over 25 years and have come through other periods of economic turbulence largely unchanged (e.g., in the 1970s and 1980s). Why were their reactions to those economic downturns not as drastic as they became in the late 1980s and early 1990s? Throughout the 1960s and 1970s, the same demographic trends and lifestyle changes were in evidence, yet these too were not met with the same sense of gloom and panic as in recent years. To understand these complexities, another factor needs to be considered: the radical changes *within* the nature of public ownership that redefined newspapers during the late 1980s and early 1990s.

THE CHANGING CONSEQUENCES
OF PUBLIC OWNERSHIP

In theory, executives of publicly held firms are always supposed to act on behalf of shareholders; however, views of "the shareholder's best interest" and of appropriate and legitimate management practices have changed since newspapers first went public. The particular historical and economic conditions of the 1980s and early 1990s have altered the meaning of public ownership for executives in all American industries, including newspapers, and have forced many of them to adopt new approaches to managing their organizations (Useem, 1993). Indeed, a broad transformation in the organization of ownership and in managerial control has occurred. Worried about losing their companies to hostile raiders, managers have begun basing strategic decisions and organizational designs on expected impact on shareholder value—a combination of stock dividends and share appreciation accumulated over a number of years—rather than such criteria as serving the public, the community, or employees.

When newspaper companies first entered the world of public ownership in the 1960s and 1970s, top executives faced few pressures from capital markets beyond meeting numerous information requests from financial and market analysts. During the bullish market and takeover wave of the 1980s, however, the nature of capital markets changed to become increasingly competitive, hostile, and threatening. Throughout the 1980s, many professional managers were ousted from their jobs by corporate raiders who claimed to be able to run the companies more efficiently and to provide a higher return to shareholders. Companies with an undervalued or low share price were at risk of being taken over by raiders offering large premiums over the going price. (See Coffee, Lowenstein, & Rose-Ackerman, 1988, for an excellent treatment of hostile takeovers.) Increased demand for short-term profits from large institutional shareholders with big blocks of stock pressured newspaper executives to rethink their priorities. Executives' primary goal became the maintenance of high share prices through unprecedented attention to cost cutting and through quarterly demonstrations of strong financial performance, all for the benefit of the audience of analysts and investors.

Meeting the expectations of this new audience is critical if executives want to retain control over their organizations. Continual and steady growth in corporate earnings are necessary to enhance the value of the stock and ensure the good recommendation of analysts, thereby enabling executives to deflect hostile takeovers and to attract additional capital needed for expansion. In an important review of these developments, Kwitny (1990) notes:

> Maintaining an analyst's "buy" recommendation requires not merely maintaining high earnings, but continuing to improve upon the ever-higher earnings of each previous year. Among other things, a declining stock price could prompt a buyout attempt by an outside concern, maybe even a General Electric or American Express. Editors might be replaced, and newsgathering become less professional, more profit-driven, than ever. (pp. 21-22)

In this demanding environment, performance is continually assessed by analysts and investors using the quarterly report on earnings. Analysts use information about a firm's operations to generate forecasts about the company's long-term productivity and performance, which are reflected in the stock price.[2] "Working for the numbers" has several important consequences for how newspapers operate. Strategies and activities geared toward creating value in the long run that require heavy investment in the short run become less attractive to executives because they decrease earnings in the current period. Because goals typically associated with newspapers such as maximizing public understanding are difficult to link directly with enhanced earnings, they are less legitimate in the eyes of the financial world than objectives that have a clear and immediate impact on the bottom line. Furthermore, the growing practice of linking executives' compensation packages to stock price adds natural incentives for managers to look for ways to increase share price.

Thus the move to public ownership led to the emergence of not only a new set of stakeholders in newspapers but a new logic for managing newspapers. Performance that is measured more in terms of economic than editorial accomplishments undermines newspaper executives' autonomy to pursue nonfinancial goals. Of interest, however, the amount of pressure exerted on managers by the financial world depends on a second factor: the degree to which actual organizational control is dispersed among the owners. That is, publicly owned newspapers vary in the degree to which voting rights are distributed among the stockholders (Blankenburg & Ozanich, 1993; Meyer & Wearden, 1984; Potter, 1992). For some newspaper firms, the original family interests were already fractionated before the firm went public (Bogart, 1991). For example, the Tribune Company and Gannett sold shares to the public after diversified ownership and a professional management team were already in place. For other organizations, however, the original family control has been perpetuated by having two classes of stock with differential voting rights (e.g., the New York Times Company, The Washington Post Company, Media General, Pulitzer, McClatchy). A takeover move to extract Media General from the Bryan family in the mid-1980s provided the incentive for more companies to issue two classes of stock (e.g., Times-Mirror, Dow Jones, A. H. Belo, Affiliated Publications, and E. W. Scripps).

The distinction between family *control* versus family ownership is important. Dual classes of stock ensure that the family (those that hold the stock with more voting rights) retain control over the corporation in the sense that they can prevent a hostile takeover and enjoy the right to determine company policies. However, such a capital structure does not imply that such firms are completely free from the pressures imposed by the stock market. These firms still rely on positive recommendations from analysts to raise the capital needed for expansion or acquisitions, and therefore their financial performance must be consistent with the criteria for such recommendations. However, attention to the dispersion of ownership does account for some of the variation in behavior among publicly held papers. Media companies that have resisted the trend toward "commodification" of the news (e.g., *New York Times, Washington Post*) tend to be those with two classes of stock and more family influence, whereas the ownership pattern of those who pioneered it (e.g., Gannett's papers and *USA Today*) is more widely dispersed.

Our argument is that, under the pressures of the capital markets, which require growth in profits amidst an increasingly turbulent environment, managers of non-family controlled, public newspapers are forced to turn to the normative framework best understood by the audience of analysts and investors: the norms of financial performance. Unlike many other industries, the newspaper business has until recently been insulated from this normative system and could operate according to the dictates of publishers and owners who may have wished to attend to the norms of journalism colleagues and elite news sources in addition to those of readers. That the new normative regime imposed by securities analysts differs ideologically from the traditional theory of news production is demonstrated by Meyer and Wearden's (1984) survey of the attitudes of financial analysts and newspaper managers.[3] When asked to rate the importance of various yardsticks for evaluating the performance of newspaper companies, securities analysts rated earnings consistency, financial health represented by the balance sheet, and management quality highest, whereas publishers still bravely rated community service, editorial quality, product quality, and company image as being most important.

CORPORATE STRATEGY

To satisfy the demands of their new financial audience, newspaper executives have turned increasingly to the logic of strategic corporate management that now dominates thinking in corporate America. The logic of strategic management focuses managers' attention on the ways in which organizations can enhance their performance in terms of financial measures. It strongly endorses economic analysis as the basis of organizational decision making as opposed to such alternative value systems as reporting "all the news that's fit to print." This perspective reflects a quasi-rational and scientific conception of business based on the quantifiable logic of finance and economic analysis. The behavior of many newspapers today can be traced to this new normative framework of business strategy as these firms try to position themselves to their best advantage in their competitive and economic environment.

A brief examination of two important strategy frameworks provides an insight into how current thinking about corporate strategy is beginning to reshape newspapers and their relationship to their readers and other markets. One of the dominant approaches to strategy has been developed by Michael Porter (1980, 1985), who asserts that the profitability of any firm in an industry is determined both by the overall structure of the industry and by the firm's position in that structure. The economic attractiveness of an industry is assessed by looking at five features: ease of entry, threat of substitution, bargaining power of buyers, bargaining power of suppliers, and rivalry among current competitors. Together these factors determine the strength of competitive forces and therefore industry profitability. To succeed economically, organizations strive to develop a "sustainable competitive advantage." A firm accomplishes this by occupying a defensible position that enables it to stave off threats from each of the five competitive forces and to earn a superior return on investment, which, of course, is one of the major indicators of financial performance.

An analysis of the newspaper industry using Porter's framework would characterize the industry's recent earnings decline as stemming from changes in competitive forces. Innovations in printing technology, the development of new technologies such as cable television and fiber optics, and regulatory changes in the telecommunication industry have lowered entry barriers, increased the threat of product substitution, and thus increased the degree of competitive rivalry in the newspaper industry. In addition, the bargaining power of buyers (i.e., advertisers and readers) has increased. From an economically rational standpoint, the newspaper industry is not as attractive as it once was.

Porter presents several generic strategies for protection from competition and enhancement of earnings. The "cost leadership strategy" is to be the lowest cost producer of a product in the industry. The "differentiation strategy" is to provide a product or service that is perceived industrywide as unique. A third option is to restrict the market scope either to a smaller geographic market or else a particular buyer group. Firms adopting this "focus strategy" can compete on the basis of low cost or differentiation in the smaller market. Organizations that do not pursue one of these paths are "stuck in the middle" and will not be able to perform as well.

The ability of newspaper firms to pursue either of the first two strategies is limited. Cost alone has never been a sufficient basis of competition for newspapers, especially on the readership side, where the cost to the consumer already represents only a fraction of the total cost of the product. A differentiation strategy, which by definition is national in scope, traditionally has been logistically and economically impractical due to the diseconomies of scale created by the demands of local production and distribution. Only a few newspapers (*Wall Street Journal, New York Times,* and *USA Today*) successfully pursue a differentiation strategy by providing a product to the entire nation that is perceived to be unique.

Traditionally, newspapers have been best able to pursue Porter's generic strategy of focused differentiation. Most newspapers have concentrated on geographically focused markets but have remained "mass media" in their commitment to serve everyone within their market areas. That is, newspapers have tried to provide a product that appeals to all readers within their areas regardless of the readers' demographic profiles, lifestyles, and interests. According to Porter's strategic framework, however, changes in demographic factors, lifestyles, and interests in the market area represent important environmental developments to which newspapers must try to respond. To the extent that geographically focused markets have fragmented into still smaller and more homogeneous segments, newspapers' traditional geographic focused-differentiation strategy has become less effective. Under these circumstances, Porter's framework suggests that a narrower, *buyer group*-focused strategy is likely to be more effective in achieving higher profits.

In sum, Porter's analysis draws attention to the nature of the environmental changes confronting newspapers. It highlights how changes in advertisers' preferences and readers' characteristics may mean newspapers have to work harder to convince their customers to buy their services and products. This market-driven perspective is shared by many other strategic theorists such as Day (1990), who asserts that most consumer markets today are changing faster than ever before and that the best strategy for any firm is to track changing consumer demands and meet them quickly. This approach complements and extends Porter's framework by placing greatest emphasis on customers as the most relevant environmental entity to monitor. An obvious example of this differentiation logic is Knight Ridder's Spanish language *El Nuevo Herald* in Miami, which presents an editorial voice explicitly shaped by marketing considerations.

Another influential strategic management framework is Miles, Snow, Meyer, and Coleman's (1978) typology of "Defenders," "Prospectors," "Analyzers," and "Reactors." Most newspapers are Defenders, who follow the strategy of focusing on what they know best, seeking to refine their existing products and building on current strengths. Prospectors, on the other hand, direct more attention to developing new markets and creating new products (e.g., Gannett's launch of *USA Today*). Analyzers are hybrids of Defenders and Prospectors. They operate in stable, core markets like Defenders, but they also build upon their existing markets and products by monitoring developments among competitors and rapidly adopting those that appear most promising. Finally, Reactors bounce back and forth between these alternative approaches and do not develop organizational strengths in any one area.

Firms that are well-known examples include Rupert Murdoch's News Corporation, an entrepreneurial Prospector firm that has expanded into movies, television, and satellites; the Washington Post Company, an efficient Defender firm that focuses efforts on its existing properties; and the Knight-Ridder Company, an Analyzer firm that has innovated in Miami and Boca Raton, Florida, while retaining more traditional franchises in other cities. Among these categories, Defenders seem least likely to continue to meet the expectations of their financial audience. While it is too early to conclude that the Defenders' stance has outlived its usefulness, Defenders probably will not be able to maintain high growth rates and profit levels. Prospectors and Analyzers are probably better able to increase profitability in markets that continue to change.

With their emphasis on environmentally oriented, market-driven approaches to organizational strategy, conceptual frameworks like those of Porter and Miles et al. represent a very different perspective on the newspaper industry than that associated with the traditional values of journalism. These frameworks challenge the view of newspapers as institutional gatekeepers that collect, edit, and disseminate information based on journalists' professional judgments. These frameworks also challenge the view of newspaper ownership as offering returns different, and greater, than other investments (see Demsetz & Lehn, 1985). Even economists, the forefathers of strategy theorists, acknowledge such "nonrational" aspects of newspaper ownership by including variables in their models to allow for an "excess" (psychological) value of newspapers to owners. However, the radical changes resulting from today's form of public ownership and from the normative frameworks that such ownership has engendered redefine the news as merely another economic commodity. The journalistic ideal of serving democracy by reporting *what the community needs to know* is seen as less legitimate than using survey research to offer *what the market wants to see*.

IMPLICATIONS AND HYPOTHESES

The financial and intellectual forces of public ownership and strategic management exert a pull on the newspaper industry that will continue to reshape the industry and the firms within it in significant ways. One outcome promoted by public ownership[4] and strategic theory would be diversification and divestiture of newspaper operations by media companies when the newspaper business is thought to be in decline. Strategic theorists such as Porter recommend that rational assessments of the prospects for industry growth drive investment and divestment decisions. If the signs within an industry are negative, a firm should invest its money in other, more profitable and promising industries. While ideological considerations might preclude privately held firms from diversifying or divesting, publicly held firms would be expected to expand into different industries and ultimately sell their newspaper holdings if profitability and growth cannot be maintained.

Another outcome promoted by public ownership and strategic theory would be a realignment of power held by various departments and functional areas within newspaper companies. Departments with a market orientation such as circulation would be expected to gain power more rapidly (relative to the editorial side) in publicly held newspaper companies. Further, the influence of financial analysts would be expected to rise more quickly in publicly held companies. In addition, the functional backgrounds of top management are increasingly likely to differ between publicly and privately held companies. Publicly held papers would be expected to have more top managers with economic or finance backgrounds. Also, recruitment patterns are increasingly likely to differ. Publicly held papers would be expected to recruit more managers with little or no background in journalism or publishing.

These organizational outcomes, in turn, suggest changes and differences in the methods for analysis and allocation of organizational resources. The budgeting process would be expected to differ between privately held and publicly held newspapers in the degree to which it reflects a "rational" or economic approach to producing news. Publicly held papers would be expected to have much more formalized procedures and standards, which, in turn, would indirectly influence content. Publicly held papers, for example, likely would be more concerned with measurement of the financial payoffs accruing to such editorial expenses as major investigative reporting projects. In contrast, privately owned papers may have greater freedom to pursue such goals as winning a Pulitzer prize. Thus the *variation* in editorial content and quality of publicly held newspapers might decrease (as compared with privately held papers) as public companies all increasingly turn to news and information products that meet the demands of the most profitable market segments at the least cost.

Finally and most generally, public ownership is hypothesized to influence the degree to which newspaper organizations are responsive to immediate economic pressures. Because of their need to consistently demonstrate short-term profitability, public companies are likely to respond more quickly and more drastically to economic downturns. A drop in earnings in one time period is more likely to be associated with personnel reductions and other cost-cutting measures in a company dependent upon the financial markets. Publicly held newspapers are not likely to be different than any other companies in this regard.

In summary, the analysis of public ownership and strategic theory suggests a number of hypotheses about structural and content differences between publicly and privately held newspapers and about changes in all newspapers that could be tested now and in the future. Even now, however, there may be fewer differences between privately and publicly owned newspaper firms as well as less variation among privately held firms than would be anticipated from this analysis due to the diffusion of strategic thinking across the entire industry. Innovations and approaches first attempted by large, public chains would be expected to diffuse by imitation. Other diffusion mechanisms such as professional training, use of consultants, and cross-hiring would also serve as mechanisms to further "rationalize" the newspaper business.

Our argument in this chapter has been that those who care about newspapers must not ignore the impact of public ownership on the industry. Most research and theory are focused on how changing economic conditions or ownership concentration affect the ways in which newspapers identify and serve their traditional audience of readers. These factors alone, however, do not explain the transformation of the historical journalistic format in many papers across the nation. We have argued that, by allowing outside investors and traders to buy stock and determine the value of their companies, newspaper executives have encountered a new and different audience to be served—an audience that, especially since the turbulent 1980s, views newspaper performance entirely in terms of ever higher profits. The ideology of business strategy offers newspaper executives a rationale and a set of prescriptions for managing their businesses, but this ideology dramatically differs from the assumptions underlying journalistic tradition. By going public, newspapers have found a new audience whose demands promise to make the conflict between business objectives and journalistic ideals sharper than ever.

NOTES

1. Not all newspapers have grown into large, public corporations. Today, the industry maintains a wide range of organizational forms, including small and large, private and public. Most descriptive data break the industry down according to the independent versus the chain or group form. However, one can infer diversity in terms of public versus private from these data. For example, a recent survey by the American Society of Newspaper Editors in 1990 shows that independent papers are mostly privately held; however, some are public. Similarly, groups or chains of newspapers are private, semiprivate, and public. This diversity makes the newspaper industry a natural setting for testing hypotheses about the relationship between ownership form (i.e., public versus private) and the behavior of news media organizations.

2. The economic theory behind the relationship between a firm's current earnings, its stock price, and its future earning potential is formalized in the Capital Asset Pricing Model. Interested readers can consult "CFO's and Strategists: Forging a Common Framework" (Rappaport, 1992) or an introductory text on finance such as *Principles of Corporate Finance* by Brearley and Meyers (1991).

3. See also McManus (1992) for how the logic of profit maximization generates a different theory of news production than the maximization of public understanding.

4. As described earlier, public ownership can take different forms. The predictions outlined in this section hold most strongly for the most extreme form of public ownership, which consists of those firms characterized by diffuse ownership patterns (rather than those where control is closely held via special stock options).

REFERENCES

American Society of Newspaper Editors. (1989, April 11-14). Chief executive officers view the impact of public ownership. In *Proceedings of the American Society of Newspaper Editors*. Washington, DC: Author.

American Society of Newspaper Editors. (1990, April 3-6). 1990 issues and trends in ownership. In *Proceedings of the American Society of Newspaper Editors*. Washington, DC: Author.

Bagdikian, B. H. (1980). Conglomeration, concentration, and the media. *Journal of Communication, 30*, 59-64.

Bagdikian, B. H. (1990). *The media monopoly* (3rd ed.). Boston: Beacon.

Blankenburg, W. B., & Ozanich, G. W. (1993). The effects of public ownership on the financial performance of newspaper corporations. *Journalism Quarterly, 70*, 68-75.

Bogart, L. (1989). *Press and public: Who reads what, when, where and why in American newspapers*. Hillsdale, NJ: Lawrence Erlbaum.

Bogart, L. (1991). *Preserving the press*. New York: Columbia University Press.

Brearley, R. A., & Meyers, S. C. (1991). *Principles of corporate finance* (4th ed.). New York: McGraw-Hill.

Chandler, A. D. (1977). *The visible hand: The managerial revolution in American business*. Cambridge, MA: Belknap Press of Harvard University Press.

Child, J. (1972). Organizational structure, environment and performance: The role of strategic choice. *Sociology, 6,* 2-22.

Coffee, J. C., Jr., Lowenstein, L., & Rose-Ackerman, S. (1988). *Knights, raiders, and targets: The impact of the hostile takeover.* New York: Oxford University Press.

Compaigne, B. M. (1985). The expanding base of media competition. *Journal of Communication, 35,* 81-96.

Day, G. S. (1990). *Market driven strategy: Processes for creating value, New York.* New York: Free Press.

Demsetz, H., & Lehn, K. (1985). The structure of corporate ownership: Causes and consequences. *Journal of Political Economy, 93*(6), 1155-1177.

Fitzgerald, M. (1991). Is the glass half-full or half-empty? ANPA panel reads the tea leaves to forecast newspapers future. *Editor and Publisher, 124,* 14, 41.

Kwitny, J. (1990). The high cost of high profits. *Washington Journalism Review, 12,* 19-29.

Lacy, S. (1991, Spring). Effects of group ownership on daily newspaper content. *Journal of Media Economics,* pp. 35-47.

McManus, J. H. (1992). What kind of commodity is news? *Communication Research, 19*(6), 787-805.

Meyer, P., & Wearden, S. T. (1984). The effects of public ownership on newspaper companies: A preliminary inquiry. *Public Opinion Quarterly, 48,* 564-577.

Miles, R. E., Snow, C. C., Meyer, A. D., & Coleman, H. J., Jr. (1978). Organizational strategy, structure and process. *Academy of Management Review, 3*(3), 546-562.

Porter, M. M. (1980). *Competitive strategy: Techniques for analyzing industries and competitors.* New York: Free Press.

Porter, M. M. (1985). *Competitive advantage.* New York: Free Press.

Potter, W. (1992). Family values. *Presstime, 14*(11), 14-19.

Rappaport, A. (1992, May-June). CFO's and strategists: Forging a common framework. *Harvard Business Review,* pp. 84-89.

Roach, C. B. (1979). Media conglomerates, antitrust law and the marketplace of ideas. *Memphis State Law Review, 9,* 257-280.

Squires, J. D. (1993). *Read all about it! The corporate takeover of America's newspapers.* New York: Times Books.

Templeton, L. B. (1990, February). When bad math equals less revenue, why use it? *Newsinc.,* pp. 49-51.

Useem, M. (1993). *Executive defense: Shareholder power and corporate reorganization.* Cambridge, MA: Harvard University Press.

Weick, K. E. (1979). *The social psychology of organizing* (2nd ed.). New York: Random House.

Chapter 9

THE ROLE OF THE AUDIENCE
IN THE PRODUCTION OF CULTURE:
A PERSONAL RESEARCH RETROSPECTIVE

Muriel Goldsman Cantor

HOW INFLUENTIAL IS the audience in determining the content of popular culture? When I first became interested in the relationship between the creators of culture and their audiences, few people were even speculating about the answer to such a question. The emphasis, then, was on the impact of organizations on creators. For example, both C. Wright Mills (1953) and Robert Merton (1957) had discussed in some detail the problems intellectuals face when they work in bureaucratic settings. "Between the intellectual and his potential public stand technical, economic and social structures which are owned and operated by others," wrote Mills (1953, p. 150). "If the intellectual becomes the hired man of an information industry, his general aims must, of course, be set by the decisions of others rather than his own integrity." According to this formulation, therefore, both the creators and their publics are powerless in a system where creativity is bureaucratically controlled.

Throughout the last quarter century, with this question in mind, I have interviewed television and movie producers (Cantor, 1971/1987a); buyers and sellers of television programs in the international marketplace (Cantor & Cantor, 1986a); stage, screen, and television actors (Cantor & Peters, 1980; Peters & Cantor, 1982); television and print fiction writers (Cantor, 1989; Cantor & Jones, 1983); and publishers of popular magazines and genre fiction (Cantor, 1987b). In addition, I have conducted both qualitative and quantitative content analyses of print fiction, soap operas, and family shows on television (Cantor, 1991; Cantor & Pingree, 1983). Now,

I contend that, although organizational and occupational factors are important in determining the nature of the stories being told, the audience matters too (Cantor, 1987b; Cantor & Cantor, 1986b; Tuchman, 1988). The creation of content, especially in prime-time television and popular movies, is the outcome of a struggle with many players participating (Cantor, 1979). Over the years, I have examined a number of avenues for audience involvement in this struggle: as "reference" individuals or groups for those who actually create the stories; as interest and advocacy groups; and as target markets for distributors, advertisers, and financiers. In this chapter, I offer a brief review of my conclusions about the role of the audience in the creation of popular culture.

AUDIENCES-AS-REFERENCE GROUPS

When I wrote *The Hollywood TV Producer* (Cantor, 1971/1987a), my underlying interest was the role that producers played in the tight-knit, small community of decision makers involved in selecting the dramatic programs to be produced and in the process by which these programs were created and later distributed to viewers in the United States. My goal was then, and still is, twofold: to learn how much creative autonomy producers and other creators have within the organizational, economic, and political contexts of their work and, second, to describe what I have called elsewhere the "negotiated struggle" (Cantor, 1979, 1980), the process that producers and writers go through to get "their" content to an audience.

In pursuit of this goal, I developed a long and complex interview schedule that was administered to 59 television line producers. I asked two questions about the audience: "What kind of an audience views the show you are now on?" and "Does this audience differ from audiences for other shows of which you have been a part?" The responses to those questions were surprising and confusing. The producers' notions of who watched their shows were limited to a mixture of stereotypes and wishful thinking. Most producers had a low opinion of their audiences' intelligence and taste. They thought if a show appealed to themselves it would not appeal to the general public (or a mass audience). A few others believed just the opposite. They thought that *they* were the audience and, if the program appealed to them, it would appeal to others as well. Those in the first group explained that most shows failed because they were not directed to the right audience. Some of them maintained that shows should not be controversial or too intellectual. Those in the other group thought that a large number of people were precluded from seeing the shows that they might like because television was so lowbrow and standardized. Some of them believed that shows should have more character and originality so that television would attract a more intellectual audience. As Todd Gitlin (1983) found out almost two decades later, producers and other creators were confused and unclear about how shows actually got on the air.

Some analysts such as Herbert Gans (1957, 1974) have suggested that, because television entertainment is created by committee, creators function as representatives (albeit self-appointed) of conflicting public tastes. But my interviews showed otherwise. Occasionally, producers reported that they did engage in conflict with corporate decision makers concerning the audience—especially when they thought that a potential audience was not being tapped. More committed (or more popular) producers reported that they argued their own points of view with decision makers. Sometimes, though not often, their points of view even prevailed. Most of the time, however, producers represented no particular audience point of view.

This is not to argue, however, that the audience-as-reference-group never has an impact on producers and their work. Soap operas provide a well-known example of television production in which audience response may have an influence on content (Cantor & Cantor, 1986b; Cantor & Pingree, 1983). "Those interested viewers who communicate their opinions through letter writing or fan magazines and through face-to-face contacts are very important even though they may be a small minority of viewers," I wrote, with Joel Cantor (1986b, p. 223), of soap opera fans. "These viewers are powerful because writers and producers most often keep them in mind when initiating themes or continuing a relatively conservative view of the social world." However, these responses are not the only sort of audience influence on content. We went on to note:

In addition, ratings (another social construction of reality) are influential because they alert producers to the taste segments being reached by a program. Although decisions on soap opera content are not subject to the same trends as prime-time programs, they do often change and can even be canceled. Innovation is highest when ratings are low. Thus when networks and production organizations decide that a soap is in trouble, the creators no longer use the involved audience as its reference but rather try to reach out to those not yet captured by the traditional stories. (Cantor & Cantor, 1986b, p. 223)

Thus, while direct audience feedback has proved to be an uncertain source of influence on the work of television creators, the audience as constituted by the ratings has proved to be an enduring feature of creators' work life. In general, the interviews I conducted for *The Hollywood TV Producer* indicated that, no matter how creative producers might be and no matter which audience they wished to reach, they had little real control over their creative efforts. Which series and scripts were selected for production, what time they were broadcast, and whether they were renewed from season to season were all determined by the networks—or, perhaps more precisely, *by the markets that the networks and their advertisers wished to reach.*

AUDIENCES-AS-SEGMENTED-MARKETS

A quarter of a century after my interviews with producers, it is still true that creative control remains with those who control the means of distribution. What has changed is that the broadcast networks have lost their monopoly. Network television was at its pinnacle in 1968 when, each night, more than 80% of the potential audience was tuned in to one of the three networks. Then, cable television systems were still used only to bring broadcast programs to isolated communities. Independent stations were few, even in the largest market areas. And there were no videotape recorders. As new technologies and, in turn, new viewing opportunities have become available, ABC, CBS, and NBC are far less able to provide advertisers with a "mass" audience (Ang, 1986, 1991; Neuman, 1991) or to control the creative process (Cantor & Cantor, 1992). Along with the new technologies that have provided more choices for audiences, there are demographic and economic changes among audiences themselves that contribute to greater diversity. In particular, audiences have become more segmented. Through my observations of how content and audiences have changed during the last 25 years, it is evident to me that, if we are to understand the creation of popular culture, we must not study creators-as-workers in isolation from audiences-as-segmented-markets.

Throughout my work, I have argued that there has never been just one audience for television. From the beginning, even when producers created programs for the "lowest common denominator," there were different audiences for different kinds of shows. However, almost everyone who wrote about television in the 1960s and early 1970s considered the audience to be an undifferentiated or homogeneous "mass." Herbert Gans claimed in 1966 that the audience for TV was the most "massified" but that the audiences for other media were segmented. By 1974, however,

Gans and others recognized that television was changing. "Ever since some advertisers discovered that they could best sell their wares by reaching potential buyers rather than the largest number of viewers," he wrote (1974, p. 157), "they have been interested in programs that appeal to specific age, sex, and sometimes even income groups in the total audience." Contemporary analyses also show that different taste segments watch different kinds of programs. Such facts as these are obvious: Women as a group are more likely to watch situation comedies, men to watch action-adventure shows and sports programs, and blacks to watch shows with black stars or characters.

Network television did (and still does) target the middle and especially the lower middle economic strata as that most likely to use such everyday products as drugs, beauty aids, and packaged food; and there is no doubt that this large group makes up most of the heavy viewers of prime-time shows. However, within this larger group, there are increasingly differentiated taste segments that prefer different kinds of shows. While some programs in the 1980s (for example, *The Bill Cosby Show* and *Family Ties*) still commanded the attention of 50% of the audience, the remaining (and shrinking) audience was divided among the two other networks, independent stations, cable, and public television. Since those shows left the air, no program has dominated the ratings in the same way. *Roseanne* became popular in the early 1990s, but its ratings did not reach the peak that shows such as *Cheers, Dallas,* and other hits achieved in the late 1970s and early 1980s. Although some programs receive higher ratings than others, few network television programs generate the appeal to aggregate enough audience segments into what could be called a "mass" audience, made up of all genders, social classes, and age groups.

Over the last decade, television has come to reflect more directly the tastes and lifestyles of various audiences (Cantor & Cantor, 1986b). Soap operas provide a good example of the relationship between television content and the tastes and lifestyles of the market segments of interest to advertisers. While all soap operas try to reach 18- to 49-year-old women, they do not have identical audiences. Moreover, soap operas have changed with their audiences. For example, a content analysis of *Guiding Light* indicated that, as the number of women in the labor force increased, the number of female characters employed outside the home also increased (Cantor & Pingree, 1983). "Modern television soap operas still, if pressed, support basic and traditional values but now principally target 'emancipated' women . . . who combine sex with marriage and career," Joel Cantor and I wrote (1986b, p. 222) of these changes. "The explanation that best fits these data is that the production companies themselves recognized these social changes, and the networks then also accepted them as the now-current morality." Thus we suggested that "a complex interrelationship arises between the audience in the head of the creators and the realities of the marketplace" to form the content of programming.

THE INTERNATIONAL AUDIENCE

While television audiences have been narrowing in one sense, they have been widening in another. The overseas market for U.S. television opened in the 1950s when other countries had to import programs to fill their schedules. It is difficult to obtain exact data on how many U.S. programs sold during those years. However, it is generally agreed that, at least through the early 1970s, more of the imported programs broadcast on foreign channels were from the United States than from any other country. Many reasons have been suggested as to why U.S. programs spread so quickly overseas; but the principal ones are that these programs could be obtained quickly, in great variety and large quantity, and at reasonable prices. Also, they appeared well made and "professional," unlike the local productions made at the time. (See the chapter by Wildman in this volume.) In general, as Joel Cantor and I argued based on our interviews with program importers and exporters, it is the audience as a market for program content (and perhaps also as market for advertisers' products) that most influences world trade in television:

> For both the suppliers and importers of television entertainment (especially dramatic programs), the goal of attracting large audiences—whether for advertisers or state-run broadcasting systems—dominates program selection, with lesser attention to the political and cultural messages expressed. It is the audience in each country, with its own system of cultural values and beliefs, that ultimately decides the popularity of programs and thereby plays a decisive role in influencing the types of shows imported from the United States and other countries. (Cantor & Cantor, 1986a, p. 510)

During the heyday of network television, U.S. program producers and suppliers did not really concern themselves with the interests of audiences in foreign markets. Of course, production companies were always interested in such sales, but the creative people rarely if ever thought about overseas audiences. Only when production companies had produced enough episodes to syndicate a program did they try to sell the program abroad. This professed lack of interest in foreign sales began to change in the 1980s when the entire cultural apparatus of the commercial television industry realized that the loss of their audiences was a structural phenomenon. It had become clear that the enormous audiences of the 1970s and early 1980s were unlikely to return to the networks.

At the same time, production costs were beginning to rise in Europe. Moreover, the growth in commercial television outlets increased competition for viewers, which in turn forced more and more European production companies into deficit financing to make "expensive-looking" programs that could attract larger audiences. Producers from two, three, or more countries began to pool resources to make programs (Cantor & Cantor, 1992; Strover, 1989; Waterman, 1988). Some sought out U.S. companies as coproducers in the hope that the productions would then look more "American" and, perhaps, also sell in the U.S. market.

The internationalization of the television market is illustrated by Marches des International Programes des Television (MIP-TV), an international meeting of programmers and suppliers held in Cannes each spring. Nearly 6,000 television program buyers, sellers, and producers from 1,500 companies attended in 1990 to negotiate broadcast rights to the more than 33,000 programs offered and also to find coproduction partners for new projects. Half of the companies present were from the United States, France, and Great Britain, putting those countries in the forefront of the international television industry. Of the estimated 110 countries attending, large contingents also came from Australia, Canada, Holland, Italy, Japan, Spain, and West Germany.

Beginning in the early 1980s, there has been much talk of "pan-European" productions that would flow easily across borders. There also has been much interest in "mid-Atlantic" productions created by combinations of European and U.S. companies. In 1982, for example, more than 350 coproductions, many involving U.S. companies, were proposed or negotiated at MIP-TV. And in 1985 Granada Television of Britain, producer of *Brideshead Revisited* and *The Jewel in the Crown*, signed an agreement with RKO Pictures to develop, produce, and distribute television movies and miniseries. The U.S. networks welcomed such agreements because they increased the choice of programs for new seasons and reduced the requirements for up-front production fees. That position became obvious when, during the Writers Guild strike of spring-summer 1988, the networks announced that they would buy the programs they needed from overseas if the strike did not end in time to start the fall season.

Until recently, very few "mid-Atlantic" programs have deliberately been made to sell in both the U.S. and the European markets. Increasingly, however, U.S. production firms are realizing that, if, by making minor changes, they can increase the probability of selling a series in particular overseas markets, then, of course, it is sensible to do so. Because the pilots for new series are shown to foreign buyers soon after the networks have made their choices, it is possible to make such changes before starting production. But as one production firm official admitted to me in an interview, he always presents any such changes to the networks as his idea, never as the suggestion of foreign buyers.

Critics, in both the United States and Europe, long have been concerned about the Americanization of culture worldwide. Though U.S. productions may not dominate anywhere, they have long been available almost everywhere. Now television is changing with uncertain consequences for cultures around the world. Restrictions against buying American films have been lifted in Eastern Europe and the former Soviet Union. Large movie studios and many independent television production companies have become part of the global economy. Coproduction has become more common as U.S. program suppliers make programs with suppliers from other countries. It may be that, in the near future, popular television around the world will cater to the tastes of those societies that invest in such coproductions. The tastes of American audiences may become less influential while those of target audiences in other societies become more powerful in shaping the content of global television. Any such changes that occur will reflect the fundamental fact that "audiences worldwide have the power to watch or not watch programs that others select for them" (Cantor & Cantor, 1986a).

AUDIENCES AND CULTURAL POLITICS

"Direct censorship of drama and film has always been recognized as a political issue; the ongoing battles for control of the symbolic content of popular dramas have not," I wrote in 1979 (p. 387). "The struggles between those who own (or control) the channels of communication, citizen and pressure groups, various government agencies and departments, and those responsible for the actual creation of the content have been largely ignored by social scientists." But while sociologists of culture were slow to recognize the production of popular culture as a political process, there is a significant history of citizen participation in that process. There have always been groups and individuals who have tried to influence the content of popular culture. It was not until the civil rights movement and the racial violence of the 1960s and the reawakening of the women's movement in the same period, however, that well-organized social action groups took an interest in television content. A landmark U.S. Court of Appeals decision in 1964 gave public interest groups the right to participate directly in FCC policymaking. For the first time since commercial broadcasting began in the 1920s, a legal and organizational support system began to develop that encouraged less powerful groups, particularly minorities and women, to lobby actively on their own behalf to change media content.

Although some groups were involved with television before the 1964 decision, interest or advocacy groups did not become a concern of producers and networks until the late 1960s and early 1970s when a number of groups began trying to influence producers and networks. The goals and motivations of these groups are diverse, reflecting the social, economic, cultural, and religious diversity of American society. Prominent among these groups have been antidefamation leagues, trade associations, labor unions, feminist organizations, gay rights groups, and those interested in environmental and other social issues. Especially active were the National Organization for Women (NOW), the National Congress of Parents and Teachers (PTA), the Moral Majority, and the American Medical Association (AMA). Also, some *Fortune* 500 corporations such as Mobil Oil actively protested some of the messages being sent through prime-time television.

Action for Children's Television (ACT) was probably the best known, and possibly the most effective, social action group. Through its efforts, Congress passed the Children's Television Act in 1990 and established the National Endowment for Children's Educational Television. ACT closed shop after its final success, but it was replaced by the Campaign for Kids TV, which continues to be an advocate nationally for children's television.

These groups have used a variety of tactics to try to change television. Along with attempts to organize boycotts of advertised products, they have lobbied Congress, the FCC, and even the White House for regulatory changes. An approach used most often in the 1970s and into the 1980s was to challenge the licenses of local stations, especially those that were owned and operated by one of the three networks. At least 15 stations throughout the United States had their licenses challenged by women's groups. In 1972, when NOW petitioned the FCC to deny renewal of licenses to WABC-TV in New York City and WRC-TV in Washington, D.C., this tactic was considered the most potent weapon then available to influence the broadcast media. The ostensible objective of the women filing the challenges was, of course, to deny broadcast licenses to broadcasters they believed were discriminating against women both in terms of employment and in terms of the images (or lack of images) on the screen. Because this objective was not achieved, the tactic was deemed a failure by many. But because of my personal involvement with the WRC-TV challenge (Cantor, 1988, 1989), I know that none of the women involved was so naive as to expect that an NBC-owned and operated station would actually lose its license. Rather, the NOW representatives hoped that, if the station owners were forced to respond to the challenges, the owners would review and perhaps alter their policies on hiring and programming.

Another tactic, as Kathryn Montgomery (1989) has shown, is direct contact between social activist groups, particularly those representing gays and African Americans, and creative personnel in Hollywood. Such groups have had some success in gaining the attention of producers when their demands were not incompatible with the television industry's pursuit of its markets. As Montgomery (1989) argued:

> The prominence and influence of these groups waxed and waned over time, corresponding to changes in the political climate or shifts in television industry practices and priorities. Gay activists were more influential in network TV when prime-time television, and the society at large, were particularly open to more liberal social mores; they were less successful in the early eighties during a period of conservatism in American politics. . . . And women's groups were able to encourage some programs to feature more positive and prominent roles for women, as societal attitudes shifted and advertisers in turn sought to reach upscale female target audiences. (p. 217)

Thus the extent to which any of these groups have influenced content can be debated. The impact of these groups may seem obvious from the changes in television content since 1968 when the three broadcast networks controlled television. More women and minorities are seen in a far greater variety of roles, and previously taboo topics such as homosexuality are now discussed. There is no question that the various forms of cultural politics impinge upon the creators' work environment. It is not clear, however, to what extent the changes in content reflect the politics of social action groups rather than the economics of changing audiences as discussed above. Audiences-as-market-segments rather than audiences-as-cultural-politicians remain the most powerful source of audience influence on television content.

CONCLUSION

In this chapter, I have focused on how audiences influence the way the American entertainment industry tells stories. In the United States, where the media are driven by market forces, ultimate control over what is available rests with those who own or manage the means of distribution. But only those who are able to reach profitable markets are successful in the struggle to get their messages on the air and in print. Because audiences can and do turn away from their television sets or do not buy tickets at the box office or books and magazines at the stands and in the stores, they do—in the aggregate—have influence on what is available to view and read.

Although I have selected television and its creators for this short review, other media and other creators can be studied profitably by examining their relationship with their audiences (Cantor, 1987b). I argue that all popular cultural products will change as the social and material conditions of their audiences change. Now, such changes in audience taste and composition along with the diffusion of new technologies, the globalization of the economy, the breakdown of regulatory barriers both in the United States and abroad are all combining to produce a new media environment. And in this environment, I believe, "mass culture" is becoming extinct—a monumental change that can be understood only if we consider carefully the role and influence of audiences in the production process.

REFERENCES

Ang, I. (1986). The battle between television and its audiences: The politics of watching television. In P. Drummond & R. Paterson (Eds.), *Television in transition* (pp. 250-266). London: BFI.

Ang, I. (1991). *Desperately seeking the audience*. New York: Routledge.

Cantor, M. G. (1979). The politics of popular drama. *Communication Research, 6*, 387-406.

Cantor, M. G. (1980). *Prime-time television: Content and control* (1st ed.). Newbury Park, CA: Sage.

Cantor, M. G. (1987a). *The Hollywood TV producer*. New Brunswick, NJ: Transaction. (Reprinted with a new introduction, by Basic Books, New York, 1971)

Cantor, M. G. (1987b). Popular culture and the portrayal of women: Content and control. In B. Hess & M. Ferree (Eds.), *Analyzing gender: A handbook of social science research* (pp. 190-215). Newbury Park, CA: Sage.

Cantor, M. G. (1988, July/August). Feminism and the media. *Society, 25*, 76-81.

Cantor, M. G. (1989). The politics of culture: Feminism and the media. In A. A. Berger (Ed.), *Political culture and public opinion* (pp. 149-166). New Brunswick, NJ: Transaction.

Cantor, M. G. (1991). American families on television: From Molly Goldberg to Bill Cosby. *Journal of Comparative Family Studies, 22*(2), 205-216.

Cantor, M. G., & Cantor, J. M. (1986a). American television in the international marketplace. *Communication Research: An International Quarterly, 13*, 509-520.

Cantor, M. G., & Cantor, J. M. (1986b). Audience composition and television content: The mass audience revisited. In S. Ball-Rokeach & M. Cantor (Eds.), *Media, audience and social structure* (pp. 214-225). Newbury Park, CA: Sage.

Cantor, M. G., & Cantor, J. M. (1992). *Prime-time television: Content and control* (2nd ed.). Newbury Park, CA: Sage.

Cantor, M. G., & Jones, E. (1983). Creating fiction for women. *Communication Research: An International Quarterly, 10*, 111-137.

Cantor, M. G., & Peters, A. K. (1980). The employment and unemployment of screen actors in the United States. In W. S. Hendon et al. (Eds.), *Economic policy for the arts* (pp. 210-216). Cambridge, MA: Abt.

Cantor, M. G., & Pingree, S. (1983). *The soap opera.* Beverly Hills, CA: Sage.

Gans, H. J. (1957). The creator-audience relationship in the mass media: An analysis of movie-making. In B. Rosenberg & D. M. White (Eds.), *Mass culture: The popular arts in America* (pp. 315-325). New York: Free Press.

Gans, H. J. (1966). Popular culture in America: Social problem in a mass society or social asset in a pluralist society? In H. S. Becker (Ed.), *Social problem: A modern approach* (pp. 549-620). New York: John Wiley.

Gans, H. J. (1974). *Popular culture and high culture.* New York: Basic Books.

Gitlin, T. (1983). *Inside prime time.* New York: Pantheon.

Merton, R. (1957). *Social theory and social structure* (rev. ed.). Glencoe, IL: Free Press.

Mills, C. W. (1953). *White collar.* New York: Oxford University Press.

Montgomery, K. C. (1989). *Target: Prime time.* New York: Oxford University Press.

Neuman, W. R. (1991). *The future of the mass audience.* Cambridge: Cambridge University Press.

Peters, A. K., & Cantor, M. G. (1982). Screen acting as work. In J. Ettema & C. Whitney (Eds.), *Individuals in mass media organization: Creativity and constraint* (pp. 53-68). Beverly Hills, CA: Sage.

Strover, S. (1989). *European communication policy and integration.* Unpublished report prepared for the Commission on European Communities.

Tuchman, G. (1988). Mass media institutions. In N. Smelser (Ed.), *Handbook of sociology* (pp. 601-626). Newbury Park, CA: Sage.

Waterman, D. (1988, June). World television trade: The economic effects of privatization and new technology. *Telecommunications Policy,* pp. 141-151.

Chapter 10

MEASURED MARKETS AND UNKNOWN AUDIENCES: CASE STUDIES FROM THE PRODUCTION AND CONSUMPTION OF MUSIC

Richard A. Peterson

THE WAYS THAT MEDIA and market researchers measure audiences pervasively shape the ways that people in the media and advertising view those audiences. And at the same time, the ways that these communicators wish to view audiences shape the ways that researchers measure them. (See, for example, Ang, 1991; Haug, 1987; Turow, 1992, as well as Barnes & Thomson and Miller in this volume.) The images that communicators hold of their audiences are, then, selective. And because the audience that communicators know is constituted by the methods and categories of measurement currently being employed, it seems appropriate to reserve the term *audience* for all the people who actually receive a media message, and the term *market* for the audience as it is currently conceptualized and measured by media decision makers.[1]

Media history offers many illustrations of how audiences and markets are only tenuously related to each other and how the measurement concepts and methods of the time determine that relationship. For example, in the early 1950s when television programming decisions were based largely on the single audience characteristic of overall size, two rival tobacco companies competed for the available audience in a particular time slot. One sponsor offered a medical drama, *Medic,* and the other a situation comedy, *I Love Lucy. Lucy* regularly received a higher market

AUTHOR'S NOTE: For their comments on an earlier draft, I greatly appreciate the help of Jennifer Jasper, Claire Peterson, Andrea Press, John Ryan, and Janet Wolff.

share. The sponsor of *Medic* canceled the program because of its relatively low ratings, and *Lucy* went on to be one of the top-rated programs of all time. Subsequent research found, however, that the cigarette advertised on *Medic* gained greatly in sales, while sales of the brand advertised on *Lucy* remained flat. Apparently the broad comedy of *Lucy* attracted an audience consisting primarily of nonsmoking youngsters and older adults who did not smoke or who were set in their smoking preferences, while the tense real-life dramas of *Medic* attracted a younger adult audience more malleable in their cigarette preferences.

There is still under- and overcounting of particular segments, as is dramatically illustrated by the recent changes in the way the music industry determines hits. In 1991 *Billboard* magazine stopped measuring records' popularity by using reports from a sample of retail store managers and began using sales data automatically reported electronically from the stores. With this new reporting system, the sales of country and rap records were shown to be much greater than reported by the old system, and Garth Brooks, a country music performer, was shown to be outselling such hot acts as Guns n' Roses, Nirvana, Def Leppard, Michael Jackson, Kris Kross, and Hammer.

Researchers with a positivistic inclination may conclude from these examples that ever-more sophisticated concepts and methods have been, and will continue to be, developed so as to provide ever-more useful information about the actual audience. And in practice, simple audience counts have been augmented by demographics, geodemographics, psychographics, and sociographics[2] as well as myriad techniques intended to better describe audiences and their responses. Despite the increasing sophistication of measurement methods, however, it remains true that any image of a media audience is necessarily shaped by the particular method used. For scholars, at least, the problem of understanding the audience is not now primarily a matter of better measurement methods.[3] Rather, the problem is to explicitly distinguish between market and audience and to recognize that market is simply a convenient and always inaccurate representation of audience. What follows are four brief illustrations of that relationship and its cultural consequences.

MULTIPLE MARKETS, MISMATCHED AUDIENCES

In practice, it is often quite difficult to square market with audience. Perhaps the best example of the complex interplay between market and audience is the longtime interdependence between the radio and music industries. Since the advent of Top 40 radio in the 1950s, commercial radio and the record[4] business have been uneasily coupled.[5] While they overlap, the audiences of these two industries, and the audience for advertisers' products on which commercial radio stations depend, are not the same. The word *market* is often used in a way that obscures these differences.

Let's see how this works. Radio stations receive from record companies a continuous supply of free programming in the form of recorded music. From that supply, stations select music that fits programmers' conceptions of the music preferences of a narrowly defined market segment. These include Top 40, country, adult contemporary, and so on. Stations, in turn, receive their revenues from advertisers who pay stations to pitch products to those who have been drawn to listen to the station by the free entertainment. In this way, commercial radio (and television) stations are like medicine shows that offer entertainment free of charge to attract an audience in the hopes of selling them the products that are promoted. They are different, of course, in that, while the medicine shows' entertainment and pitch lead directly to sales, the sales of products advertised on the radio may be due to advertising in other media and a host of other factors totally unrelated to the particular mix of radio programming.

The record companies, in return, receive free promotion of their products in the form of radio airplay; and they receive their revenues from the sale of cassettes, CDs, and videos to people who may have heard the music on the radio. But in addition to radio airplay, these sales may be motivated by seeing a group perform at a concert, watching them perform on a music television program, reading about them in a fan magazine, hearing their music at a friend's house, seeing a promotion at the record store, or reading a review of the record.

The important cultural implication of this system is the creative tension caused by the differences between the *markets* sought by radio stations and their advertisers, the *markets* identified by record companies, and, finally, the actual *audiences* for music and advertising. The rise of rock music in the 1950s provides an excellent case in point.

The marriage of radio and records made for rapid innovations in popular music during the first 15 years of Top 40 radio—the era stretching from Chuck Berry and Elvis Presley through the psychedelic period of the Beatles and their cohort. New sounds were quickly given wide radio airplay, and some became hits while many more quietly faded. Since the mid-1970s, however, radio programmers in the United States have given ever greater airtime to proven hit records already in their archives. Their market research told them that the easiest way to gain and hold listeners was to recycle well-known music, and so the number of radio formats featuring one sort of "golden oldie" or another proliferated. To win acceptance by radio programmers under such conditions, new artists had to sound much like established artists. Thus, year by year, commercial radio music (in the United States particularly) became ever more predictable as the reproduction of style replaced the raw communication of feeling.

Since the late 1970s, innovations in music have increasingly become popular, not because of commercial radio exposure but despite the lack of such exposure. For example, disco gained initial popularity in dance clubs and gained further popularity through movies such as *Saturday Night Fever*. Small independent stations and noncommercial college stations, but not the major rock and pop stations, were important in the early success of punk rock and rap music. The 1980s' innovations in pop music, including the "second British invasion" led by such groups as Duran Duran and Culture Club, came via repeated exposure on music television as did the rapid rise in the popularity of country music in the early 1990s. Thus commercial radio became the rearguard rather than the avant-garde of innovation.

Moreover, the market distinctions that made sense in the 1960s—Top 40, soul, country music, sports, and talk—have been elaborated and subdivided into ever more finely differentiated radio formats, further fragmenting recorded music market segments. As a result, there is little chance for the cross-fertilization characteristic of the early days of rock radio (Ennis, 1992; Frith, 1981; Shaw, 1987). In effect, the old marketing formulas have become a dead hand guiding both radio and recording industry marketing decisions and, in the process, robbing mainstream popular music of the vital meaning it once had in the lives of young audience members.

It may well be that the current musical era is much like the late 1940s—a clear orthodoxy in pop music offered over the air and on record, but also a huge unsatisfied audience demand for music with more emotional immediacy. Certainly, young people all over the country have turned to rap and country music, and they have experimented with musical combinations (e.g., blues, country, and diverse forms of world music) and new technologies (e.g., sound sampling) that make possible the creation of new sounds. Perhaps, then, the lackluster performance of the popular music industry in recent years is a result of radio formats and record categories that do not coincide with the musical desires of actual audiences. Defining such desires is beyond the scope of this chapter, but it is clear that the mismatch between radio and record *markets* and music *audiences* imposes a constraint on the creativity and diversity of the music that is available to those audiences.

THE CATEGORIZING CONSTRAINT

Efficient production of media content is only possible because of the proliferation of formulas (Becker, 1982) and conventions, both linguistic (Cawelti, 1976) and technological (Beniger, 1986). Ironically, no one is more dependent on conventions than the news media, because they are devoted to covering unique events. Each event must be categorized and conventionalized to be communicated effectively. For example, each section of a newspaper, and each section of the local TV news, is placed in the same relation to the others and, except on extraordinary occasions, has a set length day after day, month after month. Pictures, captions, reportorial style, as much as the content, all signal to the audience the category of news. Conventionalizing devices also help reporters, photographers, and editors shape the welter of events into stories that they can present coherently and help readers and viewers to assess the nature and importance of those events. (See, for example, Gans, 1980, and Tuchman, 1978.)

The entertainment media employ cognate conventionalizing processes, and therein lies another illustration of creative constraints imposed by marketing categories. Record company producers, promoters, and distributors, for example, must decide how to categorize each new artist and record. They must decide which radio station formats, which critics, and which fan magazines to contact. And when the product is received at the record store, will it be placed in the section labeled Classical, Current Hits, Jazz, Country, Folk, Dance, Rap, New Age, or something else? These decisions determine how an artist and a record initially will be understood and received.

Most records are easy to slot into the system. This is not because the genres are so distinct, or because the audiences for each are so different, but because the categories and conventional wisdom of those in the music industry profoundly shape the selection of artists, music, stylings, promotion, and distribution. Thus the aesthetics of the music, like the content of the news, is shaped by the production and distribution needs of the industry as much as by the creativity of music makers and the tastes of audiences (Goodwin, 1992; Peterson, 1990a; Ryan & Peterson, 1982).

The categorizing constraint does not simply frustrate creative individuals by forcing them to shape their work to fit current conventions, it shapes the fundamental categories of expression. Numerous examples might be cited, but perhaps the most consequential of all in twentieth-century popular culture has been the artificial division between the blues and country music that was created by the fledgling music industry in the first quarter of this century.[6] While it is conventional to think of the blues as having its origins in the working-class African American community of the rural South, and country music as having its origins in the working-class white community of the rural South, a number of careful studies have shown that, notwithstanding the European and African origins of various techniques, turn-of-the-century working-class southerners of both races shared a wide range of musical stylings ranging from communal church singing and harmonica playing to fiddle techniques and plaintive balladry (Cantwell, 1984; Malone, 1979; Marcus, 1982).

The sharp divergence between the blues and country music can be traced to the categories created by the record industry. In the first decade of the century, the major record companies successfully marketed records to specific immigrant ethnic and nationality groups in the urban North. These records could turn a profit with very small sales because artists were paid very little, and most songs, being uncopyrighted, could be used without paying royalty fees. Based on the logic that inexpensively produced records targeted to delimited ethnic music communities could be profitable, record industry executives, following World War I, began to explore the markets for the range of musical stylings being performed in the South.

African Americans constituted the most easily identified community. Though generally poor, like European and Asian ethnics, they proved willing to buy large numbers of records, and all the major companies developed lines of records targeted at blacks. Most, but not all, of the early artists were black; the names given to bands, the names given to many tunes, and the pictorial publicity accompanying the records all accented the racial identity of the music. Indeed, up to World War II, this line of records was even called "race records."

In 1925 Ralph Peer, one of the most enterprising of the ethnic music producers, went to Atlanta to record a number of local artists in hopes of increasing regional sales, and there he was persuaded to record a white fiddle-playing notable, Fiddlin' John Carson. Though Peer thought the recording sounded awful, he agreed to release it in the Atlanta area only on the insistence of the local record distributor. The original pressing was sold out in a few days, and in the process a demand for music by working-class whites was discovered (Daniel, 1990; Peterson, 1987). In the early days, this line of records was given several designations, including "Old Time Tunes" and "Hill and Range Favorites," that evoked nostalgia for the preindustrial rural life of plantations and hill farms. "Hillbilly" soon became the industry designation. Most, but not all, of the early performers were white, and all of the publicity for the new line of hillbilly music depicted whites enjoying the music.

To simplify the marketing of records, the record producers of the 1920s coached performers, both black and white, to make music that they considered appropriate to their race (Cantwell, 1984; Oliver, 1968). Once the marketing distinction between blues and hillbilly was established, aspiring musicians had to shape their music along the aesthetic lines "appropriate" for their race so as to become commercially successful. Thus the fledgling music industry divided markets by race, even though the audience for music had not been rigidly divided along racial lines.

One indicator of the artificiality of the divided market and the racial purification of the music is that audiences have regularly rebelled by giving great acclaim to artists who have adopted stylings from the other side of the racial divide. Jimmie Rodgers, Hank Williams, Ray Charles, and Charlie Pride are but four of the most notable examples. Indeed, it is possible to see the explosive emergence of rock music in the mid-1950s as the triumph of audience demand for the racially mixed music of Elvis Presley, Chuck Berry, Jerry Lee Lewis, Little Richard, and more recently Michael Jackson, Prince, and Hammer, over the music that neatly fit into industry categories (Marcus, 1982; Peterson, 1990a; Shaw, 1987). Creative musicians of all musical stripes have complained that their music has been distorted in the process of production to fit a category or has been buried and ignored by being promoted in the wrong category. Sensitive people in the music industry are aware of the tug between creativity and category though they have given little attention to the impact of that phenomenon on the audience. However, the role of racial stereotyping in the development of twentieth-century popular music illustrates once again the difference between market categories and audience desires—and reveals the power of constructed categories to constrain the forms of cultural expression available to audiences.

A LOT OF KNOWLEDGE
IS A DANGEROUS THING

The sophisticated media executives of today, armed with a welter of market research results, might argue that they could not make the categorizing mistakes of their predecessors in the 1950s. Perhaps not, but their very sophistication can make for another sort of blindness, as illustrated by a recent consultant's report to National Public Radio (NPR).[7]

In the mid-1980s NPR set as its goal the doubling of its listenership in 5 years. The goal had seemed possible to attain because listenership had been growing rapidly for a decade, but, then, the growth curve went nearly flat. There was speculation that classical music—the programming staple of most NPR stations—was losing its draw. A look at the research revealed, however, that the number of classical music buffs had *not* declined. Rather, they had become a much smaller *proportion* of the total NPR listenership. That is, the growth in listenership had been due almost entirely to the increased proportion of news programming on NPR stations (notably *All Things Considered, Morning Edition,* and *Weekend Edition*). And now the problem was that many of NPR's newly attracted news listeners did not like classical music or the other staples of NPR stations' programming mix—opera, operetta, and jazz—and turned back to their favorite music stations after listening to the news programs.

The primary consultants retained by NPR applied their own understanding of radio listenership gained from years of work with commercial radio stations in the United States. Conventional wisdom among commercial radio programming experts is that each station has a set of core listeners and a larger set of fringe listeners. The job of the programmers, the consultants argued, was to micromanage the programming to hold the core, while converting as many of the fringe listeners to the core as possible. This commercial radio logic applied to public radio suggested that NPR stations focus their attention on the *news* listeners and play the sort of music that would keep them tuned to the station following the news programs. Garrison Keillor's *Prairie Home Companion* and blocks of New Age music were suggested as programming compatible with the news. The consultants also concluded from their studies that classical music, and particularly opera programs, should be reduced because these types of music prompt the core news listeners to tune out the NPR station.

The radio consultants' advice to NPR stations was very clear: To double the listenership, they said, get those who listen the most to listen for much greater amounts of time each day. And to do this, they said, *decrease* the range of classical music programming and air only programs that news listeners like.

This marketing strategy was not, however, the only way to increase listenership. Another way to double listenership would be to increase the number of persons who listen to the station regularly, if only for short periods of time. And the way to do this would be to *increase* the diversity of programming presented over the course of a week. Most listeners would tune out much of the programming but would be loyal followers of their favored segments. Such a policy, which might be called "mosaic programming," seems uniquely fitted to NPR's public service mission because the music and perspectives of diverse aesthetic, ethnic, and lifestyle communities could gain a hearing. Such a strategy might make sense financially as well, because many more kinds of people could be induced to become station donor-members to support their distinctive program interests. Likewise, a wider range of companies uninterested in the mass market might become underwriters of specialty programs targeted at specific audiences.

This possibility did not appeal to the well-trained and knowledgeable radio industry consultants because their experience in commercial radio (where the strategy of seeking a numerically large but demographically narrow target market has been financially successful) blinded them to an alternative conceptualization of the market for public radio. In turn, their experience blinded them to a way to better serve the interests of the actual audience. Clearly, a wealth of knowledge can be a dangerous thing when applied without concern for the differences among various markets and without recognizing the difference between markets and audiences.

RECONCEPTUALIZING THE CULTURAL HIERARCHY

Just as industry experts may make unfortunate practical decisions because of their trained incapacity to see audiences clearly through the market lens, so scholars may miss significant social changes because of the way they have conceptualized audiences. The idea of class-based lifestyles is an excellent example of a conceptual lens that may keep us from seeing systematic change that is taking place right under our noses.

One of the most pervasive images in the social theory of industrial society is that of social class. At the top are those who have power and prestige by way of their family position, wealth, education, and occupational attainments. Ranged below them are groups with successively less of these power-giving attributes. Class position, so the theory goes, is marked by participation in arts and related leisure pursuits. This assumed relationship between social class and cultural consumption has given rise to the practice of ranking genres of music, literature, drama, and visual arts, as well as sports and hobbies, from "highbrow" to "lowbrow" and then ranking people based on their more or less high- or lowbrow tastes (e.g., Bourdieu, 1984; Gans, 1980; but see Peterson, 1983). This theory-based hierarchy of music genres underlies the market categories used by culture-producing industries. Thus, for music, the image of the market is that of distinct clusters of consumers (e.g., classical buffs, country music fans, teen buyers, the urban soul market, folkies, New Agers) each of

which can be characterized in terms of its class position (usually supplemented by considerations of age, race, and gender). If the theory of
class-based lifestyles no longer fits the empirical reality, then the definitions of markets on which it is based will not fit well with the patterns of
consumption. This is an opportune moment to ask whether the poor match
between market and audience is due, at least in part, to inadequacies in
the existing social theory. Let's begin with some empirical observations.

We all know of persons who are exceptions to the accepted class-ranked
norms—the academic who likes country music, the steelworker who likes
opera—but such cases are ordinarily shrugged off as bemusing eccentrici-
ties or signs of democratic pluralism. While there have been no publicly
available systematic studies of people's record collections or other patterns of music consumption, there is mounting evidence that the orthodox
view of a taste hierarchy ranging from the highbrow snob to the lowbrow
couch potato slob presents a systematically distorted picture of actual
audience tastes. Surveys regularly show that most of those of the upper
social ranks do not patronize high-culture pursuits. One interpretation of
this finding is that the once close correlation between social class and
culture class has broken down, and that it is now fruitless to try to understand people by tracing their patterns of cultural choice (Davis, 1982).
This, however, is going too far.

Most experts agree that there is still a taste hierarchy, but they differ
widely on how to describe it accurately (e.g., Blau, 1986; Bourdieu, 1984;
DiMaggio, 1987; Gans, 1974; Hughes & Peterson, 1983; Lamont, 1990;
Lamont & Fournier, 1992; Peterson, 1983; Peterson & DiMaggio, 1975;
Peterson & Ryan, 1989). While the picture is not now entirely clear, my
research suggests that prestige in the United States today goes to persons
who are knowledgeable about not only the traditional elite arts but also
about a wide range of other popular and folk aesthetic activities (Peterson,
1994; Peterson & Simkus, 1992). Thus the exclusive highbrow is no
longer at the top of the heap; at the top is what can be called the inclusive
yet discriminating *omnivore*. The same research suggests a rather different
formulation for the bottom of the taste hierarchy. Rather than the undis-
criminating mass of lowbrow couch potatoes, the lower end of the scale
is populated by a number of discrete taste groups that recognize the
cultural superiority of those above but that claim superiority over the other
taste groups around them at or near the bottom.[8] Collectively these can be
designated *univores* because they are groups of persons who understand
and identify with only a single aesthetic rooted in some mix of ethnic,
religious, racial, regional, gender, and occupational experience.

Such an omnivore-to-univore image of the contemporary American taste hierarchy has several ramifications for defining markets and understanding audiences. Problematizing the received ideas about the hierarchy of taste groups provides a basis for understanding what Neuman (1992) calls "fragmented audiences" and what Ang (1991) refers to as "the revolt of the audience." For example, the established theory of fashion formulated by Thorsten Veblen is that the lower orders emulate those of higher prestige so that fashion innovations begin at the top and over the years trickle down the status hierarchy. However, as Davis (1992) makes clear, this theory does not fit with the evidence of the decades in the latter half of the twentieth century. Rather, the pattern in this era is that new elite fashion elements are more likely to be adopted or adapted from marginal groups in society. This fits the idea of the high-status omnivore seeking out esoteric low-status cultural elements as exemplified by the widespread embrace of rap music by affluent white suburban young people in the early 1990s as well as the cognate fascination with the more "authentic" elements of country music among midlife affluent whites.

The idea of the univore reconceptualizes the lower end of the hierarchy not as an undifferentiated mass but as a series of mutually antagonistic subcultures whose styles of music, dance, language, and clothing help to set them apart from each other. An early example of working-class antagonisms directed not against the elite but against other symbolically distinct elements of the working class was revealed in the studies of British working-class youth in which, for example, "mods" clashed with "rockers" (Hebdige, 1979). In the United States, similar distinctions are visible in the variety of current taste groups identified by such musical tastes as rap, rock, heavy metal, house, religious, and country musics (Peterson, 1992).

Even if, in the end, the omnivore/univore differentiation of the lifestyle status hierarchy does not prove to be the most useful, it is now clear that the old ideas have lost their conceptual power. It is time again to ask how we might more usefully define and measure markets and how we might better understand audience dynamics.

CONCLUDING COMMENT

This chapter has described four situations in which there is a mismatch between market and audience. These are (a) the interplay between the interests of radio programmers and the music industry, (b) the labeling of white and black musical forms by the music industry, (c) the consequences of applying commercial radio market ideas to public radio, and (d) the conceptualization of the status hierarchy. Each of the four illustrations shows the consequences of the ways in which market categories are formulated. They have not been presented to show that the market-definers have been stupid. All practical actions involve making assumptions and simplifying the complexities of human choices. Rather, the illustrations together demonstrate the necessity of clearly distinguishing between markets and audiences and regularly reviewing the fit between the two.

There is a chance of improving the fit between market and audience because a major cause of the mismatch is that media communicators often make the convenient simplifying assumption that audiences are passive "receivers" of their "messages." In fact, as ample evidence shows, people actively process and reinterpret each communication and in so doing alter its meaning to fit with what they already know and want to believe (Liebes & Katz, 1990; Press, 1991). In this sense audiences are *auto*producers of their own cultural worlds (Peterson, 1994). This view of the audience as active information interpreters rather than as a passive mass of receivers is fundamental to resolving the problems raised in each of the four cases we have reviewed here of the mismatch between measured market and unmeasured audience.

NOTES

1. Herbert Gans (1957) coined the term *audience image* in referring to the characteristics of potential moviegoers imagined by filmmakers. In the world of commercial music production, where a number of specialists in sequence work on developing a song, Ryan and Peterson (1982) found that the specialists could not afford to have an image of the final audience. To be successful, they had to have a "product image" focusing on satisfying the expectations of the next specialist in the decision chain.

2. The term *sociographics* is used here to distinguish two quite different sorts of studies that have been lumped under the rubric *psychographics.* I would use the term *psychographics* for those measures designed to record feelings and attitudes and the term *sociographics* for the measures designed to distinguish lifestyles and patterns of cultural choice (Hughes & Peterson, 1983; Peterson, 1983).

3. The lack of fit between audience and market is sometimes intentional, because media industry researchers may not be interested in measuring some parts of their audience. In the commercial media, for example, executives have reason to care only about the programming desires of those elements of the audience who are of interest to potential advertisers (Ang, 1991; Turow, 1992).

4. While the terms *record* and *record industry* have been widely used, fewer and fewer phonograph "records" are sold. The industry, which formed in the 1890s to produce cylinders, for decades produced 78 rpm disks and has for a time produced 45 rpm disks, LPs, cassettes,

videotapes, and CDs. A number of new formats are on the drawing boards, and a generic word to cover all formats is needed. The most appropriate seems to be the term *phonogram,* which is widely used in Europe to designate all forms of electronically recorded music (Blaukopf, 1982). Because, however, the term is not widely used in the United States, we will use the more generic terms *record industry* or *music industry* as the context warrants.

5. The information for this section is drawn from my consulting for *Radio & Records* magazine. See also Peterson and Berger (1975), Peterson (1990a), Frith (1981), Ennis (1992), and Goodwin (1992).

6. The prime source for the material in this section is my ongoing study of the creation of commercial country music in the first half of the twentieth century. The working title of the book is *The Fabrication of Authenticity.* See also Oliver (1968), Rooney (1971), Cook (1973), Malone (1979), Marcus (1982), and Cantwell (1984).

7. The information for this section was gathered between 1987 and 1989 while I was a consultant for the Arts and Performance Division of National Public Radio. See ARA (1988) and Peterson (1990b).

8. There is mounting, if not uncontested, evidence that most persons of all taste levels clearly discriminate among available television programming (Fowler, 1992; Greenberg & Frank, 1983; Peterson, Bates, & Ryan, 1986).

REFERENCES

Ang, I. (1991). *Desperately seeking the audience.* London: Routledge.

ARA (Audience Research Analysis). (1988). *Audience '88: A comprehensive analysis of public radio listeners.* Silver Spring, MD: Author.

Baughman, J. L. (1992). *The republic of mass culture.* Baltimore, MD: Johns Hopkins University Press.

Becker, H. S. (1982). *Art worlds.* Berkeley: University of California Press.

Beniger, J. R. (1986). *The control revolution.* Cambridge, MA: Harvard University Press.

Blau, J. (1986). The elite arts, more or less de riguer: A comparative analysis of metropolitan culture. *Social Forces, 64,* 875-905.

Blaukopf, K. (Ed.). (1982). *The phonogram in cultural communication.* Vienna: Springer-Verlag.

Bourdieu, P. (1984). *Distinction: A social critique of the judgement of taste.* Cambridge, MA: Harvard University Press.

Cantwell, R. (1984). *Bluegrass breakdown: The making of the old southern sound.* Urbana: University of Illinois Press.

Cawelti, J. G. (1976). *Adventure, mystery, and romance: Formula stories as art and popular culture.* Chicago: University of Chicago Press.

Cook, B. (1973). *Listen to the blues.* New York: Scribner.

Daniel, W. W. (1990). *Pickin' on Peachtree: The history of country music in Atlanta, Georgia.* Urbana: University of Illinois Press.

Davis, F. (1992). *Fashion, culture, and identity.* Chicago: University of Chicago Press.

Davis, J. A. (1982). Achievement variables and class cultures: Family, schooling, job, and forty nine dependent variables in the cumulative GSS. *American Sociological Review, 47,* 569-586.

DiMaggio, P. (1987). Classification in the arts. *American Sociological Review, 52,* 440-455.

Ennis, P. H. (1992). *The seventh stream: The emergence of rock and roll in American popular music.* Hanover, NH: University Press of New England.

Fowler, J. (1992). *Why viewers watch: A reappraisal of television's effects.* Newbury Park, CA: Sage.

Frith, S. (1981). *Sound effects: Youth, leisure, and the politics of rock'n'roll.* New York: Pantheon.

Gans, H. J. (1957). The creator-audience relationship in the mass media: An analysis of moviemaking. In B. Rosenberg & D. M. White (Eds.), *Mass culture* (pp. 315-324). New York: Free Press.

Gans, H. J. (1974). *Popular culture and high culture.* New York: Basic Books.

Gans, H. J. (1980). *Deciding what's news.* New York: Random House.

Goodwin, A. (1992). *Dancing in the distraction factory: Music television and popular culture.* Minneapolis: University of Minnesota Press.

Greenberg, M. G., & Frank, R. E. (1983). Leisure lifestyles: Segmentation by interests, needs, demographics, and television viewing. *American Behavioral Scientist, 26,* 439-458.

Haug, W. F. (1987). *Commodity aesthetics, ideology and culture.* New York: International General.

Hebdige, D. (1979). *Subculture: The meaning of style.* London: Methuen.

Hughes, M., & Peterson, R. A. (1983). Isolating cultural choice patterns in the U.S. population. *American Behavioral Scientist, 26,* 459-478.

Lamont, M. (1990, August). *The refined, the virtuous, and the prosperous: Exploring symbolic boundaries in the French and American upper-middle class.* Paper presented at the 85th annual meeting of the American Sociological Association, Washington, DC.

Lamont, M., & Fournier, M. (Eds.). (1992). *Cultivating differences.* Chicago: University of Chicago Press.

Liebes, T., & Katz, E. (1990). *The export of meaning: The cross cultural reading of "Dallas."* New York: Oxford University Press.

Malone, B. C. (1979). *Southern music/American music.* Lexington: University of Kentucky Press.

Marcus, G. (1982). *Mystery train.* New York: E. P. Dutton.

Neuman, W. R. (1992). *The future of the mass media.* Cambridge: Cambridge University Press.

Oliver, P. (1968). *Screening the blues.* London: Caswell.

Peterson, R. A. (1983). Patterns of cultural choice: A prolegomenon. *American Behavioral Scientist, 26,* 422-438.

Peterson, R. A. (1987). Commercializing folk culture: The case of country music. In N. Grant, W. Hendon, & V. Owen (Eds.), *Economic efficiency and the performing arts* (pp. 118-135). Akron, OH: University of Akron Press.

Peterson, R. A. (1990a). Why 1955? Explaining the advent of rock and roll. *Popular Music, 9,* 97-116.

Peterson, R. A. (1990b). Audience and industry origins of the crisis in classical music programming: Toward world music. In D. Pankratz & V. Morris (Eds.), *The future of the arts: Public policy and arts research* (pp. 207-227). New York: Praeger.

Peterson, R. A. (1992). Understanding audience segmentation: From elite and mass to omnivore and univore. *International Journal of Empirical Research on Literature, Media, and the Arts, 21,* 243-258.

Peterson, R. A. (1994). Culture studies through the production perspective: Progress and prospects. In D. Crane (Ed.), *Emerging theoretical perspectives in the sociology of culture* (pp. 162-189). London: Blackwell.

Peterson, R. A., Bates, D., & Ryan, J. (1986). Selective versus passive television viewing. *Communications, 12,* 81-94.

Peterson, R. A., & Berger, D. G. (1975). Cycles in symbol production: The case of popular music. *American Sociological Review, 40,* 158-173.

Peterson, R. A., & DiMaggio, P. (1975). From region to class, the changing locus of country music: A test of the massification hypothesis. *Social Forces, 53,* 497-506.

Peterson, R. A., & Ryan, J. (1989). The locus of sport hunting and fishing in four taste cultures: A lesson in accounting for taste. In B. Filipcova, S. Glyptis, & W. Tokarski (Eds.), *Life styles in international perspective* (Isa RC#13, pp. 256-276). Prague: Czechoslovak Academy of Science.

Peterson, R. A., & Simkus, A. (1992). How musical tastes mark occupational status groups. In M. Lamont & M. Fournier (Eds.), *Cultivating differences* (pp. 152-168). Chicago: University of Chicago Press.

Press, A. (1991). *Women watching television.* Philadelphia: University of Pennsylvania Press.

Rooney, J. (1971). *Bossmen: Bill Monroe and Muddy Waters.* New York: Hayden.

Ryan, J., & Peterson, R. A. (1982). The product image: The fate of creativity in country music song-writing. *Sage Annual Reviews of Communication Research, 10,* 11-32.

Shaw, A. (1987). *The rockin' 50s: The decade that transformed the pop music scene.* New York: DeCapo.

Tuchman, G. (1978). *Making news: The study of the construction of reality.* New York: Free Press.

Turow, J. (1992). *Media systems in society: Understanding industries, strategies, and power.* New York: Longman.

Chapter 11

THE AUDIENCE AT HOME:
THE EARLY RECORDING INDUSTRY
AND THE MARKETING OF MUSICAL TASTE

Marsha Siefert

"YOUR VICTOR TALKING MACHINES are all right," said John Philip Sousa. The comment was not exactly an advertiser's dream, but for the fledgling Victor Talking Machine Company, it was their first culturally valuable endorsement, a pragmatic down-home judgment by mainstream America's March King (see Harris, 1990). The endorsement was printed in the second week of January 1902 (*Music Trade,* p. 45), just a month after the 1900 court injunction against the U.S. manufacture and distribution of the Victor talking machines had been lifted. Sousa's endorsement was backed by something even more valuable: recordings of some of his own marches. The trouble was that he had also recorded for the far and away leading rival, Edison's National Phonograph Company, which all but controlled the market. With a late start, little capital, and legal troubles, the Victor company needed to be more than "all right" to compete, especially against a well-known hero-inventor, Thomas A. Edison.

This chapter will analyze how the Victor company, by seeking to competitively market their talking machines, actively participated in "audiencemaking." The story hinges on a technological point: Victor

AUTHOR'S NOTE: I would like to thank Kay Youngflesh, Division of Engineering & Industry, National Museum of American History, Smithsonian Institution; Emmett D. Chisum of the American Heritage Center; and the staffs of the Free Library of Philadelphia and the Rodgers & Hammerstein Archives of Recorded Sound at the Lincoln Center Library of the Performing Arts for their generous assistance in providing access to the collections of advertisements, brochures, catalogues, and magazines from the early talking machine companies.

talking machines played only prerecorded discs and Edison phonographs played only cylinders. In 1902 that was a disadvantage to Victor, given Edison's reputation and commercial head start. But this technological advantage could be turned into an advantage if Victor could monopolize a particular type of recorded content and could convince potential customers that they wanted to hear the content available *only* on disc. The strategy was to sell talking machines by selling the recordings, which, in turn, required a strategy for selling the content of those recordings.[1] For several reasons, as this chapter will show, the Victor company chose grand opera as their special content and put tremendous resources into persuading potential customers of the wisdom of this choice. This story, then, tells how the marketers of Victor talking machines used expensive recordings of European opera singers to merchandize that exclusive content-technology link and, in the process, how they used image and text to *discursively* transform potential customers into an "audience" for what they called "opera at home."

Victor claimed to have done more than discursively identify a home audience, however. Through advertising and promotional materials, they claimed to have participated in the creation of an actual audience for opera by offering the best star performances to those who might not otherwise attend a live performance. According to Victor, being a member of the home audience for opera was just as good as being at the opera house.[2] In fact, "opera at home" actually had some advantages because the home performances were more convenient and the choice of repertoire was more diverse—if you owned a Victor talking machine. Victor also took credit for increasing the actual audience for live opera performance. Their promotional copy claimed that the creation of a home audience amplified interest in live performance. (Indeed, they assured their most important opera performers that the live performances and their reproductions were not a substitution for one another, as some promoters had feared.) Live performances, after all, sold records too.

For Victor the link between live performance and its reproduction was essential. The Victor strategy was to use the existing hierarchy of live musical performance—in this case the high prestige of opera—to legitimate their musical reproductions. By linking opera at home to the opera house, the "audience at home" was made analogous to the socially approved, highly prestigious audience in the front row. Opera records legitimized Victor, their recordings, and by extension their home audience, and thereby helped ease the talking machine—and subsequent communication technologies—into the parlors of genteel America.

This chapter will analyze advertising and sales literature to describe how Victor and their competitors attempted to create an "audience at home." Analysis of how an industry shapes, influences, or constructs its potential users, whether they are termed the *audience,* the *market,* or the *public,* is a matter of reasoned argument rather than exact measures. However, a longitudinal view of an industry's printed and proprietary materials, to some extent, can reconstruct what the industry claimed to be doing and, by inference, can reveal how the industry intended to participate in its own "social construction" (see Bijker, Hughes, & Pinch, 1987; Douglas, 1987).

In the late nineteenth century, patent claims, articles in popular science magazines, newspaper accounts, and national magazine stories constituted the published discourse about the various mechanical prototypes of the talking machine. In the first decade of the twentieth century, when the talking machine had begun to be manufactured and distributed on a large scale, that discourse was shared by several streams of published materials: publications within the individual company such as the marketing advice and instruction offered by company memos and house organs that "sell to the sellers"; publications for the industry such as trade magazines, first in music and later in the talking machine industry itself; and publications directed to the potential consumer such as advertising in national magazines and catalogs, brochures, and sales literature. In this study,[3] trade publications are represented by *Voice of the Victor* and *Edison Phonograph Monthly,* industry publications by *Music Trade Review* and later *The Talking Machine World,* and national consumer publications by the *Saturday Evening Post,* the fastest growing national weekly magazine of the decade.[4] This intertextual organizational discourse illustrates how the idea of "audience" was used in a chain of industrial activities that aimed to produce customers for the talking machine.

The story of the talking machine contributes to an understanding of how communication industries engage in audiencemaking by revealing choices that were made in the process of building a particular industry. Too often, audiences are modeled as logical, unproblematic, and uncontested even though stories of the struggles over radio broadcasting (McChesney, 1990) and cable television (Parsons, 1989; Streeter, 1987) reveal the commercial broadcasting model of the audience not to have been inevitable. The introduction of a "new" media technology provides an important site where assumptions and argumentation about the audience are likely to surface, particularly as the invention is developed into a business (see Winston, 1986).

Commercialization of a new technology requires market definition of potential users or purchasers. It also requires positioning of that technology vis-à-vis any existing media technologies that it seems to complement or challenge. It is in this process that the value of a discursive strategy becomes apparent. One way a new technology can be commercialized is to define it, through advertising and marketing techniques, as an "innovation" in an existing technology or industry. The talking machine was positioned, through such techniques, within the music industry. As an "innovation" in home music making, the talking machine could enter an existing market for pianos, sheet music, and other musical instruments. The rhetorical construction of the talking machine as a "musical instrument" therefore allowed its purchasers to be discursively constituted as a "musical audience" (see Siefert, 1995).

The talking machine is often undervalued in communication histories because it does not fit smoothly into the trajectory of "electrical communication" from telegraph to "wireless." But it is important to the history of audiencemaking through mass communication because it provided an important consumer base for mass-produced home entertainment upon which the radio and television industries were built. The talking machine made several important contributions to the definition of the audience for mass-produced home entertainment.

First, the talking machine played a role in the transformation of leisure activity from production into consumption (see Fox & Lears, 1983; Susman, 1973). The availability of professional musical entertainment on records tended to erode the amateur cultivation of talents for producing home entertainment, particularly parlor singing and playing. Advertising for the talking machine industry emphasized the advantage of this transformation as offering the opportunity to hear the "best" in music without the "necessity of constant study or practice" (see H. S. Jones, 1905, p. 9). However, the availability of professional entertainment on records also undermined the appreciation and tolerance for the developmental stages required to produce the "best" entertainment. Turning on the record player required less effort and brought more instantaneous results. And so, music making became music listening.

Second, with a talking machine, listeners no longer needed to be in the presence of strangers to experience professional entertainment. Indeed, talking machine owners were not required to leave home at all. Moreover, by purchasing a record, they could construct, through consumption, their own individualized audience experience. Thus standardized performance on records privatized the experience of musical reception. As Sennett

(1978) has argued with reference to other public activities, this change can be conceived as the transformation of the musical audience from a primarily public collectivity, as in the opera house or theater, to a collection of individuals.

Simultaneously, the privatization of musical experience through technology replicated the privatization of that experience through patronage and, later, through the opera "box." The aristocratic box seats privatized the reception of opera to familiars but displayed the listeners to the rest of the audience. In its way, so too did the "music box" known as the talking machine; it privatized musical experience through individual consumption but, as will be shown, left in place an observable hierarchy of cultural value.

Third, by centralizing the reproduction of identical musical performances and commodifying them for home consumption, the talking machine industry assisted in the further nationalization of the musical entertainment industry as a whole. Recording provided musicians with instantaneous national tours on the grooves of shellac. At the same time, the audience for the performances was expanded in size, and the monthly record publications and new record issues emphasized the nationwide sharing of the latest performances. For almost two decades, just a few companies made the same performances available at the same time across the country—a profound form of audiencemaking on a national and, eventually, international scale.

Fourth, by preparing the way for "reproduction" as the normal mode of receiving entertainment, the sound recording industry also affected aesthetic standards and perceptions of music in general (see Siefert, 1995). Listeners became accustomed to hearing mass-produced sound as a normal occurrence in the home, easing the acceptance of the sound quality of early radio broadcasts. Rather than complaining about the sound quality of early recordings, which were advertised as "natural sounding," listeners later demanded that live performances more closely match their reproductions (see Siefert, 1989). The transformation of musical performance into a "technologically mastered" reproduction eventually had a profound impact upon how much music would be composed, produced, and packaged as well as consumed (see S. Jones, 1992).

Finally, the talking machine industry managed to project, through product and discourse, an apparent solution to the tension between American values of democratic access to cultural materials and the achievement of success and distinction. The Victor company's advertising strategy emphasized the democratic nature of the talking machine technology by offering "the world's greatest artists" to all Victor talking machine owners while at the same time providing the opportunity for the display of discriminating taste through the purchase of (expensively priced and distinctively packaged) "high-class" records. Thus Victor's link between technology and its cultural content embodied, in image and prose, the paradox of cultural power in America.

SELLING SOUND
RECORDING TECHNOLOGY

By the close of the nineteenth century, the "talking machine" industry had two incompatible technological solutions to the problem of sound recording. Edison had announced his *cylinder* phonograph in 1877. After an initial flurry of publicity in both the popular scientific press and the national magazines, the phonograph languished, in part because it was still too fragile to withstand more than limited public demonstration and in part because, as Edison later explained, he was busy with the electric light (Edison, 1888; Josephson, 1959). Eleven years later, in response to a competing prototype invention,[5] Edison again went public with his "perfected phonograph," which received the accustomed, attendant publicity.

Edison had originally envisioned his prime market as businesses rather than individual consumers. Buoyed by the successes of the telephone industry, he had proffered his phonograph primarily as a dictating machine to record the "Washington Senate and the New York Press" (*Scientific American,* November 17, 1877) and had set up a series of companies to market it to business in the late 1880s and early 1890s. The enterprise was defeated by the combination of a strong stenographers' union and the still-fragile mechanism. However, the Washington, D.C., licensee, Columbia, managed to stay afloat by purchasing a patent from the parent company and by identifying a viable market. It seemed that, when cylinder players were placed in public places, individuals were willing to put "a nickel in the slot" to hear a song of their choice.

The second technological solution to sound recording was proposed to the scientific community in the late 1880s: Emile Berliner's *disc* player. The Philadelphia-based inventor, using the analogue of a photographic negative, created a sound "record" whose initial advantage was easy reproduction (Berliner, 1888). Unlike the cylinders, which had to be recorded individually by a performer who repeated the selection, the original disc recording was used to make a "master" from which up to 1,000 discs could be reproduced. This feature of the disc was attractive to performers and producers for obvious reasons.

The cylinder machine also offered an attractive feature, however. It was capable of recording as well as playing back previously recorded sound. The disc machine could only play back. But what Edison had originally thought would be of most interest to the public—the ability to record sound themselves—turned out to be of little interest. What the public seemed to want, as suggested by nickelodeons, was repeat performances of music.[6] Thus, despite the "empowering" potential of the cylinder technology for individualized production of sound recordings, that technology, from its commercial beginnings, was used to constitute *audiences*.

Although the disc player seemed to have several technological advantages, the cylinder player had a head start and one overwhelming advantage: Edison himself. Edison's celebrity as the inventor-hero and his publicized entrepreneurial spirit gave him the ability to raise capital, reach potential distributors, and attract public attention (Wachhorst, 1981). Once he was convinced that individuals might buy phonographs, he determined to make one that they could afford and began marketing cylinder machines and cylinder recordings for individual consumers. Significantly, one of Edison's first models was named "the home phonograph." By 1899 there were 2,763,300 cylinder recordings manufactured in the United States (Sterling & Haight, 1978, table 150-A). And by 1900 the reported value of the sound recording industry was $2 million, surpassing photographic apparatus, which had been available for decades (U.S. Bureau of the Census, 1904, p. 315, table 154).

And what of Berliner's disc player? Berliner had brought the gramophone to a commercially viable position with the manufacturing aid of Eldridge Johnson, a machine-shop owner in Camden, New Jersey. But by 1898 Berliner's advertising agent in New York had made Berliner's machine all but invisible and in 1900 obtained an injunction to prevent Berliner from distributing his own gramophones (Aldridge, 1964/1983, p. 33). Not coincidentally, the Columbia interests chose this moment to sue Berliner over a patent dispute. When the injunction was finally lifted and the patent adjudicated in their favor late in 1901, Johnson effectively consolidated his and the Berliner interests under the name Victor Talking Machine Company. But having lost almost 5 years on the competition, they seemed to be the victor in name only—except for one small irony. The very events that had kept Victor out of the U.S. market, and thereby forced their dependence upon a British licensee, began to yield unexpected rewards.

In 1898 the gramophone interests had licensed a separate London company, the Gramophone Company, to assemble gramophone parts imported from the United States.[7] A key element of the plan was that, although the machine parts were imported, the Gramophone Company would make its own recordings of European musicians. To sell the machines, the Gramophone Company had to convince European customers that their player would play "their music," especially the music preferred by those wealthy enough to purchase the machines. So, with a new London recording studio and a record pressing plant in Hanover, the Gramophone Company began recording, producing, and marketing recognized European musicians.

The success of the London-based Gramophone Company and its other European branches, including Deutsche Grammophon, provided the capital-strapped Victor company with an outlet for U.S.-manufactured gramophone parts during the injunction. Victor also now had access to a large repertoire of hitherto unavailable recorded material: European stars singing opera's "greatest hits." According to subsequent accounts (see Gelatt, 1965), Johnson gambled on a strategy that would link the Victor technology with this prestigious content, thereby differentiating Victor from its American rivals, who sold, in both Europe and the United States, almost exclusively American recordings of American music (Dearling & Dearling, 1984, p. 56). But it remained to be seen whether Victor could identify, reach, and persuade Americans to become gramophone customers just to have the European opera arias "available only on Victor."

SELLING OPERA

In early twentieth-century America, selling opera records was not quite as formidable as it might seem to our age and our ears. Touring opera companies and solo artists had spread opera music and opera singing across the country (see Horowitz, 1987, chap. 1). Opera arias were performed in recitals and symphony concerts, as incidental music to theatrical performances, and by mechanical reproduction on music boxes and street pianos. They were also available through best-selling sheet music for the ubiquitous parlor piano (see Loesser, 1954). Even after the establishment of more permanent musical institutions for the performance of complete operas, much operatic music was sung and played in bits and pieces with a mix of other music.

The technological constraints and peculiarities of early sound recording also benefited the popular packaging of opera. Early discs and cylinders could play for a maximum of 2 minutes, much like a music box. Discs were extended to 4 minutes with the introduction of the 12-inch record by 1904, though Edison's cylinder would not last 4 minutes until October 1908 (Gelatt, 1965, p. 163). Thus sound recording continued the nineteenth-century tradition of the "greatest hits" of opera, usually the arias whose melodies were already in circulation in other musical forms. On record, opera continued to resemble popular songs in length and format.[8]

Moreover, operatic singing was more amenable to recording than some other musical forms. A trained singer's vibrato (the slight wavering of a tone increasing in volume) recorded well because the force of the vibrato, as amplified through the recording horn, aided the mechanical "etching" of the sound onto the master wax disc. So opera singers sounded good, technologically speaking, especially the tenors whose pitch range fit the best into the tonal registers picked up by the early recording apparatus. And in the absence of electric amplification for live performances, opera vocal style was not unlike the singing style used in other live performances ranging from Gilbert and Sullivan to home-grown musicals. Opera singing therefore was not unfamiliar even to those who heard it rarely.

What sold was not only the singing but the star. Stars had always been central to attracting live audiences to opera performances (see Martorella, 1982, chaps. 2 and 6). In America, European opera singers had been known to have star potential since P. T. Barnum's merchandizing of the Swedish opera star Jenny Lind in 1859, and published predictions for the phonograph in the 1870s, 1880s, and 1890s consistently mentioned opera singers such as Adelina Patti along with Grant and Lincoln as "the voices to be preserved" (Siefert, 1995). In this pre-Hollywood era, opera stars also represented a world of glamour and high society in national magazine stories. So it was not surprising that Victor recording impresarios, like opera impresarios, recognized the necessity of stars to build a home audience for opera.

But for all these explanations that opera singing was not quite as "foreign" as its sound and language might suggest, opera was still rather limited in live performance relative to other popular forms of musical entertainment. Operatic music in popular form was familiar, but there was little evidence that opera singing would attract large numbers of customers except as a novelty. As a commercial proposition, it was, in fact, risky.

In terms of sales, it turned out to be exactly that. According to a business historian of the music industry, during this period celebrity opera recordings "generally accounted for less than one fifth of all Victor production and about three percent of total disc sales" (Sanjek, 1988, Vol. 2, p. 391). Yet Victor persisted in using opera stars as its primary advertising strategy to sell disc players even into the 1920s. For example, in this important first decade of the cylinder and the disc, almost half Victor's full-page ads in the *Saturday Evening Post* featured opera singers. The continued use of opera star advertising in the face of such meager sales, it appears, must be explained on broader grounds.

One such explanation draws upon opera's perceived value as cultural capital during this important transitional period in American musical cultural life. In the nineteenth century, the growing professional and middle classes had championed the cultivation of genteel culture as exemplified by such aesthetic sensibilities and attainments as piano playing (see Loesser, 1954; Trachtenberg, 1972, p. 143). This vision of culture for the middle classes was reflected in increased national magazine commentary on cultural events, particularly music and particularly in New York (Musselman, 1971).[9] This musical commentary, as Levine (1988) argues, also had the effect of discursively "sacralizing" certain types of musical experiences (primarily symphonic but also opera) and devaluing others. Music critics prescribed not only musical taste but also appropriate audience behavior (Levine, 1988). Promoters of this "higher" culture, while preserving these distinctions, also felt the need to reach out to those who might not yet appreciate these values by "sowing the seeds of culture" in the name of moral order (Levine, 1988, pp. 200, 206).

Sound recording technology offered a democratic way to sow the seeds of culture and to preserve the social order. The hierarchy of cultural values was becoming concretized—literally—in the building of opera houses and symphony halls (DiMaggio, 1986) and other institutions. To those excluded by place and price, sound recording technology offered access, and yet it preserved social order both inside and outside the institutions of live performance. The nouveau riche could purchase cultural capital in the form of real estate: a private box in the "golden horseshoe" at New York's Metropolitan Opera (Davis, 1980; Kolodin, 1953). And middle-class aspirants were told by Victor advertising that they could purchase a reproduction of exactly what was heard there—if they bought a box with a horn.

The Victor strategy for selling opera records domesticated opera's appeal and democratized its accessibility without destroying its value as a mark of "distinction" (Bourdieu, 1984). The Victor company, in pursuing what it perceived to be good business practices, made their records both discursively and physically distinctive and readily available as items of "conspicuous consumption" (Veblen, 1899/1953). By equating sound reproductions to Metropolitan-performed opera, with all its attendant cultural connotations, Victor advertising and sales literature portrayed their customers as the "opera audience at home." And in the process, Victor offered a technological solution to the tension between democracy and distinction in America.

SELLING DISTINCTION

The Victor strategy for selling opera records was carefully crafted. In 1900 Johnson added the first paper labels to gramophone disc records. (Previously, recordings were identified only on the cylinder casing or by etching on the mass-produced disc.) The British Gramophone Company picked up on the idea of paper labels, with one addition: The opera recordings would have a distinctive identity—labels of red paper. Thus, through the protective sleeve of the record, the content of the disc continued to be visible after the purchase was made. With the Red Seal recordings, as Johnson called them, the record had only to be seen and not heard to denote the elevated taste of its owner.[10]

For Red Seal records, it was not only the owner's taste that was elevated. Red Seal records cost at least twice as much as other recordings, initially $1 apiece. Rather than justifying the higher cost of these recordings directly, the Victor company enhanced their implicit value through separate and superior treatment. The first Red Seal catalog, issued in May 1903, was printed lavishly and promoted extensively in national magazine ads. It offered the imported recordings of several stars. By the next year, Victor had set up a Red Seal recording studio at Carnegie Hall and issued a new set of Red Seal opera recordings from "local," Metropolitan Opera stars. In new record lists printed in magazines and newspapers, Red Seal records were always listed separately; and in the yearly catalogs of all Victor recordings, they were eventually listed in a separate section on pink paper.

If the Red Seal signified Culture and Expense, then the Victor trademark, which without exception appeared on all records and ads, signified Everyday Democracy.[11] The familiar trademark, also imported from Britain, was a white terrier with black ears, head cocked in quizzical attention to the black horn of a gramophone, presumably listening to "his master's voice."[12] The mascot was registered by Berliner in 1900, and by 1902 it was used to identify all Victor products and featured prominently in all advertising. The trademark embodied rich connotations of fidelity ranging from the high technical standard of recording that allowed a dog to recognize "his master's voice" to the Anglo-American conception of a dog as "man's best friend." Nipper, as he was called, turned out to be the perfect audience icon: He was allowed into parlors, was domesticated, and belonged to no particular class. So the ideal audience for the Victor talking machine was never iconographically constrained by picturing particular human listeners or particular situations.

Another imported ingredient was the voice and face of Victor's best-selling and best-sounding opera star: Enrico Caruso. During spring 1902, this rising tenor of La Scala in Milan had recorded 10 arias for the London Gramophone Company.[13] His recorded, and subsequent live, debut in the United States in 1903 marked the beginning of a sound relationship—literally, financially, and symbolically—between the Victor company and an image of technical and cultural quality. Caruso's voice, in its timbre, range, and method of tone production, was ideally suited for, and demonstrated the potential of, sound recording (Steane, 1974). Moreover, his proven celebrity in the musical world substantiated Victor's claim that its machine was "A Real Musical Instrument" (*Saturday Evening Post,* January 31, 1903, back cover). Although his success attracted more stars to the Victor opera cast, Caruso reigned supreme in his lifetime and beyond as Victor's cultural endorsement—and best moneymaker.

The terrier and tenor were joined with the red seal of distinction on April 25, 1903, in the first double-page, across-the-fold advertisement in the *Saturday Evening Post.* The Nipper trademark dominated the spread, surrounded by textual nuggets and nine identified faces of opera stars.[14] The "living voices of the world's greatest artists," as the copy read, "can now be heard, whenever you choose, in your own home." Because "these famous artists have heretofore been heard only in crowded opera houses in the great cities of Europe and America," hearing them reproduced at home would provide an uncrowded, private concert. By extension, the correspondence between the live performance and its reproduction also linked the live audience and the gramophone audience.

The recorded version was not only more convenient—it was just as good as a live performance. Sara Bernhardt as well as Adelina Patti, the most famous diva of the past 20 years, said so: "In listening to the records of Caruso, Plancon, etc., it seemed as if those artists were actually singing in my salons." And "at a reception given under the Queen's patronage, in London, on New Year's Day . . . the guests thought that the great Caruso was actually in the room." If the greatest actress, greatest soprano, and the Queen's guests thought that "the greatest tenor in the world" was "in the room," then what more authoritative testimony (or discriminating audience) could be desired. "This is indeed an age of wonders."

The display of opera stars as well as the text, design, and aggressive size of this ad and the choice of national magazine advertising were indicative of Victor's attempts in the years to come to "create desire for the product."[15] Johnson, as Victor's president, took a personal interest in the ads, which he later described in an autobiography as "artistic in sentiment as well as practical in effect" (reprinted in Aldridge, 1964/1983, p. 119). Victor may have selected the weekly *Saturday Evening Post* for some of their most lavish advertising displays in these early years because of the magazine's dramatically rising subscription figures (700,000 by early 1904 and 1 million by late 1908; Mott, 1957, pp. 691-692). But most if not all of the other national circulation magazines carried these same ads in various sizes and permutations. As witnessed by entries in the *Readers Guide* and the contents of the *Post,* editorial content reinforced the operatic substance of these full-page ads, with profiles, interviews, stories, and reviews by such resident critics as William Armstrong for the *Post* and William J. Henderson for the monthly *Ladies Home Journal,* the first magazine with a million subscribers in 1903 (Mott, 1957, p. 545).[16]

The opera star advertisement was not the only type of advertising appeal used by the Victor company but, judging by the *Post* and other extant advertising samples from other magazines, it was the one that was treated to the most lavish display and frequent emphasis. This analysis is confirmed by the company's own post hoc analysis:

> The general problem [of creating desire for the product was] continuously attacked from four separate, carefully ratioed angles: (1) the excellence and superior performance of the product; (2) the pleasure and advantages (entertainment and education) of ownership; (3) the availability of the world's best artists; and (4) the gift idea ("the gift that keeps on giving"). The availability of the world's best artists was thought by the company to be the most effective.[17] (Aldridge, 1964/1983, p. 49)

One reason artist appeal was judged to be the most effective may be that it was the appeal that made the Victor company distinctive. The other three appeals were also used by the Edison National Phonograph Company and to a lesser extent by Columbia during these early years. Taking the year 1903 as an example, the Edison Phonograph Company ads in the

Post stressed that "the Phonograph is distinguished from other talking machines by its absolute freedom from scratching and pure, natural tones of music or voice" (May 23, p. 30); that "the Phonograph is the most delightful of all home entertainments" (September 19, p. 40; October 24, p. 32); and that "the Phonograph is the best present because of its inexhaustible variety and its education value" (December 5, p. 44). However, these ads were at most one-quarter page and often only one sixteenth of a page. In the same issues, Victor ran a full-page (October 24, p. 33) and a double-page spread (December 5, pp. 28-29) featuring the dog, surrounded by the praise of critics and, of course, a portrait of Caruso. And in 1904, not only did Victor place a profusion of ads announcing the new, recorded-in-America Caruso records complete with dog and Caruso portrait, they also used a back cover of the *Post* to publish a facsimile of their exclusive contract with him. Edison ads, while equally frequent, were smaller, and their iconography during this period had only one star: a portrait of Edison's face reflected in the horn.

SELLING DISTINCTION
TO THE SELLERS

Even though Edison phonographs clearly dominated talking machine sales through 1909 (see Millard, 1990, table 9.1), there were early signs that the Victor challenge was taken seriously—especially Edison's inauguration of grand opera cylinder recordings in 1906 (see *Saturday Evening Post,* February 10, 1906, inside cover). "Grand Opera Records a Great Success" proclaimed the *Edison Phonograph Monthly* in February of 1906: "We are confident that these new records will not only please present owners of Edison Phonographs but attract to the Edison standard many whose musical tastes have kept them from buying because our catalogues have not until now contained high class compositions sung by artists of the highest rank" (p. 3).

They were also priced lower than Victor's at 75 cents and provided better profit margins. But by December, despite these incentives, the Edison company lamented that they could not "help feeling that the trade in general, especially the smaller dealers, are not paying attention to [the grand opera records] that their high quality deserves" (p. 3).

The *Edison Phonograph Monthly* sporadically reminded dealers to push these records to people "of cultured tastes" who "seem to think all phonographic music is of the 'coon' variety" (June 1907, p. 10).[18] But these exhortations were primarily textual, almost didactic, and devoid of evidence of sales. And with the exception of reproducing the March 1907 national magazine ad for grand opera records (February 1907, p. 23), the *Monthly* used no visual items or aids and pictured no stars—with the exception of Edison himself (June 1905, p. 13).

Victor's advertising and sales philosophy, especially with regard to opera records, differed substantially from Edison's. Rather than looking for maximum effect in sales from minimum expenditure, Victor advertised in "every publication for which there was any justification" in part to be perceived in the same way as other important companies of the day (Aldridge, 1964/1983, p. 49). "High-class" records added to that image. In the last of an unprecedented series of four full-page ads in the first year of the new trade magazine *The Talking Machine World,* Victor proclaimed its philosophy: "There are four *Victor* pages in this issue. Three show pictures of operatic artists; one shows pictures of popular artists. Three to one—our business is just the other way, and more, too; but there is good advertising in Grand Opera. Are you getting your share?" (*The Talking Machine World,* October 15, 1905, p. 36).

Their explicit acknowledgment to the trade of opera's relative value in advertising and in actual sales affirms the conclusion that Victor was aiming for image as well as market share. But whatever the parent company's faith in the implicit value of high-culture advertising, the Victor dealers evidently also had some reservations about the sales value of the Red Seal line. In that same year, the New York distributor for Victor was more direct:

> DON'T FAIL to let *every* customer hear [the new Caruso records]. Most dealers don't realize how many VICTOR RED SEAL Records are sold. The price seems high until your customer hears them. Then he is surprised to be able to buy such marvelous records at any price. Even those who cannot afford it buy many of them. THESE ARE FACTS—TRY IT.
>
> High class Records have been the means of selling large outfits when the customer could not have been interested with any other class of Record. (*Talking Machine World,* May 15, 1905, p. 11)

To aid the dealer, the ad also offered an 11- by 14-inch picture of Caruso to be sold at $2.50.

In May 1906 the company began publishing *The Voice of the Victor* for its dealers. As compared with the *Edison Phonograph Monthly,* its layout, design, and tone showed some of the graphic sophistication and imagery of Victor advertising. But the *Voice* was equally impressive for the assistance offered to dealers. In the industrywide journal *Talking Machine World,* Victor merely offered exhortations; but in the *Voice,* it offered help in the style and substance of salesmanship.[19] "Sales promotion," including record catalogues and supplements, instrument catalogues, and other brochures, constituted about a third of Victor's advertising expenditures, which averaged 8.24% of sales for Victor's history (Aldridge, 1964/1983, pp. 49, 75). These materials were distributed to dealers who sold at least $300 worth of merchandise at a cost of about $25 to $35 per dealer. While these dealers were appointed by the distributors, each was recognized individually by the Victor company.

In its first year, for example, the *Voice* not only offered necessary information on contracts, new records, and so on but also featured the results of its sponsored contests: "How to Increase the Record Business" and "Prize-Winning Window Displays." In addition, new Victor booklets such as "The Victor for Every Day in the Week" recognized "the desirability of reaching families through the junior members" and suggested coordinated window displays (January 1907, p. 9).[20] Self-help for dealers also included a "Pronouncing Table of Composers and Singers" that was reprinted from the *Victor Opera Index,* one of the many handouts and brochures that helped sell opera to the sellers.

Unlike Edison's National Phonograph Company, the Victor company treated opera records consistently, especially through iconography, and built a number of selling aids around the opera records. In addition to the special catalogs and brochures, for example, one of a set of four streetcar cards in the July 1906 *Voice* pictured the familiar opera cast who "sing only for the Victor" (p. 4). Two Victor "hangers," 25- by 35-inch lithographs, with portraits of grand opera artists and popular artists, were offered to all Victor dealers "who agree to display them conspicuously" (*Voice,* May 1908, p. 7).

Any doubt about Victor's intended association with grand opera was dispelled in January 1906 with the erection of the "largest and most expensive sign in the world" on the roof of an office building at 37th Street and Broadway. The January 1907 *Voice* featured day and illuminated night photographs of this 40- by 50-foot reproduction of the Nipper trademark containing 1,000 electric lights. The *Voice* reported the sign to be a New York City landmark "passed by more people, and by more different people, every week, than probably any other spot in the United States." It was not an accident that the sign was located in the vicinity of the Metropolitan Opera House for its motto was "The Opera at Home."

Caruso also figured largely in these pages: his "Large Profits" on "the costliest songs ever sung in this country" (*Voice,* June 1906, p. 3), the story of his life (July 1907), and an offer of his life-size figure for dealers' window displays (March 1910, p. 4). His concert tour in spring 1911 was a prime opportunity for advertising, and dealers were to assume a responsibility for "the crowding of the theatre or auditorium on the evening of Caruso's appearance as it was never crowded before" (January–February 1911, p. 7). By now, the relationship between the live audience and the home audience had become mutually causal: Reproductions should create desire for the original.

In April 1908 a picture of Caruso "Listening to His Own Voice" on a Victor Victrola inaugurated a series of *Voice* cover photos lasting for several years that featured opera stars singly or together. (A variant of the photo was also used as the April 17, 1909, back cover of the *Saturday Evening Post.*) In this photo, Victor iconography had come full circle. Caruso's full-body pose in street clothes portrayed him next to the gramophone with its lid open, his head slightly cocked in a "listening pose." This analog of Nipper listening to "His Master's Voice" carries rich connotations. Not only does the "master" recognize his own voice, but the opera star becomes an individual member of the audience. If the star listens, can the listener at home be less than flattered?

A tribute to Caruso's starring role in the talking machine business was paid by Victor's competitors. In 1909 Edison once again tried to launch grand opera with new operatic tenors and a series of 4-minute Amberol records at $1 to $2 for an Amberola machine costing $200 (Gelatt, 1965, p. 162). First was Riccardo Martin, "a remarkably fine tenor voice, but little inferior to the famous Caruso" (*Edison Phonograph Monthly,* July 1909, p. 1). Then another tenor, Leo Slezak, was offered on the back cover of the *Saturday Evening Post* (February 19, 1910). During that month, the *Edison Phonograph Monthly* explained to their dealers how taking care of the two "classes" of customers would equip them "to take out all the profit there is in the business": "While . . . the Grand Opera lovers are saving up to buy more Records, the good old 'ragtime-coon songs-Sousa-Herbert-monologues-sentimental ballads' crowd will still be on the job buying Phonographs of the other styles, and Standard . . . Records, until there's frost on the sun" (*Edison Phonograph Monthly,* February 1910, p. 1).

Columbia too put forth opera singers—tenors, of course—to challenge Caruso: Constantino, "the great Spanish tenor"; Alessandro Bonci, "the world's greatest tenor"; and John McCormack, "the great Irish tenor" (*Post,* October 30, 1909, back cover; November 20, 1909, pp. 28-29;

January 15, 1910, back cover). The large size and prominent placement of the advertisements, their timing at the beginning of the opera/Christmas season, and the poses of the tenors all spoke of an intended Caruso challenge. So too did the price of "under a dollar" as compared with the $3 or more price for Caruso. For Victor, on the other hand, it was advertising and business as usual during this period.

For several critical years, however, business really had not been "usual." After the financial panic in fall 1907, sales dropped for all the talking machine companies. The Edison company was having a tough time recovering its business. At the end of their respective sales years in 1909, the Victor company had for the first time sold more dollars worth of talking machines (excluding recordings) than Edison (Millard, 1990, table 9.1). While that figure was only about 25% higher in 1909, by 1910 Victor outsold Edison by 80% on machines alone, with 94,557 sold (Millard, 1990, p. 210).

Some of this success has been attributed to the introduction of the Victrola (see Gelatt, 1965; Millard, 1990, p. 211). The important innovation of the Victrola was that the large (and, to many consumers, unsightly) amplifying horn was enclosed in a more genteel cabinet that resembled fine furniture. Introduced in late 1906, the standing cabinet model disc player went into mass production in 1907 and sold for the impressive price of $200. Comparatively speaking, horn-type models, which continued to dominate the Victor sales until 1911, sold for between $15 and $45. It was not until table model Victrolas costing under $100 were introduced (see Aldridge, 1964/1983, App. IV) that the Victrola came into its own. Table Victrolas accounted for about one quarter of all sales in 1910. However, not unlike grand opera records, the very availability of this upscale model and its appeal for the middle-class parlor established the top of the line—and the name Victrola—for record players for years to come (Millard, 1990, p. 211).[21] By 1910, according to the Edison sales force, the affluent urban markets were "Victrola crazy" (Millard, 1990, p. 212).

Did this luxury machine designed to accompany "high-class" records, along with Caruso's star status, actually mean that the audience for opera records was growing? To judge by Victor's messages to their dealers, they were not any happier than other producers of grand opera: "Red Seal Records have not always been understood by either the Dealer or his customers." Presumably because operas were numerous but expensive and heard only in the large cities, they were impossible to thoroughly understand.

To solve this problem, in April 1911, Victor introduced "Descriptive Labels" on the reverse side of records to explain the story of the aria and sometimes the words. Not only would these descriptions bring "a musical awakening that will make the great operatic arias as familiar in American homes as they are in the music centres of Europe" but they would also give "music lovers an appreciation greater than could be acquired by actually sitting in the opera house or concert hall and hearing the selections by the artists themselves" (*Voice of the Victor,* March-April 1911, p. 3). Listening to records not only was as good as being in the concert hall but allowed for even greater audience appreciation than actually being there. To persuade the dealers of the importance of their role in this coming musical awakening, the local dealer was dubbed "the impresario of his neighborhood."

While these descriptive labels did not last long, their informational intent was codified the next year in a more efficient and convenient form, *The Victor Book of Opera.* Repeating almost verbatim the promise of "equal if not greater" music appreciation to be gained from listening to records, the book offered to the "home audience" the "Stories of Seventy Grand Operas, with over Four Hundred Illustrations and Descriptions of Seven Hundred Victor Records." The illustrations were familiar from Victor advertising: cutout figures of singers and scenes from operas. Several versions of the more famous arias were noted. The cost of the book was 75 cents (50 cents to dealers)—less than the price of one Red Seal record.

Listing 700 records, *The Victor Book of Opera* provided a guide to consumable opera—a sales tool that kept on selling. Produced as a "fine book," it appeared as an adjunct to the luxury line of Victor goods. In its advertising copy, Victor described a "widespread recognition of [their] work which has carried these famous operatic records into hundreds of thousands of homes where such music was absolutely impossible in any other way," thereby "helping toward America's musical uplift" (*Voice,* June 1912, pp. 4-5).[22]

In the "Foreword" to the book, Victor again made their claims about the home opera audience, this time to that audience itself:

The Victor is an Excellent Substitute for the Opera. For every person who can attend the opera there are a hundred who cannot. However, many thousands of lovers of the opera in the latter class have discovered what a satisfactory substitute the Victor is, for it brings the actual voices of the great singers to the home, with the added advantage that the artist will repeat the favorite aria as many times as may be wished. (Victor Talking Machine Company, 1912, p. 9)

The Victor could more than substitute for the opera, however, it could increase the enjoyment of opera even for those "fortunate enough to be able to attend": "Do you think Caruso the greatest of tenors? Then do not be satisfied with an occasional hearing of his glorious voice at the opera, but let him sing for you and your friends by means of the Victor" (p. 9). In fact, favorite singers could be heard "*at home* as often as desired and their voices will be just as natural as in life."

And in much the same way, the text also put the home audience at the center of Victor's cultural contribution. Victor claimed responsibility for the awakened interest in opera in America that had taken opera beyond "merely the pastime of the well-to-do in New York City and vicinity":

During the recent season several hundred performances of grand opera, at an estimated cost of millions of dollars, were given in the United States. This great outlay for dramatic music alone would not have been possible had it not been for the increased interest aroused in opera by the wide-spread distribution by the Victor during the past ten years of hundreds of thousands of grand opera records, at widely varying prices. (Victor Talking Machine Company, 1912, p. 5)

Thus Victor promoted the idea that the audience at home could enjoy the opera—indeed, could enjoy it more fully than the audience for live performances. Nonetheless, the audience at home was creating a demand for live performances as well. Such rhetorical moves incorporated the audience for the live performance into the audience at home and vice versa, thereby drawing the performance-reproduction linkage ever tighter.

Victor's resolution of the tension between cultural distinction and democratic accessibility was reiterated and contextualized in a new format for the Victor record catalog inaugurated in 1912. The catalog indexed the whole of Victor's offerings but listed the Red Seal artists (75 opera singers and eight instrumentalists) separately (and, as mentioned before, within a few years the Red Seal section was printed on pink paper). Thus the catalog embodied the three-to-one ratio of all other music to opera recordings in the Victor output while preserving opera's distinctive place.

As "first aid" for New Victor Owners, the catalog listed recommendations for a beginning library: 12 instrumental records (including the 3-record version of the *William Tell* Overture), 8 standard songs and 8 sacred songs (including a $3 version of "Silent Night" by Ernestine Schumann-Heink), 11 popular and musical comedy selections, and, in the largest category, 17 operatic numbers, all "at widely varying prices." Once again, the Victor formula supplied this democratic range of music with a conspicuous touch of class.

THE CONSUMER AND THE AUDIENCE

Most commentators assign the triumph of the disc over the cylinder to the year 1912. Sales of Victor talking machines had topped the $10 million mark and Columbia ceased all cylinder production in that year. Significantly, in December 1912, the Edison National Phonograph Company introduced its own disc-playing machines to the public (Wile, 1990). The company had begun work on a disc as early as 1909, even though cylinders manufactured in that year outnumbered disc recordings by more than two to one (18,611,200 to 8,572,800). By 1914 less than 4 million cylinders were manufactured as compared with almost 23 million discs from all companies (Sterling & Haight, 1978, table 150-A).

As described here, some of the credit for the technological triumph of the disc must be given to Victor's product selection, business practices, and advertising strategy. Most narratives of the development of the recording industry, even those told from Edison's point of view (Millard, 1990; Read & Welch, 1959/1976), pay tribute to the impact of Caruso, the development of the Victrola, and the quantity of Victor advertising.[23] Memoirs (Gaisberg, 1942; Johnson in Aldridge, 1964/1983), company accounts (Aldridge, 1964/1983; *Voice of Victor,* June 1912, p. 4), and histories by musically inclined commentators (Gelatt, 1965) put even more stress on the "firsts" in Victor recordings of grand opera. And a simple count of grand opera advertisements suggests that, to quote Victor, "Grand Opera must be Good Advertising." Through July 1910, 6 of the 18 Victor company back covers featured Caruso and/or other opera stars. Of the 30 full-page ads, most in the early years, 14 featured opera stars. And the next most numerous category of full-pagers, holiday ads, also tended to mention the availability of the world's greatest artists.[24] The 1912 advertising campaign featuring Red Seal artists cost $1.5 million (Sanjek, 1988, Vol. 3, p. 26).

So, did these 10 years of expensive, consistent, and ubiquitous Victor advertising create "an audience" for "opera at home"? Here we must return to Sanjek's claim that, during those years when the cylinder accounted for two thirds of all prerecorded music sales, "the Red Seal line generally accounted for less than one fifth of all Victor production and about three percent of total disc sales" (Sanjek, 1988, Vol. 2, p. 391). As Victor continually stressed to its dealers, Red Seal records provided high profit margins despite high artist fees because they sold for so much more: $1.50 for a standard celebrity disc, $3 for a 12-inch Caruso solo, $6 for the quartet from *Rigoletto,* and $7 for the sextet from *Lucia*—opera recording "firsts" that were heavily advertised. Nonetheless, 3% is 3%—a figure that includes Caruso's best-selling records. Was it all hyperbole and "high-blown dedication to culture" (Sanjek, 1988, Vol. 2, p. 392)?

In response, one can point to the value of Red Seal records as an entry into an already competitive market and their coupling with the Victrola to sustain the luxury image and market during the recession years of 1907-1908. These records helped Victor establish a history, create a legend, and maintain mission for the company. Moreover, a "backlist" of records that sell over the long term is an industry strategy in use to this day—as attested to by the reissue of Caruso and other Red Seal artists on CD. But 3% is 3%. Can an audience exist without customers? Can an audience exist primarily in discursive terms—the audience for the opera at home?

Even though advertising grand opera was not only uneasy but rather unsuccessful persuasion in terms of actual sales, it had a symbolic function and an influence on certain aspects of American culture that might lend it historical and theoretical importance (see Schudson, 1984). Even if customers had no intention of listening to or purchasing Red Seal recordings, they took them "as proof of [the] quality of Victor's recording technology" (Millard, 1990, p. 201), the very aspect of his own machine of which Edison was most proud (Siefert, 1995). For those who did purchase them, a collection of Red Seal records established one as a person of taste and property. *These* records could be displayed in the refined American parlor with pride, alongside leather-bound sets of Dickens, Thackeray, and Oliver Wendell Holmes (Gelatt, 1965, p. 149).

By celebrating opera star performances, Victor drew on the existing cultural hierarchy for live music of the day to legitimate the talking machine as a "good musical instrument" (see Siefert, 1995).[25] The proclaimed distribution of the best performances of the best music, renewed the first of each month with new record announcements in major magazines and newspapers, compressed the time between hearing about a performance and actually hearing it. The advertised "firsts"—both in technological developments and in recorded selections—linked "firsts" with "best" in musical achievement. In the cultural values of the day, such promotion of "cultural uplift" was both common and expected; business-men were supposed to embody moral and cultural values.[26] Victor's advertising was, then, *good* business.

Victor's consistent and ubiquitous use of opera in national advertising and promotion materials consolidated and extended nationwide images of musical stars, particularly Caruso. "Mass-producing the moment," in Boorstin's (1973, p. 359) phrase, here meant that performances were shared by those who actually bought the 3%, but it also meant that information about the performances was far more widely distributed. Because performances as well as images could be reproduced nationally, singers could became nationwide stars even if they never came to town. Like Nipper, Caruso entered many American parlors as a culturally valued guest. He was the first star performer to sell a million records (see Millard, 1990, p. 209), although the first million-selling record was that of Alma Gluck singing a concert version of Stephen Foster's "Old Folks at Home" (Sanjek, 1988, Vol. 3, p. 24). For the first decade of the talking machine, despite the more widely available and popular voices from vaudeville and theater, there were few advertised stars other than opera stars.[27]

The relative fame or importance of stars was hierarchically ranked through record pricing. In addition to the Red Seal of distinction, which was bestowed only on the top opera singers, the various recordings of a particular aria or song by different singers were priced differently. For example, in these years there were four available recordings of "The Last Rose of Summer" priced from $5 to $1.50, depending upon the singer. To the consumer, the price differential could represent the fees that a singer demanded and therefore the singer's status in the musical world. The price differential was an implicit critique of the music and an extension of the rankings made by music critics. The cultural hierarchy therefore was commodified as it was made more democratically accessible.

Thus Victor's advertising intersected the discourse on quality and culture. If one important factor in the gradual solidification of a hierarchy of cultural value during the latter nineteenth century was the estab-lishment of institutions for imported culture, then the commercialization of technologies for the reproduction of that culture represented a new and essential element in the discourse of cultural value. The more segmented and categorized audiences became, the more a technology like the talking machine offered a strong cultural appeal. It offered an alternative for the occasional and "unprepared" audience members who might be castigated by the high-culture guardians, while at the same time it satisfied the reformist and educational impulse of those who wished to bring high culture to the masses (see Levine, 1988). Through technology, the talking machine both circumvented and reinforced the hierarchy of live performance and, by extension, of the audience. And, by using the Metropolitan Opera, the talking machine offered "a sense of place" (see Meyrowitz, 1986) with high cultural value while relating that place to the audience at home.

Sound recording technology fit perfectly into the privatization of behavior and feeling and the transformation of audiences from collectives to collections of individuals. The listener became part of an audience for professional entertainment that could heretofore only be experienced in the collective of the audience for staged, live entertainment. The availability of professional entertainment in the home for the most part superseded amateur music making, turning even the intimate, social collectives of family, friends, and suitors who produced entertainment for each other into collections of individual listeners and consumers.[28]

The talking machine privatized musical experience to the level of the family in the parlor and beyond—to the level of the individual listener. In part, this was the result of technical limitations: Acoustic recording simply could not be played back at a loud enough volume to hold the public "gramophone concerts" that had often been envisioned. But the easily consumable nature of gramophone discs and the increasing segmentation of audiences for live music fitted remarkably well into the emerging consumer society and into the display of "good taste." At once, there was both the assembly of a national audience of individuals united in their consumption of the best performance and the solidification of the notion that the original *live performance* had been *exactly reproduced* (see Benjamin, 1968). With the Red Seal, one could still be "seen" at the Metropolitan Opera.

Edison resisted Victor's celebrated analogies to the last. Despite losing money, he continued to manufacture cylinders into 1922 (see Siefert, 1995). In his notes of 1912, while listening to Caruso's Victor recording of "Testa Adorata" from Leoncavallo's *La Boheme,* Edison penciled in capital letters: "The phonograph is not an Opera House" (Harvith & Harvith, 1987, p. 13). For the discursive audience, though, perhaps it was.

NOTES

1. Just as Williams (1974/1992, p. 19) noted with reference to the broadcasting industry, here also the invention of a means of communication preceded its content.

2. Spigal (1992) makes a similar point about "the home theater" as an ideological construct for the introduction of television into the home.

3. Each issue from the relevant years of each publication was examined. All talking machine advertising in the *Post* was examined for the entire decade, and analysis of the industry and trade literature began with the initial issue of each publication: *Edison Phonograph Monthly* (1903), *The Voice of Victor* (1906), and *Talking Machine World* (1905).

4. According to Mott (1957, p. 464), in 1903 *Collier's Weekly* was about even in circulation with the *Post* but by 1912 the *Post* had almost four times the circulation (about 2 million) of *Collier's* and other weekly competitors.

5. The "graphophone," developed by the Bell Telephone interests, was also a cylinder recorder/player, which incised wax rather than indenting tin foil, as Edison's phonograph did. The patent was eventually purchased by Columbia, who marketed graphophones through 1910.

6. The idea of repetition is important. As discussed in the early magazine predictions about the phonograph, people would buy what they wanted to hear more than once or what they, or some social institution, wanted to store as a memory, or "record" (see Siefert, 1995).

7. In the late 1880s, Edison had set up the Edison-Bell Company in London to import machines into England, but its prices were double those in the United States and, relative to British wages, too expensive to make much headway. Columbia set up its first foreign office in Paris in 1897 (Gelatt, 1965, pp. 101-104).

8. Opera was often, but not necessarily, sung in English. Sheet music often provided translations. But it is also useful to keep in mind that, in the large cities like Chicago and New York, there was a large, non-English-speaking immigrant population. In the first decade of the twentieth century, for example, over a half million of the $4\frac{1}{2}$ million New Yorkers were immigrant or first-generation Italian (Kolodin, 1953, p. 211), the language of most operas performed at this time.

9. By the turn of the century, New York housed most of the music business in the form of live performances from Broadway to the opera houses, booking agencies, music publishing houses, and national magazine publishers (Sanjek, 1988).

10. The Victor company was not the first to market opera records. Columbia preempted Victor's Red Seal catalog by 1 month, issuing 32 recordings of "local" Metropolitan Opera singers in April 1903 *on disc only* (Dearling & Dearling, 1984, p. 34). Evidently desiring a quick return to offset the high singers' fees, however, they abruptly halted production and sale of these records after a few months of advertising. Even the idea was not unique to Victor. The nineteenth-century discourse surrounding the potential of the talking machine, including Edison's predictions, stressed the importance of recording opera stars for posterity (see Siefert, 1994).

11. In fact, in his large work on advertising between 1920 and 1940, Marchand (1985) quotes a lament by *Printer's Ink* in June 1935 (pp. 19, 61) to the effect that the Victor company's dog was still "advertising's great art" for the masses.

12. This trademark was taken from a painting by a Frenchman, Francis Barraud, that had been offered to the Gramophone Company after Edison's London agent had rejected the painting. A disc-playing gramophone was painted over the original cylinder-playing phonograph.

13. The story of Caruso's coming to the Metropolitan Opera has been told, in many versions, as being a result the 1902 recordings. In one version, Heinrich Conried, the new manager, used a recording to convince his New York directors to offer Caruso a contract (Lowe, Miller, & Boar, 1982, p. 65). In another, Conried was convinced to extend the number of Caruso's already contracted performances after hearing a record (Scott, 1988, p. 69).

14. A tenth star, Kubelik, "one of the greatest violinists of modern times," was also pictured. This nine-to-one ratio of singers to instrumentalists was even more pronounced in favor of singers in the catalogs and recorded selections. One of the major reasons was that violins and pianos, the favorite solo instruments, did not record nearly as well as the human voice using the early acoustic method.

15. It is noteworthy that, in the years between 1901 and 1905, when Victor began its aggressive advertising campaign in national magazines, they placed no ads in *Music Trade Review,* which published a regular column on "the talking machine trade." Columbia advertised regularly to potential distributors and therefore received article coverage as well. The Victor Talking Machine Company did receive occasional coverage—if their export company happened to advertise, usually gramophone horns. Coverage then consisted of a paraphrase of a brochure received at the editorial office. During this time, Edison phonograph interests appeared primarily in regard to lawsuits.

16. Victor also chose *Ladies Home Journal* in which to print its monthly announcements of new records in 1903, another way in which the cultural ideal of refinement and domesticity for women was enlisted in the sales effort.

17. The phrase "the gift that keeps on giving" appears to be a later advertising slogan, in use by 1926, that Aldridge would have known when writing his 1964 history of the Victor Talking Machine Company. The Christmas ads through 1912 did emphasize the gift motif but without using that exact phrase.

18. The Victor record catalog of 1912 defined "coon songs" as "up-to-date comic songs in negro dialect. The humor of many of these songs cannot be called refined, and for that reason we have distinguished them from old-fashioned darky humor, these songs being listed under 'Fisk Jubilee Quartet,' 'Negro Songs' and 'Tuskegee'." All three companies included "coon songs" in their catalogs.

19. Beginning in 1906, the Victor company took one full page each month in the *Talking Machine World,* primarily to tell the trade how well they were doing. Edison's Phonograph company did likewise. Victor wasted little design or graphic extravagance on these ads. The copy simply exhorted the dealers to follow up the intensive national advertising with local ads. Because many dealers advertising in the *TMW* were distributors for both Edison and Victor, both companies' advertising creativity was expressed primarily in the invention of new metaphors for success.

20. Two items offered to Edison customers, by contrast, were a 17- by 25-inch reproduction of a painting depicting the "delighted amazement of an old couple upon hearing a Phonograph for the first time" (offered in the *Post,* March 24, 1906) and a booklet, "The American Nights Entertainment," which suggested "many ways of making home more desirable than the club" (August 25, 1906, p. 20). Using the phonograph to keep the men at home was mentioned more than once.

21. Edison, for example, introduced his own $200 Edison Amberola in October 1909 (Gelatt, 1965, p. 165) to complement his new grand opera records, and Columbia had earlier offered the Grafonola to copy the success of the Victrola (see Aldridge, 1964/1983, p. 63).

22. Continuing "cultural uplift" under the auspices of its educational department established in 1910, Victor published *What We Hear in Music* in 1913, a music appreciation text for schools that consisted of 36 lessons keyed to 350 Victor recordings (Horowitz, 1987, p. 206; Keene, 1982/1987, chap. xiv).

23. According to Pope (1983, table 2.5), during 1913-1915, the Victor company ranked fourth or fifth in advertising expenditures, though only 170th in 1917 assets. Columbia managed to rank 19th and 20th in two of those years, though 290th in 1917 assets. Edison did not enter the picture.

24. Edison did not take a full-page ad until 1907 and took only four back covers during this period, beginning in 1908. His most notable ad campaign used a series of etchings of various everyday or unusual listening situations that looked remarkably like magazine editorial illustrations. Columbia did not really have an advertising presence until a double-page spread appeared in 1908 announcing double-sided disc records. All of their ads were for discs, and many of the full pages were for their opera tenor challengers.

25. The contested American impulse toward cultural enlightenment as a component of education has played a historical role in the introduction of new media. "High culture," even opera, was a legitimating force, certainly in discourse, for radio (Horowitz, 1987) and television (Jackaway, 1990) and has also been the spur for much technological innovation in the recording industry (Frith, 1987).

26. In an article written for *The Etude* (July 1915, p. 497), Johnson explained "What Music Should Mean to the Business Man": "The appreciation of music . . . clears the mind, . . . puts us in touch with humanity . . . and makes us better business men."

27. Of all advertising in the *Post* through 1910, and copy in the company magazines for that matter, the ads for named nonopera stars can be itemized on one hand. Victor tried to capitalize on vaudeville in 1907 by presenting six named vaudeville stars (*Post,* November 9). In 1909 Edison offered nine tiny portraits of entertainers at the bottom of an ad (*Post,* May 29, 1909, p. 31). At about the same time, Victor offered eight portraits: "The Victor not only presents the world's greatest opera stars, but the most famous bands and instrumentalists and leading vaudeville artists" (*Post,* October 16, 1909, p. 64). All these ads were quite small. Edison even tried to sell Bryan and Taft during the 1908 presidential election but they seemed to have had less star value after November.

28. According to Toll (1982, p. 104), the mass production of the same performance by professionals affected popular music as well. By the 1890s most popular songs of the Tin Pan Alley variety were written with the expectation that they would be performed by amateurs, hence simple choruses that could be learned in repeated hearings. However, after 1910, songs were written primarily for professionals and therefore were more complex. It was also during the 1910s that dance music, ragtime, and other Latin and African American rhythms were adapted to middle-class taste for mass production on records. The first jazz record was produced in 1917.

REFERENCES

Aldridge, B. L. (1983). The Victor Talking Machine Company. In T. Fagan & W. R. Moran (Compilers), *The encyclopedic discography of Victor Recordings* (pp. 1-65). Westport, CT: Greenwood. (Original work published 1964)

Benjamin, W. (1968). The work of art in the age of mechanical reproduction. In *Illuminations* (pp. 217-251). New York: Harcourt, Brace.

Berliner, E. (1888, June). The gramophone: Etching the human voice. *Journal of the Franklin Institute,* pp. 425-447.

Bijker, W. E., Hughes, T. P., & Pinch, T. J. (Eds.). (1987). *The social construction of technological systems.* Cambridge: MIT Press.

Boorstin, D. (1973). *The Americans: The democratic experience.* New York: Random House.

Bourdieu, P. (1984). *Distinction: A social critique of the judgement of taste* (R. Nice, Trans.) Cambridge, MA: Harvard University Press.

Davis, R. L. (1980). *A brief history of music in American life: Vol. 2. The gilded years, 1865-1920.* Huntington, NY: Robert Krieger.

Dearling, R., & Dearling, C. (with Rust, B.). (1984). *The Guinness book of recorded sound.* London: Guinness Books.

DiMaggio, P. (1986). Cultural entrepreneurship in nineteenth century Boston: The creation of an organizational base for high culture in America. In R. Collins, J. Curran, N. Garnham, P. Scannell, P. Schlesinger, & C. Sparks (Eds.), *Media, culture & society: A reader* (pp. 194-211). London: Sage.

Douglas, S. J. (1987). *Inventing American broadcasting: 1899-1922.* Baltimore, MD: Johns Hopkins University Press.

Edison, T. A. (1888, June). The perfected phonograph. *North American Review.*

Fox, R. W., & Lears, T. J. J. (Eds.). (1983). *The culture of consumption: Critical essays in American history, 1880-1980.* New York: Pantheon.

Frith, S. (1987). The industrialization of popular music. In J. Lull (Ed.), *Popular music and communication* (pp. 53-77). Newbury Park, CA: Sage.

Gaisberg, F. W. (1942). *The music goes around: An autobiography.* New York: Macmillan.

Gelatt, R. (1965). *The fabulous phonograph 1877-1977* (2nd rev. ed.). New York: Macmillan.

Harris, N. (1990). John Philip Sousa and the culture of reassurance. In *Cultural excursions: Marketing appetites and cultural tastes in modern America* (pp. 198-232). Chicago: University of Chicago Press.

Harvith, J., & Harvith, S. E. (Eds.). (1987). *Edison, musicians, and the phonograph: A century in retrospect.* Westport, CT: Greenwood.

Horowitz, J. (1987). *Understanding Toscanini: How he became an American culture-god and helped create a new audience for old music.* New York: Knopf.

Jackaway, G. (1990). Initial reactions to the introduction of the television, 1938-1953. In S. Thomas & W. A. Evans (Eds.), *Communications and culture: Language, performance, technology and media.* Norwood, NJ: Ablex.

Johnson, E. R. (1915, July). What music should mean to the business man. *The Etude,* p. 497.

Jones, H. S. (1905, March 15). Will replace cheap piano: This is the mission of the talking machine. *Talking Machine World,* p. 9. (Reprinted from the *Columbia Record*)

Jones, S. (1992). *Rock formation.* Newbury Park, CA: Sage.

Josephson, M. (1959). *Edison: A biography.* New York: McGraw-Hill.

Keene, J. A. (1987). *A history of music education in the United States.* Hanover, NH: University of New England Press. (Original work published 1982)

Kolodin, I. (1953). *The story of the Metropolitan Opera, 1883-1950: A candid history.* New York: Knopf.

Levine, L. (1988). *Highbrow, lowbrow: The emergence of cultural hierarchy in America.* Cambridge, MA: Harvard University Press.

Loesser, A. (1954). *Men, women & pianos: A social history.* New York: Simon & Schuster.

Lowe, J., Miller, R., & Boar, R. (1982). *The incredible music machine.* London: Quartet/Visual Arts Books.

Marchand, R. (1985). *Advertising the American dream: Making way for modernity, 1920-1940.* Berkeley: University of California Press.

Martorella, R. (1982). *The sociology of opera.* New York: Praeger.

McChesney, R. W. (1990). The battle for the U.S. airwaves, 1928-1935. *Journal of Communication, 40*(4), 29-57.

Meyrowitz, J. (1986). *No sense of place.* New York: Oxford University Press.

Millard, A. (1990). *Edison and the business of invention.* Baltimore, MD: Johns Hopkins University Press.

Mott, F. L. (1957). *A history of American magazines: Vol. 3. 1865-1885.* Cambridge, MA: Harvard University Press.

Musselman, J. (1971). *Music in the cultured generation: A social history of music in America, 1870-1900.* Evanston, IL: Northwestern University Press.

Parsons, P. R. (1989). Defining cable television: Structuration and public policy. *Journal of Communication, 39*(2), 10-26.

Pope, D. (1983). *The making of modern advertising.* New York: Basic Books.

Read, O., & Welch, W. L. (1976). *From tin foil to stereo: Evolution of the phonograph* (2nd ed.). Indianapolis: Howard W. Sams. (Original work published 1959)

Sanjek, R. (1988). *American popular music and its business: Vol. 1. The first four hundred years; Vol. 2. From 1790 to 1909; Vol. 3. From 1900 to 1984.* New York: Oxford University Press.

Schudson, M. (1984). *Advertising, the uneasy persuasion: Its dubious impact on American society.* New York: Basic Books.

Scott, M. (1988). *The great Caruso.* London: Hamish Hamilton.

Sennett, R. (1978). *The fall of public man.* New York: Random House.

Siefert, M. (1989). Opera. In the *International encyclopedia of communications.* New York: Oxford University Press.

Siefert, M. (1995). How the talking machine became a musical instrument: Technology, aesthetics and the capitalization of culture. In A. J. Rieber & M. Siefert (Eds.), *Technology: Culture, aesthetics, politics* (special issue of *Science in Context*).

Spigal, L. (1992). *Make room for TV: Television and the family ideal in postwar America.* Chicago: University of Chicago Press.

Steane, J. B. (1974). *The grand tradition: Seventy years of singing on record.* London: Duckworth.

Sterling, C. H., & Haight, T. R. (1978). *The mass media: Aspen guide to communication industry trends.* New York: Praeger.

Streeter, T. (1987). The cable fable revisited: Discourse, policy, and the meaning of cable television. *Critical Studies in Mass Communication, 4*(2), 174-200.

Susman, W. I. (1973). *Culture as history: The transformation of American society in the twentieth century.* New York: Pantheon.

Toll, R. C. (1982). *The entertainment machine: American show business in the twentieth century.* New York: Oxford University Press.

Trachtenberg, A. (1972). *The incorporation of culture: Culture and society in the gilded age.* New York: Hill and Wang.

U.S. Bureau of the Census. (1904). *Abstract of the twelfth census of the United States 1900* (3rd ed.). Washington, DC: Government Printing Office.

Veblen, T. (1953). *The theory of the leisure class.* New York: Mentor. (Original work published 1899)

Victor Talking Machine Company. (1912). *The Victor book of opera.* Camden, NJ: Author.

Wachhorst, W. (1981). *Thomas Alva Edison: An American myth.* Cambridge: MIT Press.

Wile, R. R. (1990). *Edison disc artists and records, 1910-1929* (2nd ed.). Brooklyn: Antique Phonograph Monthly Press.

Williams, R. (1992). *Television: Technology and cultural form.* Hanover, NH: New England University Press. (Original work published 1974)

Winston, B. (1986). *Misunderstanding media.* Cambridge, MA: Harvard University Press.

Chapter 12

THE VAUDEVILLE CIRCUIT:
A PREHISTORY OF THE MASS AUDIENCE

Robert W. Snyder

IN HER YOUTH, Frances Sinow was one of millions of Americans who participated in one of the most significant developments in American history: the creation of a national audience for popular entertainment through vaudeville theater. But while it was a mass audience in its proportions, it was simultaneously composed of myriad individuals—as Sinow recognized in a letter written decades after she attended vaudeville shows:

> I loved it—I miss it—neither film nor TV has the warmth, the excitement or the life of vaudeville—it moved you with an emotion quite missing in other entertainment—it reached and touched you, individually, and also caught you up in a communal happening—a sharing together of a common, wonderful experience. Nothing has taken its place. It moved fast, had a wide range that kept you always absorbed . . . a kind of entertainment audiences could lose themselves in, individually and collectively. (personal, written communication with F. Sinow, 1984)

Sinow grasped the duality that defined vaudeville: it reached people as individuals yet knit them into an audience of massive proportions. The ramifications of this phenomenon would have a profound influence on American popular culture. The mass audience, which Sinow and millions of other Americans entered into, is the definitive characteristic of American culture. But the construction of a mass audience, its meaning for the individual, and its role in the creation of culture changed drastically from the nineteenth to the twentieth century. Vaudeville was the linchpin of the transition.[1]

Through the middle of the nineteenth century, the audience for popular entertainment was constituted in highly public places, like the Bowery of New York City, with its saloons and cheap theaters. Custom and vigorous interaction between artists and audiences exerted a strong influence over cultural production. Audiences sometimes seemed like part of the show. In the twentieth century, however, popular culture came to be defined by records, film, radio, and television—the products of a centralized entertainment industry that disseminates what it produces to a nationwide, and increasingly international, audience. These new forms of popular culture created a large commercial mainstream that shaped and sustained mass audiences and undermined the local bases of culture. Audiences went from being coproducers to consumers. They could be creative and discerning consumers, but they necessarily worked with products created, for better or worse, by someone else.[2] And as these homebound forms of popular culture replaced the theater, that old focal point of popular entertainment lost much of its public quality.

Thriving from the 1880s to the 1920s, vaudeville participated in this transition. Vaudeville was, as David Marc (1989, p. 72) observed, "the biblical era of modern show business." Films, radio, the music industry, television—all trace at least part of their origins to vaudeville. The links range from performers to entrepreneurs to routines to theaters—to audiences. Indeed, vaudeville created the national audience that was later exploited by the electronic media. Of course, by the middle of the nineteenth century, large numbers of Americans shared an appreciation of artists such as Jenny Lind. But vaudeville was an organized entertainment industry that cultivated stars and fed them to a vast public week in and week out, creating a sustained audience that did not depend on the appeal of one single performer.

And vaudeville did this in an era of rising ethnic diversity, class differences, and questioning of gender roles—all of which made the construction of an entertainment mainstream problematic. Vaudeville could do this because it was not a monolithic steamroller of mass culture. In a process rich with irony, this centralized and bureaucratic industry knit people into a national audience through styles of performance that were calculated to seem direct and intimate. To use the language of classical sociology, vaudeville used *gemeinschaft* means to reach *gesellschaft* ends. Vaudeville's inextricable mixing of the intimately communal and the impersonally bureaucratic was the key to its success and its long-term influence on American culture (Marc, 1989, p. 42).

VAUDEVILLE AS A CULTURAL FORM

Vaudeville first appeared in the 1880s. Composed of separate acts strung together to make a complete bill, vaudeville drew deeply on forms of performance that predated the Civil War, such as blackface minstrelsy, circuses, melodrama, and variety. In form, it was the direct descendant of mid-nineteenth century variety theater, which had often catered to carousing middle-class and working-class men in music halls and barrooms called concert saloons that furnished alcohol and entertainment.

In the first half of the nineteenth century, American theater audiences were defined by their heterogeneity and their vocal responses to the action onstage. As late as the 1850s, George G. Foster, a New York City journalist, visited the Bowery Theater and found a mixture of quiet, respectable families and children in the dress circle. "Rowdies," "fancy men," "working girls of doubtful reputation," and "the lower species of public prostitutes" inhabited the upper tiers and galleries. Their "noisy lung-exercise," as he put it, swelled into a "merry and riotous chorus." "Compared with the performances in the audience," he concluded, "the ranting and bellowing and spasmodic galvanism of the actors on the stage are quite tame and commonplace" (see Foster, 1857, pp. 143-145, 1849, p. 120).

By the middle of the nineteenth century, however, differences of class, ethnicity, and gender made heterogeneous public gatherings distinctly combustible, as in the Astor Place Riot of 1849, which took 22 lives. Superficially, the Astor Place Riot was a conflict over whether an American or an Englishman should play Shakespeare. More fundamentally, it was a protest of working men, Irish immigrants, and American nationalists against New York's Anglophile elite. Astor Place signified the difficulty of creating a form of theater that could accommodate the different peoples of New York under one roof.

The problem reached beyond problems of ethnicity and class, both apparent in the Astor Place episode, to questions of gender. Immigrant women, especially Germans, were no strangers to beer halls. But ideals of domesticity, women's virtue, and family-centered leisure made raucous theaters and boozy saloons distinctly unattractive to most native-born, middle-class women. While heterogeneous gatherings of middle-class and working-class men were a well-established fact in the city's concert saloons from the 1860s on, the codes of gender made such establishments off-limits to most women.

Enter the creators of vaudeville, who constructed a broad and lucrative audience by creating an inclusive form of theater that could appeal to people in all their diversity. Vaudeville was old-time variety mass marketed by entrepreneurial showmen with a veneer of middle-class morality. Above all, their goal was to attract carousing men's wives and families. To that end, they banned liquor and prostitution from their houses. They jettisoned the older name, "variety," with its stigma of vice and alcohol, and adopted the classier-sounding name "vaudeville." On stage, they censored some of the bawdier acts—or at least promised to—all the while trying to maintain the energy and spark of variety theater. In the audience, they did their best to restrain the most vigorous outbursts—such as rioting and showering unpopular performers with rotten vegetables—without extinguishing the dynamic relationship between artist and audience that made variety shows so attractive.

B. F. Keith and E. F. Albee were proprietors of a string of theaters allegedly so proper that they were known as the "Sunday School Circuit." The duo worked overtime trying to subdue rowdy audiences accustomed to the old ways of variety. They took special aim at the boisterous men in the upper seats, the "gallery gods," and went so far as to issue cards printed with the following requests:

> Gentlemen will kindly avoid the stamping of the feet and pounding of canes on the floor, and greatly oblige the Management. All applause is best shown by the clapping of hands.
>
> Please don't talk during the acts, as it annoys those about you, and prevents a perfect hearing of the entertainment. (Royle, 1899, p. 488)

Backstage, Keith and Albee took the chaotic, informal booking procedures that characterized much of nineteenth-century variety theater and put them on a bureaucratic basis, centralized in New York City. Recognizing theater managers' need to hire acts and performers' need for bookings, they set themselves up as middlemen and charged vaudevillians a percentage of their salary for the privilege of using their booking office.

In a move that complemented their centralization of booking in New York, vaudeville entrepreneurs organized their theaters into nationwide chains of theaters, called circuits, that radiated out from New York City in the East and Chicago in the West. Circuits were generally identified as big time or small time. Big time specialized in stars, and usually charged higher prices. Lower priced, small time featured acts on their way up or way down. They amounted to theatrical versions of baseball's major and minor leagues. As performers toured the circuits, bringing their acts to the entire country, theater managers filed regular reports with the central office in New York City about audience response. Critics likened the system to an octopus, with a brain in Times Square and tentacles reaching far into the country.

With brilliance and audacity, the founders of vaudeville looked at the different peoples, classes, and sexes of the turn-of-the-century city and recognized constituencies that could be forged into a mass audience. Yet a mass audience of so many different components was bound to be volatile, because offering something for everyone in such a diverse country was bound to present people with the unexpected—particularly with regard to ethnicity and gender roles. In vaudeville, immigrants encountered a commercial ethnic culture that was more attuned to the New World than to the Old. Native-born Americans encountered theatrical representatives of America's immigrants in the form of singers, dancers, and comedians who wisecracked their way out of tenements in pursuit of national stardom. In such performers, middle-class audience members encountered a brash working-class spirit and a sensual expressiveness that undermined their own straitlaced Victorianism.

The appeal to the audience, in all its diversity, was fundamental. Audiences were not coerced into vaudeville houses; they were enticed. In 1922 in the magazine *The New Republic,* Mary Cass Canfield wrote about the "unforced and happy communion" between artists and audiences in the vaudeville house. To Canfield (1922), the vaudevillian was

> an apparent, if not always an actual improviser. He jokes with the orchestra leader, he tells his hearers fabricated confidential tales about the management, the other actors, the whole entrancing world behind the scenes; he addresses planted confederates in the third row, or the gallery, and proceeds to make fools of them to the joy of all present. He beseeches his genial, gum-chewing listeners to join in the chorus of his song; they obey with a zestful roar. The audience becomes a part of the show and enjoys it. And there is community art for you. (p. 335)

Vaudevillians worked tirelessly to put their acts over. As George Jessel recalled of his vaudeville years, "You lived by the reaction of the audience" (Smith, 1976, p. 29). More than its theatrical contemporaries, vaudeville consistently reached out to make the people in the seats feel like part of the show. Drama and opera could be enthralling, but essentially they created their own reality that people witnessed from their seats. Burlesque and early musical comedy reached out to audiences, but their appeal was narrower than vaudeville's.[3] In preserving the importance of the audience in the totality of the show, vaudeville perpetuated some of the blurring of the distinction between performer and spectator that made American theater so compelling in the middle of the nineteenth century.

Above all, vaudevillians faced a heterogeneous audience. The entrepreneurs had constructed a conglomeration of spectators with divergent tastes and desires. As performers worked their way cross-country on the circuits, they encountered crowds of middle and working class, immigrant and native born. Vaudeville's audience was a mass audience in its size, but it was not a rationalized audience. Legitimate theater audiences were generally alike, noted journalist Marian Spitzer in 1924, "but vaudeville audiences are different all the time": "It's almost impossible to set a performance and then play it that way forever. Each town, seems to be different; every neighborhood in the city needs different handling. So a vaudevillian has to be forever on the alert, to feel out his audience and work accordingly" (p. 6).

Vaudevillians learned to establish a fine-tuned rapport by presenting a standard act that was customized for the audience at hand. Even though they performed the same routine for weeks and even years on end, they had to sound fresh and original. The demands were apparent even to a legitimate theater star who toured in vaudeville, Ethel Barrymore. "The vaudeville public is an exacting one," she wrote, "and nothing must ever be slurred for them—perfect in the afternoon and perfect at night, over and over again for weeks and weeks" (Barrymore, 1955, p. 177).

There was nothing rote or routine in their craft. In a 1914 book, Carolyn Caffin recognized

> that genial familiarity, that confiding smile which seems to break out so spontaneously, the casual entrance and glance round the audience—all have been nicely calculated and their effect registered, but with the artist's sympathy which informs each with the spirit of the occasion and robs it of the mechanical artifice. (pp. 216-217)

During the vaudeville years, immigration transformed American cities. In 1920, for example, more than three quarters of the inhabitants of New York City were immigrants or children of immigrants.[4] Ethnicity had to be taken into account. A young Eddie Cantor flopped when he presented an English language act in a theater where most of the patrons spoke Yiddish. He translated his routine into their language and scored. He noted later (Cantor, 1928):

> We simply talked to them in the wrong language, and this in a way is every actor's problem in adapting himself to his audience. Drifting as I did into every conceivable type of crowd, I trained myself to the fact that "the audience is never wrong," and if a performance failed to go across it was either the fault of the material or the manner of presentation. By carefully correcting the one or the other or both with an eye to the peculiarities of the audience I could never fail a second time. I proved this to myself on many occasions later on, when in the same night I'd perform at the Vanderbilt home and then rush down to Loew's Avenue B and be a hit in both places. (p. 76)

Successful performers like Cantor learned to acknowledge audience mood and local custom. Sometimes vaudevillians used references to local geography, which they modified to fit the location they were playing. "I went from bad to worse, from Jersey City to Hoboken," said a character in a 1918 sketch. The script explicitly noted that two different localities could be inserted outside the New York area. As vaudevillian Frank Rowan observed, "If you're playing Bushwick, you make fun of Flatbush; if you're playing Flatbush, you make fun of Bushwick. That's an old, old game" (personal interview with Rowan, Englewood, New Jersey, February 7, 1986; see also Page, 1915, p. 489).

Local appeal sometimes involved appreciation of mood. Jewish comedian Billy Glason explained that, if he played Loew's Avenue B theater on the Lower East Side, he would give his act a "hamish," or homey, Jewish quality, perhaps by using Yiddish expressions, to make the audience feel like "family." If he played a top Times Square theater like the Palace, he would trade in the Jewish themes for more complicated, sophisticated material (personal interview with Billy Glason, New York City, January 18, 1984).

Always the vaudevillian's ultimate goal was to make it to the Palace and to become a nationwide star. A generation of hoofers, warblers, and wise guys used vaudeville as a way to escape the penury and isolation of performing in cheap saloons and isolated theaters. Like its successors in jazz, country music, and rock 'n roll, vaudeville was a way to go from being an outsider to being an insider.[5] And to improve the odds of getting there, acts worked to balance intimacy with national appeal. In her autobiography, Sophie Tucker (1945) explained how her song "My Yiddisha Mama" could be used for people of all faiths:

> "My Yiddisha Mama" was written for me by Jack Yellen and Lou Pollack. I introduced it at the Palace Theater in New York in 1925 and after that in many key cities of the U.S.A. where there were many Jews. Even though I loved the song, and it was a sensational hit every time I sang it, I was always careful to use it only when I knew the majority of the house would understand the Yiddish. However, I have found whenever I have sung "My Yiddisha Mama" in the U.S.A. or in Europe, Gentiles have loved the song and have called for it. They didn't need to understand the Yiddish words. They responded just as the hearts of Jews and Gentiles of every nationality responded when John McCormack sang "Mother Machree." You didn't have to have an old mother in Ireland to feel "Mother Machree," and you didn't have to be a Jew to be moved by "My Yiddisha Mama." Mother in any language is the same thing. (p. 260)

The ethnic cultures of the audience were among the most important factors that vaudevillians had to address. But at least as important were questions of sexuality and gender. Vaudeville was the product of an awkward meeting between rough, racy, male-oriented entertainment and middle-class ideals of propriety, female purity, and family-centered leisure. The audience, with its vacillating mixture of desires, likes, and dislikes was an integral part of this equation.

There had always been a contradiction between managers and middle-class patrons' professions of decency and the realities of the vaudeville stage, but by the years around 1910 that tension was becoming impossible to ignore. The increasingly divergent mores of middle-class patrons, a consequence of the decline and fragmentation of Victorian culture, made it harder to appeal to the comparatively more coherent sense of wholesomeness that Keith had aimed for in his early days.[6]

The Keith-Albee commitment to moral purity wavered. They revived a variety-era staple: pretty and shapely women posing in full-body tights pretending to impersonate classical statues. An updated version of this ploy was the big-time act of Annette Kellermann, a diver and swimmer who was best known for her figure and bathing apparel. She surrounded herself with a musical stage show, but as a reviewer who saw her at Keith's Riverside in Manhattan in 1918 noted, there was no mistaking the real source of her appeal:

It is all very well for her to present a diversified musical comedy tabloid, but the fact remains that the audience associates in its mind Miss Annette and union suits, and until the slim, graceful diver came to her feats in the tank the Riverside crowd was restless. Miss Kellermann's dance numbers were interesting and picturesque, and her patriotic number was well devised, but it was only when she appeared in an orange union suit and went into her old specialty that they displayed real interest and enthusiasm. It is the finish which really puts the turn over, the rest of it, much of it clever stage manipulation, being merely a time filler working up to the Kellermann specialty.[7]

The people at the Riverside knew what they wanted and what they were watching. That they had gathered for this show in a big-time Keith house was a testament to the crumbling of Victorianism, a condition that made standards and their enforcement erratic.

In autumn 1923, at the insistence of a priest working for Cardinal Patrick Joseph Hayes, the Keith organization canceled "The Unknown Lady," a short play at the Palace that was critical of divorce laws. (It was replaced by a comedy sketch, "The Cherry Tree," about one George Washington Cohen, who could not tell a lie. Five years earlier, "The Cherry Tree" had been canceled at the Palace because it showed Cohen talking with St. Peter at the gates of heaven.) Though "The Unknown Lady" was canceled at the Palace, there remained on the same bill a duet that asserted a highly sexual vision of marriage: "Mamma loves squeezin', Papa does too / Nothing can break us, / Nothing can make us blue . . . / Spooning, crooning, sweet honey mooning, / And the secret's this: / Mama says yes and Papa says yes, / and people who say yes are happy, I guess" (Spitzer, 1924, pp. 35-39).

If big-time vaudeville was so wholesome, what about this act on the opening bill of the Palace Theater in 1913? *The Billboard* (Anonymous, 1913) noted:

LaNapierkowska is offered as a pantomimist and dancer. The truth of the matters is that LaNapierkowska is a mighty good-looking and shapely dancer of the "cooch" variety, formerly so often seen in the Oriental shows on the mid-way of a fair. But the lady is some dancer of the kind. There isn't a portion of her body that she can not make wriggle at will, and there is very little of it that isn't constantly wriggling during the time which she spends on the stage in her offering, The Captive. She is supposed—so the story program runs—to have been stung by a bee and the gyrations that follow are consequent of the pain she feels. It must be some pain for such wriggling has never before been seen on a high-grade vaudeville stage. (p. 4)

Offering a belly dancer in the guise of portraying a woman suffering from a bee sting was clearly being disingenuous. So too, probably, were the people at the New Brighton Theater in August 1916. There, "The World of Dancers" promised "prehistoric barbarians," "the flesh pots of Egypt," and a finale in which "dancers of the ages past become acquainted with syncopation."[8] The resulting impression is that of an entire city walking around with tongue in cheek.

In his manual explaining how to run a vaudeville theater, Edward Renton (1918) advised managers that

> in advertising a group of classical dancers, the fact that their wardrobe is scant should not be featured; rather the aesthetic and beautiful points should be emphasized—and this may result in securing not only the patronage of those who might come with an idea of looking at nude limbs but as well of those who have a sincere appreciation for and knowledge of art and the beautiful. The latter *will not* be drawn by advertisements and stories of the attraction in which the feature of nudity is vulgarly or coarsely handled. (pp. 226-227)

In sum, vaudeville audiences were of more than two minds concerning questions of sex and gender. As one observer noted (Caffin, 1914), "There must be something for everyone, and, though the fastidious may be a little shocked (the fastidious rather like to be shocked sometimes), they must not be offended, while the seeker for thrills must on no account be bored by too much mildness" (p. 18).

Such volatility, however, was matched by an element of standardization. Vaudevillians carried Tin Pan Alley songs from Manhattan publishing offices to the farthest corners of the country. Song publishers and vaudeville lived off each other; vaudevillians took songs from Tin Pan Alley, and Tin Pan Alley used vaudeville to boost sheet music sales. Together, they made songs into nationwide hits and singers into nationwide stars.

Jokes and sketches became trademarks of popular acts and were performed from one end of the country to the other. Indeed, part of vaudeville's appeal was built on these acts' familiarity. Smith and Dale first performed "Dr. Kronkhite" around 1906 and presented it successfully for decades. Old lines evoked laughter and recognition for many performers. "I luff you, Meyer" could mean only Weber and Fields. "Is everything copacetic?" was the trademark question of dancer Bill "Bojangles" Robinson.

VAUDEVILLE AS A SYSTEM

The mechanism that made nationwide appearances possible was the vaudeville circuit system. Headquartered in New York and Chicago, the booking offices at the center of the circuits sent performers touring on carefully planned routes that crisscrossed the country. A typical tour might begin in New York City, then head north through Hartford, Providence, and Boston, west through Albany, Syracuse, Buffalo, Cleveland, and Chicago, south to Indianapolis, then back east through Columbus, Pittsburgh, Washington, D.C., and Philadelphia.

The biggest of the circuits was the Keith-Albee. It was synonymous with the big time, just as Marcus Loew's signified small time. At its height, the Keith-Albee offices were located above the Palace Theater on Times Square—the New York City theater district that was the heart of vaudeville—and they were the nerve center of vaudeville, the place where representatives of theaters all around the country organized their shows. The Keith-Albee booking system, which first appeared in 1900 and dominated vaudeville into the 1920s, thrived by playing middleman to theater managers and performers. Vaudevillians twice struck against their near-monopoly, but the Keith-Albee system outlasted all significant competition. Theater managers traded on the Keith-Albee booking office's reputation for high-class vaudeville. The booking office became a metropolitan arbiter of taste, and the Keith-Albee seal of approval became a passport to success (Bernheim, 1923, p. 39).

Bookers, each of whom represented a cluster of specific theaters, created bills to be eventually presented hundreds of miles away.[9] In seeking to gratify the desires of an individual theater's audience, bookers were aided by the basic structure of the vaudeville show: It was assembled from separate and distinct acts. Hundreds of vaudeville shows were presented in any given week in America, but all were unique combinations of acts. Individual acts might try to cultivate a wide appeal, but the shows in which they appeared were anything but a standardized product.

Bookers and theater managers tried to pick acts that would be popular with their audiences, mindful that what was successful in one theater might not work in another. An act might be too refined for a house whose patrons had rough-edged tastes or too dependent on topical political jokes for a placid municipality. In a 1907 report on singer Bessie Wynne, theater manager H. A. Daniels noted that she was a hit in New York but a comparative flop in Cleveland. "Personally, I like her work immensely," he wrote. "She is dainty, clever and artistic. But as I do not pay to see the show, it's not good policy to force my likes and dislikes on the Cleve-landites."[10]

The Keith-Albee booking system facilitated the collection of records on the popularity of acts. Bookers, of course, wanted to hire popular acts because they attracted the largest crowds and made the most money for the theater. Theater managers' reports from all across the Keith-Albee circuit, filed with New York booking agents, helped to determine which acts were hired. Few acts would last long if they flopped, as Crimmins and Gore did when they performed a sketch at a vaudeville house in Sacandaga Park, New York, in 1910. The theater manager conveyed their reception to his booker on a standard evaluation form: "Rottem (sic): 920 Paid admittance. All of 500 people left the theater before act finished completely disgusted with this act. Has killed our business for the next two days."[11]

Records of popularity pressured performers to consistently please their audiences. An anonymous vaudevillian's letter in *The New York Morning Telegraph* in 1915 complained of this rating system (Revell, 1915): "This vaudeville has gotten to be too hard a game. Every Monday you go on trial. Every week a report goes in and you wonder what it says. You have stood the test of every kind of audience and yet you must constantly show your wares all over again" (p. 2).

Booking office records also facilitated control of acts' bawdiness, or use of ethnic slurs, a system that helped maintain Keith's reputation for censorship. Obscenities and the ridicule of physical defects were forbidden everywhere. But beyond these restrictions, control was largely left to the discretion of individual managers. The result was a kind of city- and nationwide geography of the risqué: Certain jokes or songs would be allowed in one theater and not another.[12] Theoretically, within a single city, material could be banned in one Keith theater but permitted in another. And, it seems, more material did have to be cut from shows to be performed in Boston.

The enforcement of nationwide censorship regulations was aided by the centralized Keith bureaucracy. In 1919 the Philadelphia YMCA complained that it was slighted in an act at a local Keith's theater. The organization responded by sending every Keith theater instructions forbidding criticism of the YMCA. In 1922 a newspaper noted a policy forbidding references to Prohibition in all Keith theaters and houses booked through the Keith Vaudeville Exchange.[13]

The local theater managers sent information about the material cut from shows to the Keith booking offices in New York, where it was filed for future reference. Sophie Tucker (1945) recalled the procedure, which began at a Monday matinee when managers viewed the acts, noted the offending material, and sent their instructions to performers in blue envelopes. "There was no arguing about the orders in the blue envelopes. They were final. You obeyed them or quit. And if you quit, you got a black mark against your name in the head office, and you just didn't work on the Keith circuit anymore" (p. 149).[14]

Similar measures were sometimes applied to the ethnic stereotypes that were standard conventions of the American theater at the turn of the century. Stereotypes provided simple characteristics that roughly explained immigrants to native-born Americans and introduced immigrant Americans to each other. They were identifying markers on a bewildering cityscape of races, nationalities, and cultures. They were also often bigoted and racist, a trait that occasionally roused the aggrieved to protest portrayals of black chicken thieves, Jewish cheapskates, and drunk Irishmen. Sometimes the complaint was as subtle as a rabbi's backstage visit to a Jewish comedian who lampooned his own people; sometimes it was as shrewd as a threat of a boycott; sometimes it was as smashing as the boos, hisses, and vegetable matter that the Ancient Order of Hibernians used to silence the Russell Brothers' spoof of two Irish servant girls. The United Booking Office files contain repeated references to cuts of ethnic spoofs and nastier expressions such as "kike," "wop," and "dirty little Greek."[15]

VAUDEVILLE AS A TRANSITION

Performers who could survive this pressure and scrutiny and who could be a hit in vaudeville theaters nationwide became stars. Big time was the standard by which all vaudeville was judged; and, thanks to the circuit system, stars (or, at least, their small-time imitators) could shine on people in cities, towns, and neighborhoods far from the Great White Way. As one vaudeville fan, Murray Schwartz (personal interview, New York City, January 11, 1984), said of those stars, "They were out of this world; they were out of *our* world." But as everyone's gaze turned toward nationwide stars, popular culture turned toward the centralized and the standardized. The local dimension of popular culture began to erode as the rowdy spirit of the Bowery was transformed into a portable, marketable commodity (personal interviews with Harold Applebaum, Jack Gross, Murray Schwartz, Arthur Kline, and Howard Basler, all conducted in New York City, 1983-1984).

Vaudeville did not make otherwise different people the same. But it gave them something in common despite all their other differences. And it did that with a generous, human touch. In vaudeville houses, Americans enjoyed the gregarious experience of going to the theater (afterward to become a luxury in America), the intense interaction between artists and audiences, the mix of novelty and familiarity. In its direct appeal to the audience, which acknowledged the particularities of place, mood, and custom, vaudeville was the last of an older American entertainment. However, in its broad audience, its bureaucratic organization, and its mass marketing of leisure, it was the beginning of a new phase in American popular culture, one that would be most fully articulated in radio, film, and television. These newer media were probably at their best when they expressed the humanity and vitality of vaudeville. The Jimmy Cagney swagger and the Groucho Marx sarcastic aside owed much to vaudeville apprenticeships. These media were at their worst, however, when they furthered the bureaucratic control and moneygrubbing of vaudeville. After vaudeville, the economic and organizational template of modern entertainment was set.

But, for a few decades, the vaudeville entrepreneurs created an embracing form of theater that lifted people out of intimate communities and placed them in a mass audience. In effect, they created a vast mainstream. But in a heterogeneous society, that mainstream was not all blandness. The vaudeville industry's back offices may have been as rationalized as possible, but the audience they assembled were diverse and complex. Theater that appealed to clerical workers and suburban matrons, Bowery toughs and businessmen, immigrants and the native born continually presented people with the unexpected. The heterogeneity of acts and audience gave vaudeville its life and variety, making it one of the last expressions of popular culture that thrived in a living, communal atmosphere.

"The vaudeville theater belongs to the era of the department store and the short story," wrote Edwin Royle (1899, p. 495). "It may be a kind of lunch-counter art, but then art is so vague and lunch is so real."

NOTES

1. My thinking on the fundamental characteristics of popular culture has been influenced by Lawrence Levine (1984) and Carlo Ginsburg (1982). My understanding of the transformation of American popular culture at the turn of the century has been influenced by Susan Davis (1988), Daniel Czitrom (1986), and conversations with William R. Taylor.

2. On radio and the creation of a commercial mainstream, see Marc (1989, p. 36).

3. On the appeal to the audience that was characteristic of vaudeville, burlesque, minstrelsy, the circus, and Harrigan and Hart productions, see Wilson (1976, pp. 179-184). For a magazine writer's analysis of vaudeville's appeal to the audience, see Denton (1909).

4. The passage of time and the lack of comprehensive historical sources make it very difficult to identify the vaudeville audience that both shaped and was created by vaudeville. The ethnic composition of the audience in vaudeville's biggest years, 1890 to 1920, was almost certainly influenced by the great immigrant presence in New York. Carpenter (1927, p. 27) notes that "foreign born white stock," defined as foreign-born whites and native-born whites of foreign or mixed parentage, constituted 77.2% of the city's population in 1890, 76.6% in 1900, 78.6% in 1910, and 76.4% in 1920. Immigrants and their children established an important presence in vaudeville as entrepreneurs, performers, and audiences. See Snyder (1983, p. 61) and Couvares (1983, p. 147).

5. On this point in the history of popular music, see Marsh (1987).

6. My thinking on these points has been influenced by Marybeth Hamilton (1990), whose Princeton dissertation on Mae West deals with many of these issues.

7. All materials cited (except the New Brighton theater program) are in the University of Iowa, Keith-Albee Collection, Iowa City, Libraries Special Collections: For Kellermann, see review clipping dated January 31, 1918, in New Act Book 4, p. 217; on "temptation," see report on Keith's Union Square, July 14, 1913, Iowa Report Book 15, p. 113; on "two nice looking shapely girls" on a tightwire, see October 5, 1906, report by C. J. Stevens on Keith's New York, Report Book 5, p. 137; for a report on an act called "The Bathing Girl," in which a woman in full tights was a big hit, see May 6, 1907, Lindsay Morrion report on Keith's Union Square, Report Book 6, p. 113; for "dancers," see New Brighton Theater program, week of August 14, 1916, p. 9, Harvard Theater Collection, Harvard University.

8. From New Brighton Theater program, week of August 14, 1916, p. 9, Harvard Theater Collection, Harvard University.

9. On the importance of the order in the show, see Samuel Hogdon entry, report book for September 21, 1903, to March 17, 1904, p. 74, Keith-Albee Collection, University of Iowa, and Page (1915, pp. 7-10).

10. See Report Book 6, p. 169, in the Keith-Albee Collection.

11. From August 9, 1910, report to Frank Melville in vaudeville file, box 14, Warshsaw Collection of Business Americana, National Museum of American History, Smithsonian Institution.

12. For examples of acts' being censored, see interview with anonymous woman performer born 1904, Hardey interview, DeWolfe interview, Engel interview, Tucker (1945, p. 148); on the geography of censorship, see Spitzer (1924, p. 36) and B. Smith (personal communication, New York City, 1983).

13. From "No Jibes at 'Y' Allowed on Keith Circuit" (unnamed Philadelphia newspaper, April 28, 1919) and, on the prohibition policy, unnamed newspaper clipping in the Keith clipping file, New York Public Library.

14. See also Spitzer (1924, pp. 38, 133).

15. From Howe (1976, pp. 401-405). Also, the backstage visit from the rabbi was described for me in 1984 by a Jewish man who toured vaudeville with his father. For examples of cuts, see the following from the UBO report books in the University of Iowa collection: "Kike," Keith's Boston, September 16, 1907, Report Book 6, p. 241; references to a "Jew boat" and "Jews running away from a sale," Keith's Boston, July 22, 1918, Report Book 20, p. 85; "wops," Keith's Providence, Rhode Island, Theater, December 29, 1919, Report Book 21, p. 123; "dirty little Greek," Keith's Boston, August 22, 1921, Report Book 22, p. 203.

REFERENCES

Anonymous. (1913, March 24). Opening of the Palace. *The Billboard,* p. 3.

Barrymore, E. (1955). *Memories.* New York: Harper.

Bernheim, A. (1923, November). The facts of vaudeville. *Equity, 8,* 39.

Caffin, C. (1914). *Vaudeville.* New York: Mitchell Kennerley.

Canfield, M. (1922, November 22). The great American art. *The New Republic, 32,* 334-335.

Cantor, E. (1928). *My life is in your hands.* New York: Harper.

Carpenter, N. (1927). *Immigrants and their children: 1920* (Census monograph 8). Washington, DC: Government Printing Office.

Couvares, F. (1983). Triumph of commerce. In M. Frisch & D. Walkowitz (Eds.), *Working-class America: Essays on labor, community and American society* (pp. 123-152). Urbana: University of Illinois Press.

Czitrom, D. (1986). *Media and the American mind: From Morse to McLuhan.* Chapel Hill: University of North Carolina Press.

Davis, S. (1988). *Parades and power: Street theater in nineteenth-century Philadelphia.* Berkeley: University of California Press.

Denton, H. (1909, May). The technique of vaudeville. *The Green Book Album, 1,* 1068-1074.

Foster, G. (1849). *New York in slices: By an experienced slicer.* New York: W. F. Burgess.

Foster, G. (1857). *New York naked.* New York: DeWitt and Davenport.

Ginsburg, C. (1982). *The cheese and the worms: The cosmos of a sixteenth century miller.* New York: Penguin.

Hamilton, M. (1990). *When I'm bad, I'm better: Mae West and American popular entertainment.* Unpublished doctoral dissertation, Princeton University.

Howe, I. (1976). *The world of our fathers.* New York: Harcourt Brace Jovanovich.

Levine, L. (1984). William Shakespeare and the American people: A study in cultural transformation. *American Historical Review, 89,* 46.

Marc, D. (1989). *Comic visions: Television comedy and American culture.* Boston: Unwin Hyman.

Marsh, D. (1987). *Glory days: Bruce Springsteen in the 1980s.* New York: Pantheon.

Page, B. (1915). *Writing for vaudeville.* Springfield, MA: Home Correspondence School.

Renton, E. (1918). *The vaudeville theater: Building, operation, management.* New York: Gotham.

Revell, N. (1915, October 24). News and gossip of the vaudeville world. *New York Morning Telegraph,* sec. 4, p. 2.

Royle, E. (1899, October). The vaudeville theater. *Scribner's, 26,* 485-495.

Smith, B. (1976). *The vaudevillians.* New York: Macmillan.

Snyder, F. (1983). *American vaudeville—Theater in a package: The origins of mass entertainment.* Unpublished doctoral dissertation, Yale University.

Spitzer, M. (1924, May 24). The people of vaudeville. *Saturday Evening Post,* pp. 18-19, 125, 129-130, 133.

Tucker, S. (1945). *Some of these days.* Garden City, NY: Doubleday.

Wilson, G. (1976). *A history of American acting.* Bloomington: Indiana University Press.

INDEX

ABOUT THE CONTRIBUTORS

BETH E. BARNES is Assistant Professor in the School of Communications, Pennsylvania State University, where she teaches and conducts research on the advertising industry. She received her Ph.D. in Communication Studies from Northwestern University.

JAMES R. BENIGER is Associate Professor in the Annenberg School for Communications, University of Southern California. His research interests include information technology, communication theory, and societal change. His books include *The Control Revolution: Technological and Economic Origins of the Information Society.*

MURIEL GOLDSMAN CANTOR is Professor Emerita in Sociology at American University, Washington, D.C. Among her books on the production of popular culture are *The Hollywood Television Producer* and *Prime-Time Television: Content and Control* (with Joel M. Cantor). She received her Ph.D. from the University of California at Los Angeles.

JAMES S. ETTEMA is Professor in the Department of Communication Studies, Northwestern University, where he teaches and conducts research on the social and cultural consequences of mass communication and telecommunication. He received his Ph.D. from the University of Michigan and previously taught in the School of Journalism and Mass Communication, University of Minnesota.

SUSAN HERBST is Associate Professor of Communication Studies and Political Science at Northwestern University. She is the author of *Politics at the Margin: Historical Studies of Public Expression Outside the Mainstream* and *Numbered Voices: How Opinion Polling Has Shaped American Politics.*

PAUL M. HIRSCH is the James Allen Distinguished Professor of Strategy and Organization at Northwestern University's Kellogg Graduate School of Management and Departments of Communication Studies and Sociology. He has published numerous articles on the organization of mass media in the United States and the social effects of television. He has taught at Stanford and Indiana universities, the University of Arizona, and (from 1973 to 1988) the University of Chicago and has coedited *New Strategies for Communication Research* (the sixth Sage Annual Review of Communication Research).

PETER V. MILLER is Associate Professor of Communication Studies and Journalism at Northwestern University. He has taught at Purdue University, the University of Illinois at Urbana-Champaign, and the University of Michigan. He has served as the chair of the Standards Committee of the American Association for Public Opinion Research. He received his Ph.D. from the University of Michigan.

RICHARD A. PETERSON is Professor of Sociology at Vanderbilt University and Founding Chair of the Culture Section of the American Sociological Association. His research on the music industry has been instrumental in the development of the "production of culture" perspective in sociology and communication. Currently, he is completing a book titled *The Fabrication of Authenticity,* which details the creation of commercial music in the first half of the twentieth century.

PATRICIA F. PHALEN is a doctoral student in the Department of Radio/Television/Film at Northwestern University. She received an M.B.A. from Boston College and worked in audience research at WTTW/Chicago. Her research interests include audience behavior and media coverage of U.S. foreign policy.

MARSHA SIEFERT teaches communications at Muhlenberg College. She was the associate editor of the *Journal of Communication* from 1975 to 1985 and the editor from 1986 to 1991. She has edited several books including *Mass Culture and Perestroika in the Soviet Union* and *The*

Information Gap. She holds graduate degrees in folklore from Indiana University and in communications from the University of Pennsylvania.

ROBERT W. SNYDER is the author of *The Voice of the City: Vaudeville and Popular Culture in New York* (Oxford, 1989). Currently an independent writer and historian, he has taught at Rutgers, Princeton, and New York University. He was a 1989-1990 research fellow at the Freedom Forum Media Studies Center at Columbia University.

TRACY A. THOMPSON received her Ph.D. in organizational behavior from Northwestern University and is Assistant Professor at the University of Washington at Tacoma. Her work on investor activism and corporate control has been published in journals such as *Administrative Science Quarterly.* Her current research examines how environmental forces and organizational characteristics combine to influence strategic adaptation in the daily newspaper industry.

LYNNE M. THOMSON is Manager of Marketing Research, Long Distance and Multi-Media, Ameritech Corporation. She received her doctorate in communication studies from Northwestern University and worked for the DDB Needham Worldwide advertising agency before assuming her current position.

ELLEN A. WARTELLA is Walter Cronkite Regents Chair and Dean of the College of Communication at the University of Texas at Austin. She is the author and editor of seven books on mass communication and her particular research specialty is children and mass media. She received her Ph.D. from the University of Minnesota.

JAMES G. WEBSTER is Professor in the Department of Radio/Television/Film and Associate Dean in the School of Speech at Northwestern University. His research has focused on audience behavior and the impact of new communication technologies. He is coauthor (with Lawrence Lichty) of *Ratings Analysis: Theory and Practice.* He received his Ph.D. from Indiana University.

D. CHARLES WHITNEY is Professor in the Department of Journalism and the Department of Radio-Television-Film at the University of Texas at Austin. His research is in media sociology and public opinion and political communication. He received his Ph.D. from the University of Minnesota.

STEVEN S. WILDMAN is Associate Professor of Communication Studies and Director of the Program in Telecommunications Science, Management and Policy at Northwestern University. He holds a Ph.D. in economics from Stanford University and is the author of two books and numerous articles on the economics of communication industries and technologies.